Annie's Favorite

Designer Fashions™

Annie's Attic®

Product Development Director
Andy Ashley

Publishing Services Director
Ange Van Arman

Crafts Design Manager
Deborah Levy-Hamburg

Product Development Staff
Mickie Akins, Darla Hassell, Sandra Miller Maxfield,
Alice Mitchell, Elizabeth Ann White

Senior Editor
Donna Scott

Crochet Editorial Staff
Shirley Brown, Liz Field, Skeeter Gilson,
Sharon Lothrop, Nina Marsh, Lyne Pickens

Graphic Artists
Debby Keel, Betty Holmes

Color Specialist
Betty Holmes

Cover Design
Lois Sullivan, Sullivan Rothe

Photography Manager
Scott Campbell

Photographers
Tammy Coquat-Payne,
Andy J. Burnfield

Photo Stylist
Martha Coquat

Production Coordinator
Glenda Chamberlain

Library of Congress Cataloging-in-Publication Data
ISBN: 0-9655269-9-2
First Printing: 2001
Library of Congress Catalog Card Number: 00-135311
Published and Distributed by
Annie's Attic, Big Sandy, Texas 75755
AnniesAttic.com
Printed in the United States of America

Contents

Dear Friends,

One of my greatest pleasures is to crochet clothing and fashion accessories. There are so many opportunities and occasions to wear these creations. It's always exciting to wear a new sweater, hat or a simple hair adornment and become the focus of everyone's attention. It's a great ego-boost to be able to say that I made it myself and bask in all of the compliments and admiring comments.

Within these pages we have selected a variety of projects to adorn you from head to foot, along with accessories to enhance your existing wardrobe. From casual to elegant, there's just the right touch to add that extra something to your fashion lifestyle.

Annie

Elegant Evenings

CHAPTER ONE

Shoulder Wrap

Designed by Ann Parnell

Finished Size: One size fits all.
Materials:
- ❏ 10 oz. off-white sport yarn
- ❏ H hook or hook size needed to obtain gauge

Gauge: We are not responsible for lack of materials due to project not being worked to gauge. Gauge for this pattern: 1 V st and 1 sc = 1"; 6 rows = 2½".

Basic Stitches: Ch, sl st, sc, dc.

Wrap

Row 1: Ch 62, sc in second ch from hook, *ch 1, skip next ch; for **V stitch (V st), (dc, ch 1, dc)** in next ch, ch 1, skip next ch, sc in next ch; repeat from * across, turn. *(30 ch-1 sps, 16 sc, 15 V sts made)*

Row 2: Ch 4, sc in second ch from hook, ch 1, skip next ch, V st in next ch, ch 1, skip next sc, (*V st in next ch 1 sp, ch 1, skip next V st, V st in next ch-1 sp, ch 1*, skip next sc and next ch-1 sp, V st in ch sp of next V st, ch 1, skip next ch-1 sp and next sc) 7 times; repeat between **, sc in last sc, turn. *(25 ch-1 sps, 24 V sts, 2 sc)*

Row 3: Ch 4, sc in second ch from hook, ch 1, skip next ch, V st in next ch, ch 1, skip next sc, sc in next ch-1 sp, ch 1, V st in next V st, (ch 1, sc in next ch-1 sp, ch 1, V st in next V st) 24 times, ch 1, skip next ch-1 sp, sc in last sc, turn. *(25 V sts)*

Row 4: Ch 4, sc in second ch from hook, ch 1, skip next ch, V st in next ch, ch 1, (V st in next V st, ch 1) across, sc in last sc, turn. *(27 ch-1 sps, 26 V sts, 2 sc)*

Rows 5-11: Repeat rows 3 and 4 alternately, ending with row 3 and *(66 ch-1 sps, 34 sc, 33 V sts).*

Row 12: Ch 4, sc in second ch from hook, ch 1, skip next ch, V st in next ch, *(ch 1, V st in next V st) 3 times, ch 1, skip next ch-1 sp and next sc, V st in next ch-1 sp, ch 1, skip next V st, V st in next ch-1 sp; repeat from * 7 more times, ch 1, V st in next V st, ch 1, sc in last sc, turn. *(43 ch-1 sps, 42 V sts, 2 sc)*

Rows 13-19: Repeat rows 3 and 4 alternately, ending with row 3 and *(98 ch-1 sps, 50 sc, 49 V sts).*

Row 20: Ch 4, sc in second ch from hook, ch 1, skip next ch, V st in next ch, *(ch 1, V st in next V st) 3 times, ch 1, skip next ch-1 sp and next sc, V st in next ch-1 sp, ch 1, skip next V st, V st in next ch-1sp; repeat from * 11 more times, ch 1, V st in next V st, ch 1, sc in last sc, turn. *(63 ch-1 sps, 62 V sts, 2 sc)*

Rows 21-27: Repeat rows 3 and 4 alternately, ending with row 3. At end of row 27, fasten off. *(69 V sts, 3 chs)*

Row 28: Ch 24, sc in first ch on row 27, ch 1, skip next ch, V st in next ch, ch 1, (V st in next V st, ch 1) across, sc in last sc, ch 23, turn. *(71 ch-1 sps, 70 V sts, 47 chs, 2 sc)*

Row 29: Sc in second ch from hook, (ch 1, ski next 2 chs, V st in next ch, ch 1, skip next 2 chs, sc in next ch) 3 times, ch 1, skip next 2 chs, V st in next ch, ch 1, skip next sc, sc in next ch-1 sp, ch 1, V st in next V st, (ch 1, sc in next ch-1 sp, ch 1, V st in next V st) 69 times, ch 1, skip next ch-1 sp, sc in next sc, (ch 1, skip next 2 chs, V st in next ch, ch 1, skip next 2 chs, sc in next ch) 4 times, turn. *(78 V sts)*

Row 30: Ch 4 *(counts as first dc and ch-1)*, (V st in next V st, ch 1) across to last sc, dc in last sc, turn. *(79 ch-1 sps, 78 V sts)*

Row 31: Ch 1, skip first st, sc in next ch-1 sp, (ch 1, V st in next V st, ch 1, sc in next ch-1 sp) across leaving last dc unworked, turn. *(79 sc, 78 V sts)*

Rnd 32: For **edging,** working around outer edge, ch 4, (V st in next V st, ch 1) across with (dc, ch 1) 3 times in last sc, **do not turn;** skip row 30, (dc, ch 1) 3 times in end of row 29; working in chs on opposite side of row 28, (V st in same ch as next V st, ch 1) 4 times; working in ends of rows, (skip next row, V st in end of next row, ch 1) 14 times; working in chs on opposite side of row 1, (V st in same ch as next sc, ch 1) 15 times; working in ends of rows, V st in end of next row, ch 1, (skip next row, V st in end of next row, ch 1) 13 times; working in chs on opposite side of row 28, (V st in same ch as next V st, ch 1) 4 times, (dc, ch 1) 3 times in end of row 29, skip row 30, (dc, ch 1) 2 times in same st as ch-4, join with sl st in third ch of ch-4, **turn.** *(141 ch-1 sps, 129 V sts)*

Rnd 33: Ch 4; working in ch-1 sps and in ch sps of V sts, sc in first sp, ch 1, V st in next sp, ch 1, (sc in next sp, ch 1, V st in next sp, ch 1)

Continued on page 28

Cotton Gloves

Designed by Ann Parnell

Finished Sizes: Slightly stretched: **Lady's small** 7" around palm; **large** fits 8" around palm.

Materials:
- 400 yds. size 10 crochet cotton thread
- 4 bobby pins for markers
- Steel hook stated below or hook size needed to obtain gauge for size

Gauges: We are not responsible for lack of materials due to project not being worked to gauge. Gauge for **small size using No. 7 steel hook**: 5 extended sc clusters =1"; 8 rows = 1". For **large size using No. 4 steel hook,** 9 extended sc clusters =2"; 6 rows = 1".

Basic Stitches: Ch, sl st, sc, hdc.

Special Stitches: For **extended sc cluster in ch (escl-ch),** (insert hook in next ch, yo, pull through ch) 2 times, yo, pull through 2 lps on hook, yo, pull through last 2 lps on hook.

For **extended sc cluster (escl),** insert hook in ch-1 sp before next st *(see illustration),* yo, pull through sp, insert hook in sp before vertical strand of same st, yo, pull through sp, (yo, pull through 2 lps on hook) 2 times.

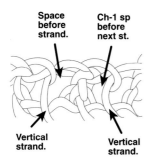

Space before strand. Ch-1 sp before next st. Vertical strand. Vertical strand.

For **extended sc decrease (escl dec),** (insert hook in sp before vertical strand of next st, yo, pull through st) 2 times, yo, pull through all 3 lps on hook.

Right Glove

Row 1: Beginning at wrist on little finger edge, ch 79, skip first 2 chs, **(escl-ch**—*see Special Stitches,* ch 1) across to last ch, hdc in last ch, turn. *(38 escl-ch made)*

Rows 2-5: Ch 2, **(escl**—*see Special Stitches,* ch 1) across to last st, hdc in top of ch-2, turn. *(38 escl)*

Row 6: Ch 2, (escl, ch 1) 28 times, escl leaving remaining escl unworked; for **ring finger,** ch 29, turn. *(29 escl)*

Row 7: Skip first 2 chs, (escl-ch, ch 1) across to last ch, insert hook in last ch, yo, pull through ch, insert hook in sp before vertical bar of next st, yo, pull through sp, complete as escl, ch 1, (escl, ch 1) across to last st, escl, hdc in top of ch-2, turn. *(42)*

Rows 8-11: Repeat row 2.

Row 12: Ch 2, (escl, ch 1) 29 times, escl leaving remaining sts unworked; for **middle finger,** ch 31, turn. *(30 escl)*

Row 13: Repeat row 7. *(44)*

Rows 14-17: Repeat row 2.

Row 18: Ch 2, (escl, ch 1) 29 times, escl leaving remaining sts unworked; for **index finger,** ch 27, turn. *(30 escl)*

Row 19: Repeat row 7. *(42)*

Rows 20-22: Repeat row 2.

Row 23: Ch 2, (escl, ch 1) 19 times, escl leaving remaining sts unworked; for **thumb,** ch 24, skip first 2 chs, (escl-ch, ch 1) 10 times, escl-ch, sc in same sp as last escl on finger section, (escl, ch 1) 21 times, escl, hdc in top of ch-2. *(53 escl, 1 sc)*

Row 24: Ch 2, (escl, ch 1) 22 times; working on thumb, (escl, ch 1) 11 times, sc in end of thumb on row 23, ch 1; working on opposite side of ch on thumb, (escl-ch, ch 1) 11 times; working across finger section, (escl, ch 1) 19 times, escl, hdc in top of ch-2, turn. *(64 escl, 1 sc, 1 hdc)*

Row 25: Ch 2, (escl, ch 1) 31 times, insert hook in next ch-1 sp, yo, pull through sp, insert hook in next sc, yo, pull through st, complete as escl, ch 1, (3 escl, ch 1) across to last st, escl, hdc in top of ch-2, turn. *(65 escl)*

Rows 26-28: Repeat row 2.

Row 29: Ch 2, (escl, ch 1) 30 times, escl, **escl dec** *(see Special Stitches),* mark st just made, escl; fold thumb in half with part of row already worked at back; working on back with inside facing you, insert hook in marked st, yo, pull through st, remove marker, insert hook in sp before vertical strand of next st, yo, pull through st, complete as escl; (for **side seam**

Continued on page 26

1911 Puritan Collar

Designed by Emily Garside

Finished Size: Fits 20" neckline.

Materials:
- ❑ 400 yds. size 20 crochet cotton thread
- ❑ ⅝" pearl shank button
- ❑ Sewing needle and thread
- ❑ No. 10 steel hook or hook size needed to obtain gauge

Gauge: We are not responsible for lack of materials due to project not being worked to gauge. Gauge for this pattern: Widest point of pineapple between clover leafs = 1¼"; 2 dc rows and 8 ch sp rows at center of pineapple = 1¾"; 1 clover leaf = ¾" wide x ½" tall including base.

Basic Stitches: Ch, sl st, sc, dc.

Special Stitches: For **beginning clover leaf (beg clover leaf),** ch 1; for **petals,** (sc, 4 dc, sc) in each of next 2 ch sps, (sc, 4 dc) in next ch sp, sc in next dc. *(3 petals)*

For **clover leaf,** sc in next dc; for **petals,** (4 dc, sc) in next ch sp, (sc, 4 dc, sc) in next ch sp, (sc, 4 dc) in next ch sp, sc in next dc.

For **beginning base (beg base),** ch 3, sc in second dc of next petal, ch 3, dc in second dc of next petal. (ch 3, dc in same st) 3 times, sc in second dc of next petal.

For **ending base (end base),** ch 2, sc in second dc of next petal, dc in second dc of next petal, (ch 3, dc in same st) 3 times.

Collar

Rnd 1: Beginning at center back, ch 39, dc in seventh ch from hook, ch 3, dc in same ch, ch 3, *skip next 3 chs, sc in next ch, ch 4, skip next 4 chs, sc in next ch, ch 2, skip next 2 chs, sc in next ch, ch 4, skip next 3 chs, dc in next ch, ch 4, skip next 3 chs, sc in next ch, ch 2, skip next 2 chs, sc in next ch, ch 4, skip next 4 chs, sc in next ch, ch 3, skip next 3 chs*, (dc, ch 3) 7 times in last ch; working on opposite side of ch, repeat between **, (dc, ch 3, dc) in next ch, ch 3, join with sl st in third ch of ch-6.

Rnd 2: Ch 1, (sc, 4 dc, sc) in each of next 2 ch sps, *(sc, 4 dc) in next ch sp, sc in next st, ch 4, skip next ch sp, sc in next st, skip next ch sp, skip next st, 4 dc in next ch sp, dc in next st, 4 dc in next ch sp, skip next st, skip next ch sp, sc in next st, ch 4, skip next ch sp, sc in next st, (4 dc, sc) in next ch sp*, (sc, 4 dc, sc) in each of next 6 ch sps; repeat between **, (sc, 4 dc, sc) in each of next 2 ch sps, join with sl st in first sc, **turn,** sl st in next 3 sts, **turn.**

Row 3: Working in rows, ch 65, sc in seventh ch from hook, (ch 3, skip next 3 chs, sc in next ch) 2 times, (ch 4, skip next 4 chs, sc in next ch) 3 times, (ch 5, skip next 5 chs, sc in next ch) 3 times, (ch 6, skip next 6 chs, sc in next ch) 2 times, ch 3, skip last 3 chs, sc in second dc of next 4-dc group, **do not turn.** Fasten off.

Row 4: For **first side,** starting at top of ch-65, join with sc in fourth ch of ch-6, (ch 3, skip next ch sp, sc in next st) 3 times, (ch 4, skip next ch sp, sc in next st) 3 times, (ch 5, skip next ch sp, sc in next st) 3 times, (ch 6, skip next ch sp, sc in next st) 2 times, ch 3, skip next ch sp, sc in worked dc on next petal, ch 3, dc in third dc of next 4-dc group, (ch 3, dc in same st) 3 times, ch 2, sc in second dc of next 4-dc group, ch 2, skip next ch sp, skip next sc, dc in next dc, (ch 1, dc in next dc) 8 times, ch 2, skip next st, skip next ch sp, sc in second dc of next 4-dc group, ch 2, dc in third dc of next 4-dc group, (ch 3, dc in same st) 3 times, turn.

Row 5: Beg clover leaf *(see Special Stitches),* ch 2, sc in next dc, (ch 5, sc in next dc) 8 times, ch 2, **clover leaf** *(see Special Stitches),* ch 7, skip next ch sp, sc in next ch sp, (ch 6, sc in next ch sp) 2 times, (ch 5, sc in next ch sp) 3 times, (ch 4, sc in next ch sp) 3 times, (ch 3, sc in next ch sp) 3 times, turn.

Row 6: Ch 5, sc in first ch sp, (ch 3, sc in next ch sp) 2 times, (ch 4, sc in next ch sp) 3 times, (ch 5, sc in next ch sp) 3 times, **beg base** *(see Special Stitches),* ch 2, sc in next ch-5 sp, (ch 5, sc in next ch-5 sp) 7 times, **end base** *(see Special Stitches),* turn.

Row 7: Beg clover leaf, ch 2, sc in next ch-5 sp, (ch 5, sc in next ch-5 sp) 6 times, ch 2, clover leaf, ch 7, skip next ch sp, sc in next ch sp, 7 dc in next st, sc in next ch sp, (ch 5, sc in next ch sp) 3 times, 6 dc in next st, sc in next ch sp, (ch 4, sc in next ch sp) 3 times, 5 dc in next st, sc in

Continued on page 12

1911 Puritan Collar

Continued from page 10

next ch sp, (ch 3, sc in next ch sp) 3 times, turn.

Row 8: Ch 5, sc in first ch sp, (ch 3, sc in next ch sp) 2 times, ch 3, sc in center st of next 5-dc group, (ch 4, sc in next ch sp) 3 times, ch 5, sc in fourth st of next 6-dc group, (ch 5, sc in next ch sp) 2 times, ch 6, sc in next ch sp, ch 6, sc in center st of next 7-dc group, ch 6, sc in next ch sp, beg base, ch 2, sc in next ch-5 sp, (ch 5, sc in next ch-5 sp) 5 times, end base, turn.

Row 9: Beg clover leaf, ch 2, sc in next ch-5 sp, (ch 5, sc in next ch-5 sp) 4 times, ch 2, clover leaf, ch 7, skip next ch sp, sc in next ch sp, ch 7, sc in next ch sp, (ch 6, sc in next ch sp) 3 times, (ch 5, sc in next ch sp) 3 times, (ch 4, sc in next ch sp) 3 times, (ch 3, sc in next ch sp) 3 times, turn.

Row 10: Ch 5, sc in first ch sp, (ch 3, sc in next ch sp) 2 times, (ch 4, sc in next ch sp) 3 times, (ch 5, sc in next ch sp) 3 times, (ch 6, sc in next ch sp) 3 times, (ch 7, sc in next ch sp) 2 times, beg base, ch 2, sc in next ch-5 sp, (ch 5, sc in next ch-5 sp) 3 times, end base, turn.

Row 11: Beg clover leaf, ch 2, sc in next ch-5 sp, (ch 5, sc in next ch-5 sp) 2 times, ch 2, clover leaf, ch 7, skip next ch sp, sc in next ch sp, 7 dc in next st, sc in next ch sp, (ch 6, sc in next ch sp) 3 times, 6 dc in next st, sc in next ch sp, (ch 5, sc in next ch sp) 3 times, 6 dc in next st, sc in next ch sp, (ch 4, sc in next ch sp) 2 times, ch 3, sc in next ch sp, 5 dc in next st, sc in next ch sp, ch 3, sc in last ch sp, turn.

Row 12: Ch 5, sc in first ch sp, ch 3, sc in center st of next 5-dc group, ch 3, sc in next ch sp, (ch 4, sc in next ch sp) 2 times, ch 4, sc in fourth st of next 6-dc group, (ch 5, sc in next ch sp) 3 times, ch 6, sc in fourth st of next 6-dc group, (ch 6, sc in next ch sp) 2 times, ch 7, sc in next ch sp, ch 7, sc in center st of next 7-dc group, ch 7, sc in next ch sp, ch 3, sc in second dc of next petal, dc in second dc of next petal, (ch 3, dc in same st) 3 times, sc in second dc of next petal, ch 2, sc in next ch-5 sp, ch 5, sc in next ch-5 sp, end base, turn.

Row 13: Beg clover leaf, ch 2, sc in next ch-5 sp, ch 2, sc in next dc, 2 dc in next ch sp, ch 1, sl st in second dc of last petal made, ch 1, sl st in last dc made, (2 dc, sc) in same ch sp, complete clover leaf, ch 3, skip next ch sp, sc in next ch sp, (ch 7, sc in next ch sp) 2 times, (ch 6, sc in next ch sp) 3 times, (ch 5, sc in next ch sp) 3 times, (ch 4, sc in next ch sp) 3 times, (ch 3, sc in next ch sp) 3 times, turn.

Row 14: Ch 5, sc in first ch sp, (ch 3, sc in next ch sp) 2 times, (ch 4, sc in next ch sp) 3 times, (ch 5, sc in next ch sp) 3 times, (ch 6, sc in next ch sp) 3 times, ch 3, dc in next ch sp, (ch 3, dc in same sp) 3 times, ch 2, (dc, ch 5, dc) in next ch sp, ch 2, skip next ch sp, sc in second dc of next petal, dc in second dc of next petal, (ch 3, dc in same st) 3 times, skip next 2 joined clover leaf, sc in second dc of next petal, turn.

Row 15: Ch 1, sl st in first st, beg clover leaf, ch 2, dc in next ch-2 sp, ch 2, 8 dc in next ch sp, ch 2, dc in next ch-2 sp, ch 2, clover leaf, ch 7, skip next ch sp, sc in next ch sp, (ch 6, sc in next ch sp) 3 times, 7 dc in next st, sc in next ch sp, (ch 5, sc in next ch sp) 2 times, ch 4, sc in next ch sp, 5 dc in next st, sc in next ch sp, (ch 3, sc in next ch sp) 3 times, turn.

Row 16: Ch 5, sc in first ch sp, (ch 3, sc in next ch sp) 2 times, ch 4, sc in center st of next 5-dc group, (ch 4, sc in next ch sp) 2 times, ch 5, sc in next ch sp, ch 5, sc in center st of next 7-dc group, ch 5, sc in next ch sp, (ch 6, sc in next ch sp) 3 times, ch 3, sc in second dc of next petal, dc in second dc of next petal, (ch 3, dc in same st) 3 times, sc in second dc of next petal, ch 2, skip next ch sp, skip next dc, skip next ch sp, dc in next dc, (ch 1, dc in next dc) 7 times, end base, turn.

Row 17: Beg clover leaf, ch 2, sc in next dc, (ch 5, sc in next dc) 7 times, ch 2, clover leaf, ch 7, skip next ch sp, sc in next ch sp, (ch 6, sc in next ch sp) 2 times, (ch 5, sc in next ch sp) 3 times, (ch 4, sc in next ch sp) 3 times, (ch 3, sc in next ch sp) 3 times, turn.

Row 18: Ch 5, sc in first ch sp, (ch 3, sc in next ch sp) 2 times, (ch 4, sc in next ch sp) 3 times, (ch 5, sc in next ch sp) 3 times, (ch 6, sc in next ch sp) 3 times, beg base, ch 2, sc in next ch-5 sp, (ch 5, sc in next ch-5 sp) 6 times, ch 5, sc in same ch sp, end base, turn.

Row 19: Beg clover leaf, ch 2, sc in next ch-5 sp, (ch 5, sc in next ch-5 sp) 6 times, ch 2, clover leaf, ch 7, skip next ch sp, sc in next ch sp, (ch 6, sc in next ch sp) 2 times, 7 dc in next st, sc in next ch sp, (ch 5, sc in next ch sp) 2 times, ch 4, sc in next ch sp, 6 dc in next st, sc in next ch sp, (ch 4, sc in next ch sp) 2 times, ch 3, sc in next ch sp, 5 dc in next st, sc in next ch sp, ch 3, sc in last ch sp, turn.

Row 20: Ch 5, sc in first ch sp, ch 3, sc in center st of next 5-dc group, ch 3, sc in next ch sp, (ch 4, sc in next ch sp) 2 times, ch 4, sc in fourth st

Elegant Evenings - page 12

of next 6-dc group, (ch 5, sc in next ch sp) 3 times, ch 6, sc in center st of next 7-dc group, (ch 6, sc in next ch sp) 2 times, ch 7, sc in next ch sp, beg base, ch 2, sc in next ch-5 sp, (ch 5, sc in next ch-5 sp) 5 times, end base, turn.

Row 21: Beg clover leaf, ch 2, sc in next ch-5 sp, (ch 5, sc in next ch-5 sp) 4 times, ch 2, clover leaf, ch 7, skip next ch sp, sc in next ch sp, ch 7, sc in next ch sp, (ch 6, sc in next ch sp) 3 times, (ch 5, sc in next ch sp) 3 times, (ch 4, sc in next ch sp) 3 times, (ch 3, sc in next ch sp) 3 times, turn.

Row 22: Ch 5, sc in first ch sp, (ch 3, sc in next ch sp) 2 times, (ch 4, sc in next ch sp) 3 times, (ch 5, sc in next ch sp) 3 times, (ch 6, sc in next ch sp) 3 times, (ch 7, sc in next ch sp) 2 times, beg base, ch 2, sc in next ch-5 sp, (ch 5, sc in next ch-5 sp) 3 times, end base, turn.

Row 23: Beg clover leaf, ch 2, sc in next ch-5 sp, (ch 5, sc in next ch-5 sp) 2 times, ch 2, clover leaf, ch 7, skip next ch sp, sc in next ch sp, (ch 7, sc in next ch sp) 2 times, 7 dc in next st, sc in next ch sp, (ch 6, sc in next ch sp) 2 times, ch 5, sc in next ch sp, 6 dc in next st, sc in next ch sp, ch 5, sc in next ch sp, (ch 4, sc in next ch sp) 2 times, 5 dc in next st, sc in next ch sp, (ch 3, sc in next ch sp) 3 times, turn.

Row 24: Ch 5, sc in first ch sp, (ch 3, sc in next ch sp) 2 times, ch 4, sc in center st of next 5-dc group, (ch 4, sc in next ch sp) 2 times, ch 5, sc in next ch sp, ch 5, sc in fourth st of next 6-dc group, ch 5, sc in next ch sp, (ch 6, sc in next ch sp) 2 times, ch 6, sc in center st of next 7-dc group, (ch 7, sc in next ch sp) 3 times, ch 3, sc in second dc of next petal, dc in second dc of next petal, (ch 3, dc in same st) 3 times, sc in second dc of next petal, ch 2, sc in next ch-5 sp, ch 5, sc in next ch-5 sp, end base, turn.

Rows 25-26: Repeat rows 13-14.

Row 27: Ch 1, sl st in first st, beg clover leaf, ch 2, dc in next ch-2 sp, ch 2, 8 dc in next ch sp, ch 2, dc in next ch-2 sp, ch 2, clover leaf, ch 6, skip next ch sp, sc in next ch sp, ch 6, sc in next ch sp, 7 dc in next st, sc in next ch sp, (ch 5, sc in next ch sp) 3 times, 6 dc in next st, sc in next ch sp, (ch 4, sc in next ch sp) 2 times, ch 3, sc in next ch sp, 5 dc in next st, sc in next ch sp, ch 3, sc in last ch sp, turn.

Row 28: Ch 5, sc in first ch sp, ch 3, sc in center st of next 5-dc group, ch 3, sc in next ch sp, (ch 4, sc in next ch sp) 2 times, ch 4, sc in fourth st of next 6-dc group, (ch 5, sc in next ch sp) 3 times, ch 6, sc in center st of next 7-dc group, (ch 6, sc in next ch sp) 2 times, beg base, ch 2, skip next ch sp, skip next dc, skip next ch sp, dc in next dc, (ch 1, dc in next dc) 7 times, skip next ch sp, skip next dc, skip next ch sp, end base, turn.

Row 29: Beg clover leaf, ch 2, sc in next dc, (ch 5, sc in next dc) 7 times, ch 2, clover leaf, ch 7, skip next ch sp, sc in next ch sp, (ch 6, sc in next ch sp) 3 times, (ch 5, sc in next ch sp) 3 times, (ch 4, sc in next ch sp) 3 times, (ch 3, sc in next ch sp) 3 times, turn.

Row 30; Ch 5, sc in first ch sp, (ch 3, sc in next ch sp) 2 times, (ch 4, sc in next ch sp) 3 times, (ch 5, sc in next ch sp) 3 times, (ch 6, sc in next ch sp) 3 times, ch 7, sc in next ch sp, beg base, ch 2, sc in next ch-5 sp, (ch 5, sc in next ch-5 sp) 6 times, ch 5, sc in same ch sp, end base, turn.

Row 31: Beg clover leaf, ch 2, sc in next ch-5 sp, (ch 5, sc in next ch-5 sp) 6 times, ch 2, clover leaf, ch 7, skip next ch sp, sc in next ch sp, ch 7, sc in next ch sp, 7 dc in next st, sc in next ch sp, (ch 6, sc in next ch sp) 2 times, ch 5, sc in next ch sp, 6 dc in next st, sc in next ch sp, ch 5, sc in next ch sp, (ch 4, sc in next ch sp) 2 times, 5 dc in next st, sc in next ch sp, (ch 3, sc in next ch sp) 3 times, turn.

Row 32: Ch 5, sc in first ch sp, (ch 3, sc in next ch sp) 2 times, ch 4, sc in center st of next 5-dc group, (ch 4, sc in next ch sp) 2 times, ch 5, sc in next ch sp, ch 5, sc in fourth st of next 6-dc group, ch 5, sc in next ch sp, (ch 6, sc in next ch sp) 2 times, ch 6, sc in center st of next 7-dc group, (ch 7, sc in next ch sp) 2 times, beg base, ch 2, sc in next ch-5 sp, (ch 5, sc in next ch-5 sp) 5 times, end base, turn.

Row 33: Beg clover leaf, ch 2, sc in next ch-5 sp, (ch 5, sc in next ch-5 sp) 4 times, ch 2, clover leaf, ch 7, skip next ch sp, sc in next ch sp, (ch 7, sc in next ch sp) 2 times, (ch 6, sc in next ch sp) 3 times, (ch 5, sc in next ch sp) 3 times, (ch 4, sc in next ch sp) 3 times, (ch 3, sc in next ch sp) 3 times, turn.

Row 34: Ch 5, sc in first ch sp, (ch 3, sc in next ch sp) 2 times, (ch 4, sc in next ch sp) 3 times, (ch 5, sc in next ch sp) 3 times, (ch 6, sc in next ch sp) 3 times, (ch 7, sc in next ch sp) 3 times, ch 3, sc in second dc of next petal, dc in second dc of next petal, (ch 3, dc in same st) 3 times, sc in second dc of next petal, ch 2, sc in next ch-5 sp, (ch 5, sc in next ch-5 sp) 3 times, end base, turn.

Row 35: Beg clover leaf, ch 2, sc in next ch-5 sp, (ch 5, sc in next ch-5 sp) 2 times, ch 2, clover leaf, ch 7, skip next ch sp, sc in next ch sp, 7 dc in next st, sc in next ch sp, ch 7, sc in next ch sp, (ch 6, sc in next ch sp) 2 times, 6 dc in next st, sc in next ch sp, (ch 5, sc in next ch sp) 3 times, 6 dc in next st, sc in next ch sp, (ch 4, sc in next ch sp) 2 times, ch 3, sc in next ch sp, 5 dc in next st, sc in next ch sp, ch 3, sc in last ch sp, turn.

Rows 36-97: Repeat rows 12-35 consecutively, ending with row 25. At end of last row, fasten

Continued on page 24

Nighttime Sky Vest

Designed by Mara Goodwin

Finished Sizes: Lady's small, fits 30"–32" bust. Finished Measurement: 38½". **Lady's medium,** fits 34"–36" bust. Finished Measurement: 42". **Lady's large,** fits 38"–40". Finished Measurement: 45½".

Materials:
- ❏ Amount of wool sock yarn or light fingering yarn stated for size needed:
  - 10 oz. for small
  - 11½ oz. for medium
  - 13 oz. for large
- ❏ Amount of clear/silver beads stated for size needed:
  - 1,024 beads for small
  - 1,088 beads for medium
  - 1,484 beads for large
- ❏ ⅝" shank button
- ❏ Crochet stitch markers
- ❏ Beading needle
- ❏ C hook or hook size needed to obtain gauge

Gauge: We are not responsible for lack of materials due to project not being worked to gauge. Gauge for this pattern: Large Motif is 3½" across. Half Motif is 2"x 3½". 4 sc and 3 ch sps = 2".

Basic Stitches: Ch, sl st, sc, dc, tr.

Special Stitches: For **cluster,** yo 2 times, insert hook in ch sp, yo, pull through ch sp, (yo, pull through 2 lps on hook) 2 times, *yo 2 times, insert hook in same ch sp, yo, pull through ch sp, (yo, pull through 2 lps on hook) 2 times; repeat from *, yo, pull through all lps on hook.
For sc **bead,** (sc, pull up bead, ch 1, sc) in next ch sp.

Note: Instructions are for small size; changes for medium and large sizes are in [ ].

Vest Assembly
Using the following instructions; work Motifs A, B, C, D, E and F according to assembly illustrations on page 17 for size needed.

Motif A
Rnd 1: Thread 20 beads onto yarn, pushing beads back along yarn as you work until needed; ch 10,

sl st in first ch to form ring, ch 1, 20 sc in ring, join with sl st in first sc. *(20 sc made)*
Note: For loop, drop lp from hook, insert hook in st specified, pull dropped lp through st.
Rnd 2: Ch 1, sc in first 5 sts, ch 8, work **loop** *(see Note)* in first st made, 15 sc in loop just made, (sc in next 5 sts of last rnd, ch 8, work loop in fourth st from last st made, 15 sc in loop just made) 3 times, join with sl st in first sc. *(4 15-sc groups)*
Rnd 3: Ch 9, sc in center st of first group, (ch 9, sc in next space between groups, ch 9, sc in center st of next group) around, ch 9, join with sl st in joining sl st of last rnd. *(8 ch sps)*
Rnd 4: Ch 1, 11 sc in each ch sp around, join with sl st in first sc. *(8 11-sc groups)*
Rnd 5: Ch 8, sc in sixth st of first group, *ch 5, (dc, ch 5, dc) in first st of next group *(corner ch sp made),* ch 5, sc in sixth st of same group, ch 5, (dc, pull up bead, ch 1, dc) in first st of next group *(beaded V st made),* ch 5, sc in sixth st of same group; repeat from * 2 more times, ch 5, (dc, ch 5, dc) in first st of next group *(corner ch sp made),* ch 5, sc in sixth st of same group, ch 5, dc in same st as ch-8, pull up bead, ch 1, join with sl st in third ch of ch-8.
Rnd 6: Ch 1, (sc bead—*see Special Stitches,* ch 6) in each of first 2 ch-5 sps, *(cluster—*see Special Stitches,* ch 5, cluster) in next corner ch sp, (ch 6, sc bead) in each of next 2 ch-5 sps, ch 6, skip next beaded V st, (sc bead, ch 6) in each of next 2 ch-5 sps; repeat from * 2 more times, (cluster, ch 5, cluster) in last corner ch sp, (ch 6, sc bead) in each of last 2 ch-5 sps, ch 6, join with sl st in first sc. Fasten off.

Motif B (joined on one side)
Rnds 1-5: Repeat rnds 1-5 of Motif A.
Note: For **joining,** ch 2, sc in adjacent ch sp of corresponding Motif, ch 2.
Rnd 6: Ch 1, (sc bead, ch 6) in each of first 2 ch-5 sps; for **corner joining,** (cluster, work **joining**—*see Note;* cluster) in next corner ch sp *(corner joining completed—if there are two Motifs joined at this point, sc in joining sc);* for **side joining,** (work joining, sc bead in next ch-5 sp of this Motif) 2 times, skipping next beaded V st on this Motif, (work joining, sc bead in next ch-5 sp

Continued on page 16

Nighttime Sky Vest

Continued from page 15

on this Motif) 2 times, work joining, *(side joining completed);* work corner joining, *(ch 6, sc bead) in each of next 2 ch-5 sps, ch 6, skip next beaded V st, (sc bead, ch 6) in each of next 2 ch-5 sps, (cluster, ch 5, cluster) in next corner ch sp; repeat from *, (ch 6, sc bead) in each of last 2 ch-5 sps, ch 6, join with sl st in first sc. Fasten off.

Motif C (joined on three sides)
Rnds 1-5: Repeat rnds 1-5 of Motif A.
Rnd 6: Ch 1, (sc bead, ch 6) in each of first 2 ch-5 sps, (work corner joining, side joining) 2 times, corner joining, (ch 6, sc bead) in each of next 2 ch-5 sps, ch 6, skip next beaded V st, (sc bead, ch 6) in each of next 2 ch-5 sps, (cluster, ch 5, cluster) in next corner ch sp, (ch 6, sc bead) in each of last 2 ch-5 sps, ch 6, join with sl st in first sc. Fasten off.

Half Motif D
Rnd 1: Thread 11 beads onto yarn, pushing beads back along yarn as you work until needed; ch 10, sl st in first ch to form ring, ch 1, 20 sc in ring. *(20 sc made)*
Rnd 2: Ch 1, sc in first 5 sts, ch 8, work loop in first st made, 15 sc in loop just made, sc in next 5 sts of last rnd, ch 8, work loop in fourth st from last st made, 15 sc in loop just made, sl st in each st around, join with sl st in first sc. *(2 15-sc groups)*
Rnd 3: Ch 9, sc in center st of first 15-sc group, ch 9, sc in next space between groups, ch 9, sc in center st of next 15-sc group, ch 9, skip next 7 sts on loop, sc in next worked st, sl st in each sl st around, join with sl st in joining sl st of last rnd. *(4 ch sps)*
Row 4: Working in rows, ch 1, 11 sc in each of first 4 ch sps, sc in next st leaving remaining sts unworked, turn. *(4 11-sc groups)*
Row 5: (Ch 3, pull up bead, ch 1, dc) in first st *(beaded V st made),* ch 5, sc in sixth st of first 11-sc group, ch 5, (dc, ch 5, dc) in first st of next 11-sc group *(corner made),* ch 5, sc in sixth st of same group, ch 5, (dc, pull up bead, ch 1, dc) in first st of next 11-sc group *(beaded V st made),* ch 5, sc in sixth st of same group, ch 5, (dc, ch 5, dc) in first st of next 11-sc group *(corner made),* ch 5, sc in sixth st of same group, ch 5, skip last 5 sts on this group, (dc, pull up bead, ch 1, dc) in next st on rnd 3, turn.
Row 6: Ch 6, sc bead in first ch sp, ch 6, sc bead in next ch sp, ch 6, work corner joining, working across Large Motif, work side joining, corner joining, (work joining, sc bead in next ch sp on this Motif) 2 times, work joining, tr in last dc on this Motif. Fasten off.

Half Motif E
Rnds 1-3: Repeat rnds 1-3 of Half Motif D.
Rows 4-5: Repeat rows 4-5 of Half Motif D.
Row 6: Ch 4, sc in adjacent center ch sp on side of corresponding Large Motif, ch 4, (sc bead in next ch sp on this Motif, work joining) 2 times, corner joining, (ch 6, sc bead) in each of next 4 ch sps, ch 6, (cluster, ch 5, cluster) in next corner ch sp, (ch 6, sc bead) in each of last 2 ch sps, ch 2, tr in last dc. Fasten off.

Half Motif F
Rnds 1-3: Repeat rnds 1-3 of Half Motif D.
Rows 4–5: Repeat rows 4-5 of Half Motif D.
Row 6: Ch 4, sc in adjacent corresponding ch sp on Half Motif, ch 4, (sc bead in next ch sp on this Motif, work joining) 2 times, corner joining, (ch 6, sc bead) in each of next 4 ch sps, ch 6, (cluster, ch 5, cluster) in next corner ch sp, (ch 6, sc bead) in each of last 2 ch sps, ch 2, tr in last dc. Fasten off.

Right Shoulder Seam
Row 1: With right side of right front facing you, join with sc in first corner ch sp, (ch 6, sc in next ch sp) 10 [10, 14] times, turn.
Row 2: Ch 6, sc in first ch sp, (ch 6, sc in next ch sp) 9 [9, 13] times, ch 2, tr in last st, turn.
Row 3: For **medium and large size only;** ch 6, sc in first ch sp, (ch 6, sc in next ch sp) across, turn.
Row 4: For **medium and large size only,** ch 6, sc in first ch sp, (ch 6, sc in next ch sp) across to last ch sp, ch 2, tr in last ch sp, turn.
Rows 5-6: For **large size only;** repeat rows 3-4 of large size.
Row 3 [5, 7]: Ch 1, sc in first ch sp, sc in corresponding ch sp on back, ch 2, sc in next ch sp on this side, (work joining, sc in next ch sp on this side) across, work joining, sc in same ch sp as last sc made on this side. Fasten off.

Left Shoulder Seam
With wrong side of left front facing you, work same as Right Shoulder Seam. Turn right side out.

Sleeves
Rnd 1: With right side facing you, working in sts and ch sps, join with sc in center ch sp at underarm,

evenly space (ch 6, sc) 32 [34, 36] times around, ch 2, join with tr in first sc *(joining ch sp made)*. *(33 ch sps made)* *[35 ch sps, 37 ch sps made]*

Rnds 2-4: (Ch 6, sc in next ch sp) around, ch 2, join with tr in joining tr on last rnd.

Rnds 5-7: (Ch 7, sc in next ch sp) around, ch 3, join with tr in joining tr of last rnd.

Rnd 8: (Ch 8, sc in next ch sp) 2 times, ch 8, sc next 3 ch sps tog, (ch 8, sc in next ch sp) around, ch 3, join with tr in joining tr of last rnd. *(31 ch sps)* *[33 ch sps, 35 ch sps]*

Rnds 9-11: (Ch 8, sc in next ch sp) around, ch 3, join.

Rnd 12: (Ch 8, sc in next ch sp) 3 times, ch 8, sc next 3 ch sps tog, (ch 8, sc in next ch sp) around, ch 3, join. *(29 ch sps)* *[31 ch sps, 33 ch sps]*

Rnds 13-15: (Ch 8, sc in next ch sp) around, ch 3, join.

Rnd 16: (Ch 8, sc in next ch sp) 4 times, ch 8, sc next 3 ch sps tog, (ch 8, sc in next ch sp) around, ch 3, join. *(27 ch sps)* *[29 ch sps, 31 ch sps]*

Rnds 17-19: (Ch 8, sc in next ch sp) around, ch 3, join.

Rnd 20: (Ch 8, sc in next ch sp) 5 times, ch 8, sc next 3 ch sps tog, (ch 8, sc in next ch sp) around, ch 3, join. *(25 ch sps)* *[27 ch sps, 29 ch sps]*

Rnds 21-23: (Ch 8, sc in next ch sp) around, ch 3, join.

Rnd 24: (Ch 8, sc in next ch sp) 6 times, ch 8, sc next 3 ch sps tog, (ch 8, sc in next ch sp) around, ch 3, join. *(23 ch sps)* *[25 ch sps, 27 ch sps]*

Rnds 25-27: (Ch 8, sc in next ch sp) around, ch 3, join.

Rnd 28: (Ch 8, sc in next ch sp) 7 times, ch 8, sc next 3 ch sps tog, (ch 8, sc in next ch sp) around, ch 3, join. *(21 ch sps)* *[23 ch sps, 25 ch sps]*

Rnds 29-31: (Ch 8, sc in next ch sp) around, ch 3, join.

Rnd 32: (Ch 8, sc in next ch sp) 8 times, ch 8, sc next 3 ch sps tog, (ch 8, sc in next ch sp) around, ch 3, join. *(19 ch sps)* *[21 ch sps, 23 ch sps]*

Rnds 33-35: (Ch 8, sc in next ch sp) around, ch 3, join.

Rnd 36: (Ch 8, sc in next ch sp) 9 times, ch 8, sc next 3 sts tog, (ch 8, sc in next ch sp) around, ch 3, join. *(17 ch sps)* *[19 ch sps, 21 ch sps]*

Next Rnds or until pieces measures 17" [18", 18½" long]: (Ch 8, sc) in each ch sp around, ch 2, tr in last ch sp, join.

Next Rnd: (Ch 6, sc) in each ch sp around, join.

Last Rnd: Ch 1, 2 sc in first ch sp, 4 sc in each ch sp around, 2 sc in same ch sp as first 2 sc, join with sl st in first sc. Fasten off.

Repeat Sleeve in other armhole.

Edging

Rnd 1: With right side of work facing you, starting at bottom right front corner ch sp, join with sc in ch sp, *(ch 6, sc in next ch sp) 5 times, ch 6, sc

in next joining at corner; repeat from * 2 [2, 3] more times, (ch 6, sc in next ch sp) 6 times, mark last ch sp made; *work the following steps to complete the rnd:*

A: (Ch 6, sc in next ch sp) 5 times, ch 2, tr in next cluster, tr in next joining, tr in next cluster, ch 2, sc in next ch sp;

B: (Ch 6, sc in next ch sp) 4 times, ch 6, skip next ch sp and next joining, sc in next ch sp;

C: For **medium and large sizes only**, (ch 6, sc in next ch sp) across to joining;

D: For **all sizes**, ch 2, tr in corner joining of back, ch 2, sc in next ch sp;

E: Working across back, (ch 6, sc in next ch sp) across to next joining at other side of Shoulder Seam; repeat step D;

F: For **medium and large sizes only**, repeat step C;

G: For **all sizes**, ch 2, sc in next ch sp, ch 6, skip next joining and next ch sp, sc in next ch sp, (ch 6, sc in next ch sp) 4 times;

H: Ch 2, tr in next cluster, tr in next joining, tr in next cluster, ch 2, sc in next ch sp, (ch 6, sc in next ch sp) 6 times, mark last ch sp;

I: (Ch 6, sc in next ch sp) around, ch 6, join with sl st in first sc.

Rnd 2: Ch 1, 5 sc in each ch-6 sp across to marked ch sp, 5 sc in marked ch sp, remove marker, ch

SMALL

B	D		B	C	C	C	C		F	C
B	C	D	B	C	C	C	C	E	C	C
B	C	C	C	C	C	C	C	C	C	C
B	C	C	C	C	C	C	C	C	C	C
A	B	B	B	B	B	B	B	B	B	B

↑
FIRST ROW

MEDIUM

B	D		F	C	C	C	C	D		F	C
B	C	D	E	C	C	C	C	D	E	C	C
B	C	C	C	C	C	C	C	C	C	C	C
B	C	C	C	C	C	C	C	C	C	C	C
A	B	B	B	B	B	B	B	B	B	B	B

↑
FIRST ROW

LARGE

B	C		F	C	C	C	C	C	D		B	C
B	C	C	E	C	C	C	C	C	D	D	C	C	C
B	C	C	C	C	C	C	C	C	C	C	C	C	C
B	C	C	C	C	C	C	C	C	C	C	C	C	C
B	C	C	C	C	C	C	C	C	C	C	C	C	C
A	B	B	B	B	B	B	B	B	B	B	B	B	B

↑
FIRST ROW

Continued on page 26

Irish Medallion

An Original by Annie

Finished Sizes: Finished corded chain is 26" long. Large Medallion is 3" across; Small Medallion is 2" across; Earring is 1½" across

Materials:
- ❏ 150 yds. size 10 white crochet cotton thread
- ❏ 5" square satin fabric
- ❏ 13" of round cord elastic
- ❏ One 2", two 1½" and two ⅞" covered buttons
- ❏ 2 small round white Velcro® fasteners
- ❏ White hook-and-eye fastener
- ❏ Pair of earring posts or clips
- ❏ Craft glue
- ❏ Sewing thread
- ❏ Beading and sewing needles
- ❏ No. 7 steel hook or hook size needed to obtain gauge

Gauge: We are not responsible for lack of materials due to project not being worked to gauge. Gauge for this pattern: 9 chs = 1".

Basic Stitches: Ch, sl st, sc, hdc, dc, tr, dtr *(see Stitch Guide).*

Laundering Instructions: Remove covered buttons from Medallions. Hand wash in mild detergent and cold water. **Do not** squeeze or wring. To remove excess moisture, wrap in towel and press lightly. To block, shape and pin in place. Let dry completely.

Necklace
Large Medallion
Rnd 1: For **slip ring** *(see illustration),* leaving 4"

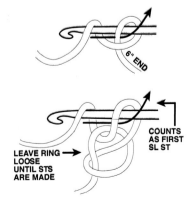

LEAVE RING LOOSE UNTIL STS ARE MADE

COUNTS AS FIRST SL ST

end on thread, lap thread over 4" end forming a loop, insert hook through loop from front to back, yo, pull through loop to form ring, yo, pull through lp on hook; ch 1, 10 sc in ring, pull end tightly to close ring, join with sl st in first sc. *(10 sc made)*

Rnd 2: Ch 1, sc in first st, ch 2, skip next st, (sc in next st, ch 2, skip next st) around, join. *(5 sc, 5 ch sps)*

Rnd 3: For **petals,** (sl st, ch 2, 4 dc, ch 2, sl st) in each ch sp around, **do not join.** *(5 petals)*

Rnd 4: Working behind last rnd in **back bar** *(see illustration)* of sc on rnd 2, (sc in next sc, ch 4) around, join with sl st in first sc. *(5 ch sps)*

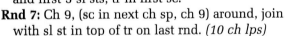

Top of Stitches

Back Bar

Rnd 5: For **petals,** (sc, hdc, 2 dc, 3 tr, 2 dc, hdc, sc) in each ch sp around. *(5 petals)*

Rnd 6: Sl st in first 3 sts on first petal of last rnd, (*sc in next st; for **double picot, ch 3, sl st in third ch from hook, ch 3, sl st in front lp and left bar of last sc made** (see illustration);* ch 5, skip next 3 sts, sc in next st, double picot*, ch 5, skip next 6 sts) 4 times; repeat between **, ending with ch 2, skip last 3 sts and first 3 sl sts, tr in first sc.

Rnd 7: Ch 9, (sc in next ch sp, ch 9) around, join with sl st in top of tr on last rnd. *(10 ch lps)*

Rnd 8: In each ch sp work (3 sc; for **single picot, ch 3, sl st in front lp and left bar of sc made;** 3 sc, single picot, 3 sc, single picot, 3 sc), join with sl st in first sc. Fasten off.

Rnd 9: Working in **back strands of sc** *(see illustration)* on rnd 7, join with sc in any sc, ch 10, (sc, ch 10) in each sc around, join with sl st in first sc. Fasten off.

Small Medallion (make 2)
Rnd 1: Make slip ring, (2 sc; for **picot, ch 5, sc in front lp and left bar of last sc made**) 5 times in ring, pull end tightly to close ring, join with sl st in **back lp** *(see Stitch Guide)* of first sc. *(10 sc made)*

Continued on page 27

Animal Print Accessories

Designed by Ann Parnell

Finished Sizes: Purse is 7" x 11½" x 2". Hat is 3" high x 7½" across. Belt is 2½" wide and fits waist to 26", 36" or 46". Scarf is 5" wide x 36" long.

Materials:

- Worsted yarn:
    - 12 oz. black
    - 9 oz. gold
- ⅓ yd. lining fabric
- 1¼" shank buttons *(optional)*
- 2" belt buckle
- 10½" x 12½" piece plastic canvas
- Bobby pins for markers
- Sewing thread to match lining
- Sewing and tapestry needles
- F, G and I hooks or hook sizes needed to obtain gauges

Gauges: We are not responsible for lack of materials due to project not being worked to gauge. Gauge for this pattern: **G hook,** 4 sc = 1"; 17 rows = 4". **I hook,** 7 sc = 2"; 4 rows = 1".

Basic Stitches: Ch, sl st, sc.

Note: For **color change** *(see Stitch Guide),* drop last color to wrong side of work, pick up again when needed. Always change to next color in last st made.

Purse

Row 1: With G hook and black, ch 43; changing colors according to row 1 of graph, sc in second ch from hook, sc in each ch across, turn. *(42 sc made)*

Rows 2-64: Changing colors according to next row on graph, ch 1, sc in each st across, turn.

Rows 65-66: For **flap,** changing colors according to Flap Graph, beginning with row 65 on graph, ch 1, sc in each st across, turn. Mark each end of row 66.

Rows 67-84: Changing colors according to next row on Glap Graph, ch 1, skip first st, sc in each st across to last 2 sts, sc last 2 sts tog, turn. At end of last row, fasten off gold. *(6)*

Row 85: With black, ch 1, sc in each st across. Fasten off.

Lining

1: Using crochet piece as pattern. allowing ½" on all sides for seams, cut two pieces from fabric; mark edge at row 1; opposite edge at last row is Flap end.

2: Allowing ½" on all sides for seams, sew Lining pieces together around all sides leaving row 1 edge unsewn. Turn right side out. Press.

3: Insert plastic canvas into Lining, fold row 1 end ½" to inside, sew folded edges together catching end of plastic canvas every 2" to prevent slipping. Sew together across other end of plastic canvas, sew again across center of plastic canvas. Lay aside.

Gusset (make 2)

Row 1: with G hook and black, ch 7, mark first ch from hook, sc in next 5 chs, 5 sc in last ch; working on opposite side of starting ch, sc in next 5 chs, sl st in marked ch, ch 8, turn. *(15 sc, 1 sl st, 8 chs made) Do not remove markers until stated.*

Row 2: Mark first ch from hook, sc in next 7 chs, sc in same ch as sl st, sc in next 6 sts, 2 sc in each of next 3 sts, sc in next 6 sts, sc in next sl st; working on opposite side of ch-8, sc in next 7 chs, sl st in marked ch, ch 9, turn. *(35 sts, 9 chs)*

Row 3: Mark first ch from hook, sc in next 7 chs, hdc in next ch, hdc in same ch as sl st, sc in next 14 sts, 2 sc in each of next 6 sts, sc in next 14 sts, hdc in next sl st; working on opposite side of ch-9, hdc in next ch, sc in next 7 chs leaving marked ch unworked. Fasten off. *(58 sts) Front of row 3 is right side of work.*

Remove markers, lay aside.

Edging

Rnd 1: With right side of Purse facing you, working in ends of rows and in sts around entire outer edge, with F hook, join black with sc in end of row 1 at left side, sc in same row, sc in each row across to marked row 66, remover marker, 2 sc in

Continued on page 22

Animal Print Accessories

Continued from page 21

row 66, (evenly space 3 sc over next 2 rows) across to last row, 2 sc in last row; for **buttonhole,** sc in next st, ch 6, skip next 4 sc, sc in next sc; 2 sc in other end of last row, (evenly space 3 sc over next 2 rows) across to marked row 66, remove marker, 2 sc in row 66, sc in each row across to row 1, 3 sc in row 1, sc in each st across row 1, sc in same place as first sc, join with sl st in first sc. *(240 sc, 6 chs made)*

Rnd 2: Ch 1, sc in first 66 sts, 2 sc in next st, sc in next 30 sts, sl st in next 8 sts and chs, sc in next 30 sts, 2 sc in next st, sc in next 9 sts, mark last st made, sc in next 57 sts, sl st in last 44 sts. **Do not fasten off.** *(196 sc, 52 sl sts)*

Assembly

1: To join first Gusset, hold Gusset behind Purse with wrong sides toether, matching sts of last rows on Gusset and Edging; beginning in first st of last row on Gusset and Edging, working through both thicknesses, ch 1, sc in each st around to last st on Gusset. Fasten off. *(58 sc made)*

2: To join second Gusset, joining in first st on Gusset and marked st on Edging and ending at corner of Edging, work same as first Gusset.

3: Insert Lining into Purse, sew row 1 edge in place, sew all edges of flap end in place from row 66 to end; working carefully so sts do not show on front, sew row 66 to Lining.

Crocheted Button (optional)

Rnd 1: With G hook and black, ch 2, 6 sc in second ch from hook, **do not join.** *(6 sc made)*

Rnd 2: 2 sc in each st around. *(12)*

Rnd 3: Sc in each st around.

Rnd 4; (Sc next 2 sts tog) around. Leaving 6" end for weaving, fasten off.

Weave end through each st around, stuff with small amount of yarn, pull end tight, secure, tack through center of rnd 1, pull tight to flatten Button, secure.

Sew purchased button or Crocheted Button to Purse under buttonhole.

Hat
Side

Row 1: With G hook and black, ch 85; changing colors according to row 1 of graph, sc in second ch from hook, sc in next 41 chs, mark last st made; repeating same row of graph, sc in last 42 sts, turn. *(84 sc made)*

Note: When working into marked st, remove mark-

er, work st, mark last st made.

Rows 2-11: Changing colors according to next row on graph as established, ch 1, sc in each st across, turn. At end of last row, fasten off both colors.

Sew ends of rows together.

Rnd 12: For **trim,** with right side of work facing you, with F hook, join MC with sc in first st on row 1 at same time, sc in each st around.

Rnd 13: Sl st in each st around, join with sl st in first sl st. Fasten off.

Crown

Note: *Work in continuous rnds, do not join or turn unless otherwise stated. Mark first st of each rnd.*

Rnd 1: With G hook and black, ch 2, 6 sc in second ch from hook. *(6 sc made)*

Rnd 2: 2 sc in each st around. *(12)*

Rnd 3: (Sc in next st, 2 sc in next st) around. *(18)*

Rnd 4: (Sc in next 2 sts, 2 sc in next st) around. *(24)*

Rnd 5: (2 sc in next st, sc in next 3 sts) around. *(36)*

Rnd 6: (Sc in next 3 sts, 2 sc in next st, sc in next st) around. *(36)*

Rnd 7: (2 sc in next st, sc in next 5 sts) around. *(42)*

Rnd 8: (Sc in next 4 sts, 2 sc in next st, sc in next 2 sts) around. *(48)*

Rnd 9: (Sc in next 7 sts, 2 sc in next st) around. *(54)*

Rnd 10: (Sc in next 3 sts, 2 sc in next st, sc in next 5 sts) around. *(60)*

Rnd 11: (2 sc in next st, sc in next 9 sts) around. *(66)*

Rnd 12: (Sc in next 5 sts, 2 sc in next st, sc in next 5 sts) around. *(72)*

Rnd 13: (Sc in next 2 sts, 2 sc in next st, sc in next 9 sts) around. *(78)*

Rnd 14: (Sc in next 9 sts, 2 sc in next st, sc in next 3 sts) around. *(84)*

Rnd 15: Sc in each st around, join with sl st in first sc.

Rnd 16: For **joining rnd,** remove lp from hook, hold row 11 of Side and rnd 15 of Crown wrong sides together with right side of Side facing you, insert hook in last st on row 11 of Side, return lp to hook, pull lp through, ch 1; working through both thicknesses, matching sts, sc in each st around, join. Fasten off.

Belt

Note: *Instructions are for waist to 26"; changes for waist to 36" and 46" are in [ ].*

Row 1: With G hook and black, ch 127 [169, 211] changing colors according to row 1 of graph, sc in second ch from hook, sc in next 41 chs, (mark last st made; repeat same row of graph, sc in next 42 sts) 2 [3, 4] times, turn. *(126 sc made) [168 sc made, 210 sc made]*

Rows 2-8: Changing colors according to next row on graph as established, ch 1, sc in each st across, turn. At end of last row, **do not turn.** Fasten off gold.

Rnd 9: For **edging**, working in ends of rows and in sts around entire piece, with F hook, join black with sc in end of last row, sc around with 3 sc in each corner.

Rnd 10: Sl st in each st around, join with sl st in first sl st. Fasten off.

Attach buckle.

Scarf

Row 1: With I hook and black, ch 127; changing colors according to row 1 of graph, sc in second ch from hook, sc in next 41 chs, (mark last st made; repeating same row of graph, sc in next 42

sts) 2 times, turn. *(126 sc made)*

Rows 2-8: Changing colors according to next row on graph as established, ch 1, sc in each st across, turn.

Row 9: Changing colors according to next row on graph as established, ch 1, sc in each st across to last 18 sts; for **buttonhole**, ch 3, skip next 3 sts; sc in each st across, turn.

Row 10: Changing colors according to next row on graph as established, ch 1, sc in each st and in each ch across, turn.

Rows 11-17: Changing colors according to next row on graph as established, ch 1, sc in each st across, turn. At end of last row, **do not turn.** Fasten off.

Rnds 18-19: With G hook, repeat rnds 9-10 of Belt.

Sew on purchased or Crocheted Button to front of row 9 on 17th st from end opposite buttonhole. ❧

COLOR CHANGE GRAPH
WORK ROWS 1-32 CONSECUTIVELY

FLAP GRAPH

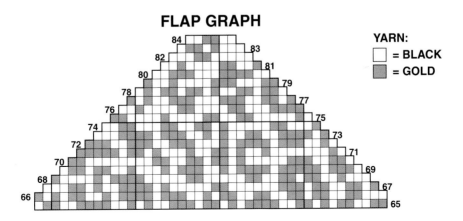

YARN:

☐ = BLACK

▨ = GOLD

Glittery Fringed Scarf

Designed by Suzanne Mitchell

Finished Size: 11" x 47½" without Fringe.

Materials:
- ❑ 335 yds. novelty metallic thread
- ❑ 24 pheasant feathers
- ❑ Tacky glue
- ❑ Large embroidery needle
- ❑ E hook or hook size needed to obtain gauge

Gauge: We are not responsible for lack of materials due to project not being worked to gauge. Gauge for this pattern: 17 tr = 4"; 11 tr rows = 7".

Basic Stitches: Ch, tr.

Scarf
Row 1: Ch 5, 2 tr in fifth ch from hook, turn. *(3 tr made)*
Rows 2-23: (Ch 4, tr) in first st, tr in each st across to last st, 2 tr in last st, turn. At end of last row *(47)*.
Rows 24-52: Ch 4, tr in each st across, turn.
Rows 53-74: Ch 4; **for tr dec, *yo 2 times, insert hook in next st, yo, pull through st, (yo, pull through 2 lps on hook) 2 times; repeat from *, yo, pull through 3 lps on hook;** tr in each st across to last 2 sts, tr dec, turn. At end of last row *(3)*.
Row 75: Ch 3, tr dec. Fasten off.

Feather (make 24)
For each feather, with embroidery needle, punch three holes evenly spaced through center of quill. With needle, leaving 3" ends for tying, weave 10" strand metallic thread through holes *(see illustration #1).* Wrap same thead around quill *(see illustration #2);* dot holes on each side of quill with glue, allow to dry.

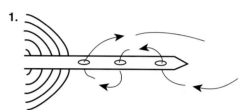

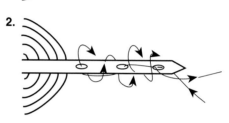

Working in ends of rows on one side of Scarf, starting with third row and working in every following third row, tie ends of thread on one feather through top st at end of row.

Fringe (make 51)
Working on same side of Scarf as feathers, cut two strands metallic thread each 9½" long. With both strands held together, fold in half, insert hook in top of st at end of row 1, pull fold through row, pull ends through fold, tighten. Skipping rows with feathers, Fringe in end of each remaining row across. ❧

1911 Puritan Collar

Continued from page 13

ending with row 25. At end of last row, fasten off.
Row 4: For **second side,** starting at top of ch-65, join with sc in third ch of ch-6, repeat row 4 of first side.
Rows 5-97: Repeat rows 5-97 of first side. At end of last row, **do not turn or fasten off.**

Row 98: Working across neckline in ch-5 sps at ends of rows and in ch sp at end of ch-65, 6 dc in first ch sp, (skip next ch sp, sc in next ch sp, skip next ch sp, 6 dc in next ch sp) across; for **button loop,** ch 10, sl st in same sp. Fasten off. Sew button opposite loop. ❧

Cotton Gloves

Continued from page 9

joining, working on front escl; working on back, escl) 8 times leaving 22 escl unworked on back, mark last sp worked into on back; working on front only, (escl, ch 1) 22 times, escl, hdc in top of ch-2, turn.

Row 30: Ch 2, (escl, ch 1) 22 times, escl, sc in same sp as last st made, sc in side of next escl on seam, sc in next marked sp, remove marker, sc in sp before vertical strand of next escl, mark sp just worked into, **turn;** working into sts just made; for **sc dec, skip first sc, insert hook next sc, yo, pull through st, skip next sc, insert hook in next sc, yo, pull through st, yo, pull through all 3 lps on hook;** mark st just made; escl dec, mark last sp worked into, **turn;** working into sts just made, skip first st, insert hook in next marked st, yo, pull through st, remove marker, insert hook in next marked sp, yo, pull through sp, remove marker, complete as escl, mark st just made, ch 1, (escl, ch 1) 8 times, escl leaving last 12 escl unworked; for **middle finger,** ch 31, turn.

Row 31: Skip first 2 chs, (escl-ch, ch 1) across to last ch, insert hook in last ch, yo, pull through ch, insert hook in sp before vertical bar of first st, yo, pull through sp, complete as escl, ch 1, (escl, ch 1) 7 times, (insert hook in ch-1 sp before next st, yo, pull through sp) 2 times, complete as escl, ch 1, (insert hook in next marked st, yo, pull through st, remover marker) 2 times, complete as escl, ch 1, (escl, ch 1) 20 times, escl, hdc in top of ch-2, turn. *(44 escl)*

Rows 32-35: Repeat row 2.

Row 36-41: Repeat rows 6-11.

Row 42: Ch 2, (escl, ch 1) 28 times, escl leaving remaining sts unworked; for **little finger,** ch 21, turn.

Row 43: Repeat row 7. *(38)*

Joining row: Fold Glove in half with row 1 on top, ch 1, sc in first st on row 1 on top, work side seam joining 38 times across to end of finger; for **end of row joining, working in end of next row on top of Glove, *insert hook in top of row, yo, pull through row, insert hook in bottom of next row, yo, pull through row, (yo, pull through 2 lps on hook) 2 times*; working in end of next row on bottom of Glove; repeat between **;** repeat end of row joining; working side seam joining in sts and working end row joining 2 times across tip of each finger, join front and back tog across to tip of index finger. Fasten off.

Cuff

Rnd 1: With right side of work facing you, join with sl st in end of last row before side seam, ch 2; working in sps on each side of seam, escl, ch 1; working in sps on each side of ends of rows, escl, ch 1, *skip next row, (escl around next row, ch 1) 2 times; repeat from * around, join with sl st in top of ch-2, **turn.** *(34 escl made)*

Rnds 2-3: Ch 2, (escl, ch 1) around, join. At end of last rnd, fasten off.

Left Glove

Rows 1-47: Repeat rows 1-47 of Right Glove.

Joining row: Turn thumb inside out; fold Glove in half with row 1 on bottom, complete same as joining row on Right Glove.

Cuff

Work same as Right Glove Cuff. ♣

Nighttime Sky Vest

Continued from page 17

8, drop lp from hook, insert hook in fourth st from last st made, 15 sc in loop just made *(buttonhole made),* (5 sc in each ch-6 sp, 2 sc in each ch-2 sp across with sc in center tr of each 3-tr group) across to next marked ch sp; *work the following steps to complete the rnd:*

A: 5 sc in marked ch sp, **turn,** remove marker;

B: Ch 1, skip first st, sc in next 4 sts, **turn.**

C: Ch 1, skip first st, sc in next 3 sts, ch 1, sl st in skipped st of 5-sc group *(button tab completed);* 5 sc in each ch sp around, join. Fasten off.

Sew button to button tab. ♣

Irish Medallion

Continued from page 19

Rnd 2: Working in **back lps**, sc in first st, (ch 3, skip picot and next st, sc in next st) 4 times, ch 3, join. *(5 ch sps)*

Rnd 3: For **petals**, (sl st, ch 2, 4 dc, ch 2, sl st) in each ch sp around.

Rnd 4: Ch 2, **working behind petal** *(see illustration)*, sc around ch sp of rnd 3 between 2 center dc, single picot, (ch 3, sc around ch sp between 2 center dc on next petal, single picot) 4 times, ch 1, dtr in first sc.

Rnd 5: (Sc, ch 4, sc) around post of dtr, *(ch 4, sc, ch 4, sc) in next ch sp; repeat from * 3 more times, ch 4, join with sl st in first sc.

Rnd 6: (3 sc, single picot, 3 sc) in each ch sp around, join.

Rnd 7: Ch 5, (sc, ch 5) in **back strand** of each sc on rnd 5, join with sl st in first ch of ch-5. Fasten off.

First Leaf

Row 1: Ch 25, 4 tr in fifth ch from hook, turn. *(5 tr made)*

Row 2: Ch 3, dc next 2 sts tog, dc in next st leaving last st unworked, turn. *(3 dc)*

Row 3: Ch 3, sc in third ch from hook, skip first st, dc in next st leaving last st unworked, **do not turn**; working down side of Leaf, ch 2, sl st in base of st at end of row 2, ch 4, sl st in same ch as 4 tr on row 1, sl st in each ch across. Fasten off.

Second Leaf

With ch 30, work same as First Leaf.

Third Leaf

With ch 35, work same as First Leaf.

Fourth Leaf

With ch 40, work same as First Leaf.

Chains

Ch 2, sc in second ch from hook; turn last st made to left *(so the back of the sc is facing you)*; sc in strand on left side of st *(see illustration No. 1)*;

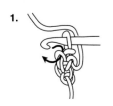

*turn last st made to left; sc in parallel strands on left side of st *(see illustration No. 2)*; repeat from * until chain measures 26". Fasten off. Make two more chains each 3½" long.

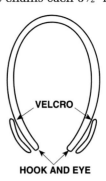

VELCRO

HOOK AND EYE

Assembly

Cover 2" and 1⅛" buttons with satin.

Cut 4" piece elastic. Place Large Medallion over 2" button. Weave elastic through ch sps of last rnd. Draw up, being careful not to stretch elastic. Tie or sew ends of elastic tog. Trim ends if necessary. *(The elastic makes the button removable for changing colors and when cleaning.)* Cut two 3" pieces elastic. Repeat with two Small Medallions.

Glue one side of one Velcro fastener to back of each 1⅛" button.

Tack edges at one end of each 3½" Chain to edge at each end of 26" Chain *(see illustration)*. Tack edge at opposite end of each 3½" Chain to edge of 26" Chain 3¼" from end.

Sew other side of Velcro fasteners to chains according to illustration. Sew hook-and-eye to ends of Chain.

Weave ends of Chains through elastic and ch sps on back of each Small Medallion. Attach to Velcro on Chains. Weave one end of Chains through ch sps on back of Large Medallion *(see illustration)*. Join ends with hook-and-eye.

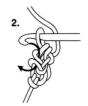

Hold ends of all Leaves together. With separate strand crochet cotton, tie around all ends.

Continued on page 28

Irish Medallion

Continued from page 27

Secure ends. Sew tied ends to back at center bottom of Large Medallion.

Earring (make 2)
Medallion
Rnd 1: Ch 2, 5 sc in second ch from hook, **do not join.** *(5 sc made)*
Rnd 2: (Sc, ch 3) in each st around, join with sl st in first sc. *(5 sc, 5 ch sps)*
Rnd 3: Sl st in next ch, sc in first ch sp, ch 4, (sc in next ch sp, ch 4) around, join.
Rnd 4: Sl st in next ch, sc in first ch sp, ch 5, (sc in next ch sp, ch 5) around, join.
Rnd 5: (3 sc, single picot, 3 sc) in each ch sp around, join.
Rnd 6: Ch 4, (sc, ch 5) in **back strand** of each sc on rnd 4, join with sl st in first ch of ch-4. Fasten off.

Flower
Rnd 1: Ch 2, 5 sc in second ch from hook, **do not join.** *(5 sc made)*
Rnd 2: (Sl st, ch 2, 2 dc, ch 3, sl st) in each st around. Fasten off.
Sew center of Flower to center front of Medallion.

Assembly
Cover ⅞" button with satin.
Cut 3" piece elastic. Place Medallion over button. Weave cord elastic and attach same as Necklace.
Glue back of button to earring post. 🐾

Shoulder Wrap

Continued from page 6

around, join with sl st in first sc, **turn.** *(270 ch-1 sps, 135 V sts)*
Rnd 34: Sl st across to center of first V st, (ch 4, dc) in same sp, (ch 1, V st in next V st) 76 times, *(ch 1, dc) 3 times in each of next 2 V sts, (ch 1, dc) 4 times in next V st*, (ch 1, dc) 3 times in each of next 2 V sts, (ch 1, V st in next V st) 49 times; repeat between **, (ch 1, dc) 3 times in next V st, (ch 1, dc) in same V st as ch-4, ch 1, join with sl st in third ch of ch-4, **turn.** *(157 ch-1 sps, 125 V sts)*
Rnd 35: Repeat rnd 34. Fasten off. 🐾

Special Touches

CHAPTER TWO

Irish Bouquet

An Original by Annie

Finished Size: Bouquet is 5½" long; Rose is 1½" across; Posy is ¾" across.

Materials:
- ❑ 60 yds. white size 10 crochet cotton thread
- ❑ Piece 2 x 12-holes 7-mesh plastic canvas
- ❑ 3"-long hair bow clip or comb
- ❑ White covered floral wire
- ❑ White quilting thread
- ❑ Spray starch
- ❑ Rustproof straight pins
- ❑ Tapestry and sewing needles
- ❑ No. 7 steel hook or hook size needed to obtain gauge

Gauge: We are not responsible for lack of materials due to project not being worked to gauge. Gauge for this pattern: 9 sc = 1"; 10 sc rows = 1"; 9 dc = 1"; 4 dc rows = 1".

Basic Stitches: Ch, sl st, sc, hdc, dc, tr.

Laundering Instructions: Remove any metal parts or wires before washing. Hand wash in mild detergent and cold water. Do not squeeze or wring. To remove excess moisture, wrap in towel and press lightly with towel. Arrange and shape on clean flat surface. Let dry completely. Replace metal parts or wires when dry.

Blocking Instructions: To block, apply starch until item is damp. Using rust proof straight pins, shape and pin in place on padded surface. Let dry completely.

Base

Row 1: Ch 20, dc in fourth ch from hook, dc in each ch across, turn. *(18 dc made)*
Row 2: Ch 3, dc in each st across, turn.
Row 3: Working in **back lps** *(see Stitch Guide)*, ch 3, dc in each st across, turn.
Row 4: Ch 3, dc in each st across. **Do not fasten off.**
Fold crocheted piece in half lengthwise around plastic canvas piece, matching opposite side of starting ch and **back lps** of sts on row 4; working through both thicknesses, sl st in each st across. Fasten off. Sew open ends of Base closed.

Rose

Rnd 1: For **slip ring** *(see Stitch Guide)*, leaving 4" end on thread, lap thread over 4" end forming a loop, insert hook through loop from front to back, yo, pull through loop to form ring, yo, pull through lp on hook; ch 3, 9 dc in ring, pull end tightly to close ring, join with sl st in top of ch-3. *(10 dc made)*
Rnd 2: Ch 1, sc in first st, sc in each st around, join with sl st in first sc.
Rnd 3: Ch 3, skip next st, (sc in next st, ch 2, skip next st) around, sc in joining sl st of rnd 2. *(5 ch sps)*
Rnd 4: For **petals**, (sl st, ch 2, 4 dc, ch 2, sl st) in each ch sp around. *(5 petals)*
Rnd 5: Working behind petals, ch 1, (sc in **back lp** of next skipped sc on rnd 2, ch 4) around, join with sl st in first sc. *(5 ch sps)*
Rnd 6: (Sl st, ch 2, 7 dc, ch 2, sl st) in each ch sp around. *(5 petals)*
Rnd 7: Working behind petals, ch 2, *sc around ch sp between center 2 dc on next petal *(see illustration)*, ch 5; repeat from * around, join with sl st in first sc. *(5 ch sps)*

Rnd 8: (Sl st, ch 2, 10 dc, ch 2, sl st) in each ch sp around. Fasten off.

Posy (make 3)

Rnd 1: Ch 4, sl st in first ch to form ring, ch 4, 11 tr in ring, join with sl st in top of ch-4. *(12 tr made)*
Rnd 2: Ch 1, sc in first st, skip next st, (sc in next st, skip next st) 5 times, join with sl st in first sc. *(6 sc)*
Rnd 3: (Sl st, ch 2, 4 dc, ch 2, sl st) in each st around. Fasten off.

Leaf Spray (make 3)

Beginning at bottom of stem, ch 16, **do not fasten off.**
Row 1: For **first leaf**, 6 tr in fifth ch from hook, turn. *(7 tr made)*
Row 2: Ch 3, (dc next 2 sts tog) 2 times, dc in next st leaving last st unworked, turn. *(4 dc)*
Row 3: Ch 1, skip first st, sc next 2 sts tog leaving last st unworked, **do not turn;** for **tip of leaf,** ch 3, sc in third ch from hook; working down side

Continued on page 56

Flower Fall

An Original by Annie

Finished Size: Arrangement is 8½" long; Small Leaf is 1½" long; Medium Leaf is 2" long; Violet is ¾" across.

Materials:
- ❏ 90 yds. white size 10 crochet cotton thread
- ❏ Piece 2 x 12-holes 7-mesh plastic canvas
- ❏ 2"-long hair bow clip or comb
- ❏ 17 white 5mm pearl beads
- ❏ White quilting thread
- ❏ Tapestry and sewing needles
- ❏ No. 7 steel hook or hook size needed to obtain gauge

Gauge: We are not responsible for lack of materials due to project not being worked to gauge. Gauge for this pattern: 9 sc = 1"; 10 sc rows = 1"; 9 dc = 1"; 4 dc rows = 1".

Basic Stitches: Ch, sl st, sc, hdc, dc, tr.

Laundering Instructions: Remove any metal parts or wires before washing. Hand wash in mild detergent and cold water. Do not squeeze or wring. To remove excess moisture, wrap in towel and press lightly with towel. Arrange and shape on clean flat surface. Let dry completely. Replace metal parts or wires when dry.

Base
Rnd 1: Ch 20, dc in fourth ch from hook, dc in each ch across, turn. *(18 dc made)*
Row 2: Ch 3, dc in each st across, turn.
Row 3: Working in **back lps** *(see Stitch Guide)*, ch 3, dc in each st across, turn.
Row 4: Ch 3, dc in each st across. **Do not fasten off.**
Fold crocheted piece in half lengthwise around plastic canvas piece, matching opposite side of starting ch and **back lps** of sts on row 4; working through both thicknesses, sl st in each st across. Fasten off. Sew open ends of Base closed.

Violet (make 17)
Row 1: Ch 2, 5 sc in second ch from hook, **do not join.** *(5 sc made)*
Rnd 2: (Sl st, ch 2, 2 dc, ch 2, sl st) in each st around. Fasten off.

Small Leaf (make 2)
Row 1: Ch 12, sc in third ch from hook, sc in each ch across to last ch; for **base,** 3 sc in last ch; working on opposite side of ch-12, sc in each ch across leaving last 3 chs unworked, turn. *(20 sc made)*
Rows 2-4: Ch 1, skip first st, sc in each st across to center st of base, 3 sc in center st, sc in each st across leaving last 3 sts unworked, turn. At end of last row, fasten off. *(14)*

Medium Leaf (make 7)
Row 1: With ch 15, repeat row 1 of Small Leaf. *(26 sc made)*
Rows 2-6: Repeat row 2 of Small Leaf. At end of last row, fasten off. *(16)*
Sew Leaves to Base according to illustration.

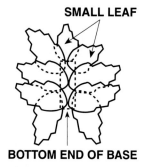

SMALL LEAF

BOTTOM END OF BASE

First Vine
Row 1: Ch 20, 4 tr in fifth ch from hook, turn. *(5 tr made)*
Row 2: Ch 3, dc next 2 sts tog, dc in next st leaving last st unworked, turn. *(3 dc)*
Row 3: Ch 3, sc in third ch from hook, skip first st, sc in next st leaving last st unworked, **do not turn;** working down side of leaf, ch 2, sl st in basde of st at end of row 2, ch 4, sl st in same ch as 4 tr on row 1, sl st in each ch across. Fasten off.

Second Vine
With ch 25, work same as First Vine.

Third Vine
With ch 30, work same as First Vine.

Continued on page 40

Hangers & Sachets

Designed by Dot Drake

Floral Hanger
Finished Size: Fits 16" garment hanger. Flower is 3" across.

Materials:
- ❏ Size 10 crochet cotton thread:
    - 225 yds. yellow
    - Small amount pink
- ❏ 16" padded garment hanger with bow
- ❏ 9 pearl 4mm beads
- ❏ White sewing thread
- ❏ Tapestry and sewing needles
- ❏ No. 8 steel hook or hook size needed to obtain gauge

Gauge: We are not responsible for lack of materials due to project not being worked to gauge. Gauge for this pattern: 4 dc = ½"; 7 rows = 2".

Basic Stitches: Ch, sl st, sc, hdc, dc.

Sleeve (make 2)
Note: Back of sts is right side of work.

Rnd 1: With yellow, ch 6, sl st in first ch to form ring, ch 4, (dc in ring, ch 1) 9 times, join with sl st in third ch of ch-4. *(10 dc made)*

Rnd 2: Sl st in first ch sp, ch 5, (dc in next ch sp, ch 2) around, join with sl st in third ch of ch-5.

Rnd 3: Ch 3, dc in next ch sp; for **picot, ch 3, sl st in top of last st made;** dc in same ch sp, dc in next st, ch 2, *dc in next st, (dc, picot, dc) in next ch sp, dc in next st, ch 2; repeat from * around, join with sl st in top of ch-3.

Rnd 4: Ch 6, *[skip next 2 sts and next picot, dc in next st, (dc, picot, dc) in next ch sp], dc in next st, ch 2; repeat from * 3 more times; repeat between [ ], join.

Rnd 5: Ch 3, *(dc, picot, dc) in next ch sp, dc in next st, ch 2, skip next 2 sts and next picot, dc in next st; repeat from * 3 more times, (dc, picot, dc) in next ch sp, dc in next st, ch 2, skip next 2 sts and next picot, join.

Rnds 6-27: Or as many rnds as it takes to fit the Sleeve over one end of hanger to center; repeat rnds 4 and 5 alternately. At end of last rnd, fasten off.

Place Sleeves on hanger, sew picots together at center.

Flower
Rnd 1: With pink, ch 5, sl st in first ch to form ring, ch 1, 10 sc in ring, join with sl st in first sc. *(10 sc made)*

Rnd 2: Ch 1, 2 sc in each st around, join. Fasten off. *(20)*

Rnd 3: Join yellow with sc in first st, sc in next 3 sts, ch 10, (sc in next 4 sts, ch 10) around, join. *(5 ch-10 lps)*

Rnd 4: *Sl st in second and third sts of 4-sc group; for **petals,** (3 sc, hdc, 13 dc, hdc, 3 sc) in each ch-10 lp around, join.

Rnd 5: *Sl st in first 2 sc on petal, sc in next sc, ch 3, skip next hdc, dc in next dc, (ch 1, skip next dc, dc in next dc) 3 times, ch 3, dc in same st, (ch 1, skip next dc, dc in next dc) 3 times, ch 3, skip next hdc, sc in next sc, sl st in next 2 sc; skipping sl st between petals, repeat from * around, join with sl st in first sl st on first petal. Fasten off.

Rnd 6: Join pink with sc in first sl st in on any petal, *[sc in next sl st, sc in next sc, 3 sc in first ch-3 sp on petal, (sc in next dc, 2 sc in next ch-1 sp) 3 times, sc in next dc, (2 sc, picot, 2 sc) in next ch-3 sp, (sc in next dc, 2 sc in next ch-1 sp) 3 times, sc in next dc, 3 sc in next ch-3 sp, sc in next sc, sc in next 2 sl sts], sc in first sl st on next petal; repeat from * 3 more times; repeat between [ ], join with sl st in first sc. Fasten off.

Glue beads in a circle around center of Flower.

Sew or glue back of Flower to center front of hanger.

Floral Sachet
Finished Size: 3¾" across.

Materials:
- ❏ Size 10 crochet cotton thread:
    - 40 yds. lavender
    - Small amount each yellow and pink
- ❏ 9 pearl 4mm beads
- ❏ Two 3½" squares tulle
- ❏ Small amount potpourri
- ❏ White sewing thread
- ❏ Tapestry and sewing needles
- ❏ No. 8 steel hook or hook size needed to obtain gauge

Continued on page 36

Hangers & Sachets

Continued from page 35

Gauge: We are not responsible for lack of materials due to project not being worked to gauge. Gauge for this pattern: 2 shells and 1 ch-2 sp = 1"; 5 rows = 1½".

Basic Stitches: Ch, sl st, sc, hdc, dc.

Flower
Reversing colors, work same as Floral Hanger Flower.

Back
Note: Back of sts is right side of work.

Rnd 1: With lavender, ch 7, join with sl st in first ch to form ring, ch 3, 3 dc in ring, (ch 3, 4 dc in ring) 3 times, ch 1, join with dc in top of ch-3 *(joining ch sp made). (16 dc, 4 ch sps made)*

Rnd 2: (Ch 3, 3 dc) in joining ch sp, *ch 2, (4 dc, ch 3, 4 dc) in next ch sp; repeat from * 2 more times, ch 2, 4 dc in same ch sp as first ch-3, ch 1, join with dc in top of ch-3.

Rnd 3: (Ch 3, 3 dc) in joining ch sp, *ch 2; for **shell, 4 dc in next ch sp, ch 2;** for **corner, (4 dc, ch 3, 4 dc) in next ch sp;** repeat from * 2 more times, ch 2, shell, 4 dc in same sp as first ch-3, ch 1, join with dc in top of ch-3.

Rnds 4-6: (Ch 3, 3 dc) in joining ch sp, (ch 2, shell across to next corner, corner) 3 times, ch 2, shell across, 4 dc in same sp as first ch-3, ch 1, join with dc in top of ch-3. At end of last rnd, fasten off.

Front
Rnd 1: With lavender, ch 6, sl st in first ch to form ring, ch 3, 3 dc in ring, *ch 2, 4 dc in ring, ch 2, (4 dc, ch 3, 4 dc) in ring; repeat from * 2 more times, (ch 2, 4 dc in ring) 2 times, ch 1, join with dc in top of first ch-3 *(joining ch sp made).*

Rnd 2: (Ch 3, 3 dc) in joining ch sp, (ch 2, shell 2 times, corner) 3 times, ch 2, shell 2 times, 4 dc in same ch sp as first ch-3, ch 1, join with dc in top of first ch-3.

Rnds 3-4: Repeat rnd 4 of Back. At end of last rnd, fasten off.

Sew all sides of tulle squares together stuffing with potpourri before closing.

Trim
Place potpourri square inside crochet squares and work Trim through both thicknesses.

Join pink with sc in first ch-2 sp after corner on any side, sc in same ch sp, *(sc in next 2 sts, picot, sc in next 2 sts, 2 sc in ch-2 sp) across side to corner, sc in next 2 sts, picot, sc in next 2 sts, 2 sc in corner ch sp, ch 5, sl st in second ch from hook, ch 1, dc in last sc made, (ch 5, sl st in second ch from hook, ch 1, dc in last dc made) 2 times, 2 sc in same corner ch sp; repeat from * 3 more times, sc in next 2 sts, picot, sc in next 2 sts, join with sl st in first sc. Fasten off.

Sew or glue Flower to center Front of Sachet.

Rose Hanger & Sachet
Finished Size: Fits 16" garment hanger. Large Rose is 2" across.

Materials:
- ❑ Size 10 crochet cotton thread:
    265 yds. white
    Small amount each green, yellow, lt. pink and dk. pink
- ❑ 16" padded garment hanger with bow
- ❑ Two 3½" squares tulle
- ❑ Small amount potpourri
- ❑ White sewing thread
- ❑ Tapestry and sewing needles
- ❑ No. 8 steel hook or hook needed to obtain gauge

Gauge: We are not responsible for lack of materials due to project not being worked to gauge. Gauge for this pattern: 1 shell = ¾"; 3 shell rows = 1¼".

Basic Stitches: Ch, sl st, sc, hdc, dc, tr.

Special Stitches: For **beginning shell (beg shell),** ch 5, tr in ch sp indicated in instructions, (ch 1, tr) 3 times in same ch sp.

For **shell,** (tr, ch 1) 4 times in third ch of next ch-5 sp, tr in same ch.

For **picot,** ch 3, sl st in top of last st made.

Sleeve (make 2)
Rnd 1: With white, ch 8, sl st in first ch to form ring, ch 3, (sc in ring, ch 3) 7 times, join with sl st in first ch of first ch-3. *(8 ch sps made)*

Rnd 2: Sl st in first ch sp, (ch 5, sc in next ch sp) around, ch 2, join with dc in first ch of first ch-5 *(joining ch sp made).*

Rnd 3: (Ch 5, sc in next ch sp) around, ch 2, join with dc in first ch of first ch-5

Rnd 4: Beg shell *(see Special Stitches)* in joining ch sp, (ch 2, sc in next ch sp, **shell**—see *Special Stitches)* 3 times, ch 2, sc in next ch sp, ch 2, join with sl st in fourth ch of ch-5. *(4 shells)*

Back of rnd 4 is right side of work.

Rnd 5: Sl st to third tr of beg shell, (ch 2, shell in next sc, ch 2, sc in third tr of next shell) 3 times, ch 2, shell in next sc, ch 2, join with sl st in same sl st as first ch-2.

Rnd 6: Beg shell, (ch 2, sc in third tr of next shell, ch 2, shell in next sc) 3 times, ch 2, sc in third tr of next shell, ch 2, join with sl st in fourth ch of ch-5.

Repeat rnds 5 and 6 until Sleeve fits one end of hanger. Fasten off.

Make second Sleeve. Place Sleeves on hanger and sew together in center.

Large Rose

Rnd 1: With yellow, ch 2, 6 sc in second ch from hook, **do not join unless otherwise stated.** *(6 sc made)*

Rnd 2: 2 sc in each st around. *(12)*

Rnds 3-4: Sc in each st around. At end of last rnd, join with sl st in first sc. Fasten off.

Rnd 5: Join lt. pink with sc in any st, ch 3, skip next st, (sc in next st, ch 3, skip next st) around, join, **turn.** *(6 ch sps)*

Rnd 6: For petals, (sc, ch 1, 5 dc, ch 1, sc) in each ch sp around, **do not join.** *(6 petals)*

Rnd 7: Ch 3, (sc around ch sp between center 2 dc on next petal, ch 3) around, join with sl st in first ch of first ch-3.

Rnd 8: For petals, (sc, ch 1, dc, 3 tr, dc, ch 1, sc) in each ch sp around, **do not join.**

Rnd 9: Repeat rnd 7. Fasten off.

Rnd 10: For petals, join dk. pink with sc in any ch sp, (ch 1, dc, 3 tr, dc, ch 1, sc) in same ch sp, (sc, ch 1, dc, 3 tr, dc, ch 1, sc) in each ch sp around, **do not join.**

Rnd 11: Ch 4, (sc around ch sp between center 2 dc on next petal, ch 4) around, join with sl st in first ch of first ch-4.

Rnd 12: For petals, (sc, ch 2, dc, 8 tr, dc, ch 2, sc) in each ch sp around, join with sl st in first sc. Fasten off.

Rnd 13: Join lt. pink with sc between any 2 petals, sc in next ch-2 sp, sc in next 5 sts, picot *(see Special Stitches)*, sc in next 5 sts, sc in next ch-2 sp, (sc between petals, sc in next ch-2 sp, sc in next 5 sts, picot, sc in next 5 sts, sc in next ch-2 sp) around, join. Fasten off.

Rnd 14: Join green with sl st around ch sp between center 2 dc on any petal, ch 6, (sl st around ch sp between center 2 dc on next petal, ch 6) around, join with sl st in first ch of first ch-6.

Rnd 15: For petals, (sc, hdc, 2 dc, 4 tr, picot, 4 tr, 2 dc, hdc, sc) in each ch sp around, join. Fasten off.

Small Rose (make 2)

Rnd 1: With yellow, ch 2, 5 sc in second ch from hook, join with sl st in first sc. *(5 sc made)*

Rnd 2: For petals, (sc, hdc, dc, hdc, sc) in each

st around, **do not join.**

Rnd 3: Ch 3, (sl st in **back strands of dc on next petal**—*see illustration*, ch 3) around, join with sl st in first ch of first ch-3. Fasten off.

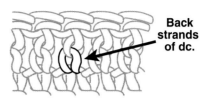

Back strands of dc.

Rnd 4: Join dk. pink with sc in any ch sp, (hdc, 5 dc, hdc, sc) in same ch sp, (sc, hdc, 5 dc, hdc, sc) in each ch sp around, **do not join.**

Rnd 5: Ch 4, (sc around ch sp between center 2 dc on next petal, ch 4) around, join with sl st in first ch of first ch-4. Fasten off.

Rnd 6: Join green with sc in any ch sp, 3 sc in same ch sp, *sc, hdc, dc, 2 tr, 2 **dtr**—*see Stitch Guide*, picot, 5 sc around last dtr made, sc) in next ch sp*, 4 sc in next ch sp; repeat between ** 2 times, join with sl st in first sc. Fasten off.

Glue all Roses to front of hanger as shown in photo.

Sachet

With white and dk. pink, work same as Flower Sachet. Make one Large Rose same as for Hanger. Sew to center Front of Sachet.

Violets Hanger & Sachet

Finished Sizes: Fits 16" garment hanger. Sachet is 3½" across.

Materials:
❑ Size 10 crochet cotton thread:
    225 yds. white
    Small amount each pink and purple
❑ 16" padded garment hanger with bow
❑ 9 pearl 4mm beads
❑ 5" square pink tulle
❑ Small amount potpourri
❑ Pink and white sewing thread
❑ Tapestry and sewing needles
❑ No. 8 steel hook or hook size needed to obtain gauge

Gauge: We are not responsible for lack of materials due to project not being worked to gauge. Gauge for this pattern: 1 shell = $\frac{1}{2}$"; 3 shell rows = 1".

Basic Stitches: Ch, sl st, sc, hdc, dc, tr.

Special Stitches: For **shell**, (2 dc, ch 3, 2 dc) in next ch sp.

Continued on page 38

Hangers & Sachets

Continued from page 37

For **picot,** ch 3, sl st in top of last st made.

Sleeve (make 2)
Rnd 1: With white, ch 8, sl st in first ch to form ring, ch 3, (sc in ring, ch 3) 7 times, join with sl st in first ch of ch-3. *(8 ch sps made)*

Rnd 2: Sl st in first ch sp, (ch 5, sc in next ch sp) around, ch 2, join with dc in first ch of first ch-5 *(joining ch sp made).*

Rnd 3: (Ch 5, sc in next ch sp) around, ch 2, join with dc in first ch of first ch-5.

Rnd 4: (Ch 3, dc, ch 3, 2 dc) in joining ch sp, **shell** *(see Special Stitches)* in each ch sp around, join with sl st in top of ch-3.

Rnd 5: Sl st in next st, (sl st, ch 3, dc, ch 3, 2 dc) in first ch sp, shell in each ch sp around, join.

Next rnds: Repeat rnd 5 until Sleeve fits one end of hanger. At end of last row, fasten off.

Place Sleeves on hanger and sew together in center.

Sachet
Violet
Rnd 1: With white, ch 2, 5 sc in second ch from hook, join with sl st in first sc. *(5 sc made)*

Rnd 2: For **petals,** (sc, hdc, dc, hdc, sc) in each st around, **do not join.** *(5 petals)*

Rnd 3: Ch 3, (sl st in **back strands** of first sc on next petal, ch 3) around, join with sl st in first ch of first ch-3.

Rnd 4: For **petals,** (sc, hdc, 3 dc, hdc, sc) in each ch sp around, **do not join.**

Rnd 5: Ch 4, (sc around ch sp between center 2 dc on next petal, ch 4) around, join with sl st in first ch of first ch-4.

Rnd 6: For **petals,** (sc, ch 1, dc, 5 tr, dc, ch 1, sc) in each ch sp around, join with sl st in first sc. Fasten off.

Rnd 7: Join pink with sc between any 2 petals, sc in next ch sp, sc in next 4 sts, **picot** *(see Special Stitches),* sc in next 3 sts, sc in next ch sp, (sc between petals, sc in next ch sp, sc in next 4 sts, picot, sc in next 3 sts, sc in next ch sp) around, join. Fasten off.

Sew three pearl beads to center of Violet.

Reversing colors, make two more Violets.

Cut one circle 4" diameter from tulle. Place potpourri in center and gather edge with thread to close into small pouch.

Sachet Holder
Rnd 1: With purple, ch 10, sl st in first ch to form ring, ch 12, (**dtr**—*see Stitch Guide*—in ring, ch 7) 6 times, join with sl st in fifth ch of ch-12. *(7 ch sps made)*

Rnd 2: Ch 1, 12 sc in each ch sp around, join with sl st in first sc. Fasten off. *(84 sc)*

Repeat rnds 1-2, **do not fasten off.**

Rnd 3: Place Holders together, working through both thicknesses in **back lps** *(see Stitch Guide)* on front piece and **both lps** on back piece, sc in each st halfway around, place potpourri pouch inside, sc in each st around, join.

Rnd 4: Ch 1, sc in first st, hdc in next st, dc in next st, tr in next st, 2 dtr in next st, dtr in next st, picot, 5 sc around post of dtr just made, (sc in next st, hdc in next st, dc in next st, tr in next st, 2 dtr in next st, dtr in next st, picot, 5 sc around post of dtr just made) around, join.

For **handle,** (ch 3, hdc in third ch from hook) 10 times, join with sl st at base of first ch-3. Fasten off.

Glue Violets over front of Sachet and place handle on hanger hook. ❧

Shell-Edged Purse

Designed by Catherine Peiter

Finished Size: 5½" across.

Materials:
- ❑ 280 yds. white size 10 crochet cotton thread
- ❑ 7" x 14" white satin fabric
- ❑ 1½ yds. white ¼" satin ribbon
- ❑ White sewing thread and needle
- ❑ No. 10 steel hook or hook size needed to obtain gauge

Gauge: We are not responsible for lack of materials due to project not being worked to gauge. Gauge for this pattern: Rnds 1-2 = 1¼" across.

Basic Stitches: Ch, sl st, sc, dc, tr.

Special Stitches: For **shell,** (3 tr, ch 1, 3 tr) in indicated ch sp.
For **picot,** ch 3, sl st in front lp and left bar of same st as ch-3 *(see illustration)*.

Side (make 2)
Rnd 1: Ch 7, sl st in first ch to form ring, ch 4, 23 tr in ring, join with sl st in top of ch-4. *(24 tr made)*

Note: *Work in continuous rnds; do not join or turn unless otherwise stated. Mark first st of each rnd.*

Rnd 2: Ch 2, 2 tr in sp between first 2 sts, (ch 1, skip next 2 sts, 3 tr in next sp between sts) 8 times, ch 4, skip next st, (sc in next st, ch 4, skip next st) 3 times, sc in same st as first ch-2, ch 4. *(27 tr, 5 ch-4 sps)*

Rnd 3: **Shell** *(see Special Stitches)* in next ch-1 sp, (ch 3, shell in next ch-1 sp) 7 times, ch 4, (sc in next ch-4 sp, ch 4) 5 times. *(8 shells, 6 ch-4 sps)*

Rnd 4: (Shell in ch sp of next shell, ch 5) 7 times, shell in ch sp of next shell, ch 4, (sc in next ch-4 sp, ch 4) 6 times. *(8 shells, 7 ch sps)*

Rnd 5: (Shell in next shell, ch 6) 7 times, shell in ch sp of next shell, ch 4, (sc in next ch-4 sp, ch 4) 7 times. *(8 shells, 8 ch sps)*

Rnd 6: (Shell in next shell, ch 7) 7 times, shell in

Continued on page 40

Shell-Edged Purse

Continued from page 39

ch sp of next shell, ch 4, (sc in next ch-4 sp, ch 4) 8 times. *(8 shells, 9 ch sps)*

Rnd 7: (Shell in next shell, ch 8) 7 times, shell in ch sp of next shell, ch 4, (sc in next ch-4 sp, ch 4) 9 times. *(8 shells, 10 ch sps)*

Rnd 8: Sc in next shell, (ch 6; for **long dc**, working around ch sps of rnds 3-7, dc in next ch-3 sp on rnd 3; ch 6, sc in next shell) 7 times, ch 4, skip next 2 dc, sc in next dc, ch 4, (sc in next ch-4 sp, ch 4) 9 times leaving last ch sp unworked. *(14 ch-6 sps, 11 ch-4 sps)*

Rnd 9: 5 tr in unworked ch sp, (9 tr in next ch-6 sp) 14 times, (5 tr, ch 4, sc) in next ch sp, ch 4, (sc in next ch-4 sp, ch 4) 10 times. *(136 tr, 12 ch-4 sps)*

Rnd 10: Tr in next 3 sts, ch 6, skip next 8 sts, tr in next 3 sts, (ch 6, skip next 6 sts, tr in next 3 sts) 13 times, ch 6, skip next 3 sts, tr in next 2 sts, tr in top of ch-4, ch 4, sc in same ch-4 sp, ch 4, (sc in next ch-4 sp, ch 4) 11 times. *(48 tr, 13 ch-4 sps)*

Rnd 11: (Shell in next ch-6 sp, ch 3) 14 times, shell in next ch-6 sp, ch 4, (sc in next ch-4 sp, ch 4) 13 times. *(15 shells, 14 ch-4 sps)*

Rnd 12: (Shell in next shell, ch 5) 14 times, shell in next shell, ch 4, (sc in next ch-4 sp, ch 4) 14 times. *(15 shells, 15 ch-4 sps)*

Rnd 13: (Shell in next shell, ch 6) 14 times, shell in next shell, ch 4, (sc in next ch-4 sp, ch 4) 15 times. *(15 shells, 16 ch-4 sps)*

Rnd 14: *[Sc in next st, **picot**—*see Special Stitches,* ch 2, sc in next ch-1 sp, picot, ch 2, skip next 2 sts, sc in next st, picot], ch 2; working around ch sps on rnds 11-13, long dc in next ch sp on rnd 11, picot, ch 2; repeat from * 13 more times; repeat between [ ] leaving ch-4 sps unworked. Fasten off. *(59 picots)*

With wrong sides together, matching sts, sew Sides together on rnd 13 leaving ch-4 sps unsewn.

Rnd 15: Join with sl st in first ch-4 sp past seam, ch 6; working around both Sides, (tr in next ch-4 sp, ch 2) around, join with sl st in fourth ch of ch-6. *(32 ch-2 sps)*

Rnd 16: Ch 3, *(2 tr, picot, 2 tr, picot, 2 tr) in next ch-2 sp, ch 2, skip next ch-2 sp; repeat from * around, join with sl st in first tr. Fasten off.

Finishing

For **lining,** using crochet Purse as pattern, allowing ½" extra on all edges for seams, keeping rnd 16 edge straight, cut two pieces from satin.

Sew pieces wrong sides together with ⅛" seam across curved edges leaving straight edge unsewn. Turn wrong side out. Press seam. Sew ⅜" seam around curved edges enclosing raw edge.

For hem, fold straight edge to wrong side ¼", fold again ¼", sew in place.

With lining right side out, insert into Purse, sew hemmed edge to ch-4 sps on rnd 13.

For **drawstrings,** cut ribbon in half; beginning and ending at same seam, weave one piece through rnd 15, tie ends in knot. Beginning and ending at opposite seam, weave second piece and tie same as first piece. &

Flower Fall

Continued from page 33

Fourth Vine
With ch 35, work same as First Vine.

Fifth Vine
With ch 40, work same as First Vine.

Assembly
With quilting thread, sew one bead to center of each Violet.

Sew one Violet to leaf at stem on Second and Fifth Vines. Tack ends of all Vines to bottom end of Base.

Tack center back of remaining Violets to Base and leaves according to illustration.

With quilting thread, sew hair bow clip or comb to back of Base. &

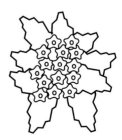

Hankie Edging

Designed by Jackie Rubenacker

Materials:
- ❑ 75 yds. white size 50 crochet cotton thread
- ❑ No. 11 steel hook or hook size needed to obtain gauge

Gauge: We are not responsible for lack of materials due to project not being worked to gauge. Gauge for this pattern: 11 sc = 1".

Basic Stitches: Ch, sl st, sc.

Edging

Note: *Number of sts in rnd 1 must be in multiples of 5.*

Rnd 1: Working around outer edge of hankie, spacing sts ⅛" apart, join with sc, sc around with 3 sc in each corner, join with sl st in first sc.

Rnd 2: Ch 1, (sc, ch 4, sc) in first st, ch 9, sl st in fifth ch from hook to form loop, ch 4, skip next 4 sts, *(sc, ch 4, sc) in next st, ch 9, sl st in fifth ch from hook to form loop, ch 4, skip next 4 sts; repeat from * around, join.

Rnd 3: Ch 1, 6 sc in each ch-5 loop around, join. Fasten off. ❧

Pearls & Flowers Pin

Designed by Andy Ashley

Finished Size: 2⅛" across.

Materials:
- ❑ 25 yds. lt. rose size 10 crochet cotton thread
- ❑ 25 yds. gold 3-ply metallic cord
- ❑ 16" of 3.5mm string beads
- ❑ 2" bone ring
- ❑ Pin back
- ❑ Craft glue
- ❑ No. 11 steel hook or hook needed to obtain gauge

Gauge: We are not responsible for lack of materials due to project not being worked to gauge. Gauge for this pattern: Rnds 1-4 of Flower = ¾" across.

Basic Stitches: Ch, sl st, sc, hdc, dc.

Ring
Join gold with **sc around ring** *(see illustration),* sc around ring covering evenly, join with sl st in first sc. Fasten off.

Flower
Rnd 1: With lt. rose, ch 2, 8 sc in second ch from hook, join with sl st in first sc. *(8 sc made)*

Rnd 2: Ch 1, sc in each st around, join.

Rnd 3: Ch 3, skip next st, (sc in next st, ch 2, skip next st) around, join with sl st in first ch of ch-3. *(4 ch sps)*

Rnd 4: For **petals,** (sl st, ch 2, 3 hdc, ch 2, sl st) in each ch sp around, **do not join.** *(4 petals)*

Rnd 5: Working behind petals, ch 1, *sc in **back lp** *(see Stitch Guide)* of next skipped sc on rnd

2, ch 4; repeat from * around, join with sl st in first sc. *(4 ch sps)*

Rnd 6: (Sl st, ch 2, 5 hdc, ch 2, sl st) in each ch sp around. Fasten off.

Leaf (make 2)
With gold, ch 6, sl st in second ch from hook, sl st in next ch, sc in next ch, hdc in next ch, 5 dc in next ch; working on opposite side of ch-6, hdc in next ch, sc in next ch, sl st in last 2 chs. Fasten off.

Assembly
Glue Leaves and Flower to front of Ring as shown in photo. Glue pin back on back of Ring. Glue five pearls to rnd 2 on Flower. Wrap remaining pearls around Ring, glue in place on back. ❧

Floral Hatband

Designed by Erma Fielder

Finished Size: One size fits all.

Materials:
- ❏ Small amount each yellow and blue variegated size 10 crochet cotton thread
- ❏ Small Velcro® fastener
- ❏ Matching sewing thread and needle
- ❏ No. 7 steel hook or hook needed to obtain gauge

Gauge: We are not responsible for lack of materials due to project not being worked to gauge. Gauge for this pattern: Each Flower is 1½" across.

Basic Stitches: Ch, sl st, sc, tr.

Hatband
First Flower
Rnd 1: With yellow, ch 6, sl st in first ch to form ring, ch 5, (sc in ring, ch 4) 6 times, join with sl st in first ch of ch-5. Fasten off.

Rnd 2: Join variegated with sl st in any ch sp, (ch 4, 3 tr, ch 4, sl st) in same ch sp, (sl st, ch 4, 3 tr, ch 4, sl st) in each ch sp around, join with sl st in first sl st. Fasten off.

Next Flower
Rnd 1: With yellow, ch 6, sl st in first ch to form ring, ch 5, (sc in ring, ch 4) 6 times, join with sl st in first ch of ch-5. Fasten off.

Rnd 2: Join variegated with sl st in any ch sp, (ch 4, 3 tr, ch 4, sl st) in same ch sp, (sl st, ch 4, 3 tr, ch 4, sl st) in next ch sp, (sl st, ch 4, tr) in next ch sp, ch 1, **turn;** with wrong side of last Flower made facing you, sl st in top of center tr of sixth petal, ch 1, **turn;** (2 tr, ch 4, sl st) in same ch sp as last tr on same Flower, (sl st, ch 4, 3 tr, ch 4, sl st) in each ch sp around on this Flower, join with sl st in first sl st. Fasten off.
Repeat Next Flower until desired length.

Tab
Row 1: Join variegated with sc in first tr of sixth petal on last Flower made, sc in next 2 sts, sc in top of ch-4, turn. *(4 sc made)*

Rows 2-4: Ch 1, sc in each st across, turn. At end

of last row, fasten off.
Cut piece of Velcro to size of Tab. Sew one piece of Velcro to right side of Tab. Sew other piece to wrong side of third petal on First Flower.
Place Hatband around hat. Fasten Velcro. 🦋

Turban Hat

Designed by Deborah Levy-Hamburg

Finished Size: Fits 20"-24" head.

Materials:
- ❏ Mohair-type worsted yarn:
    - 3 oz. purple
    - 1 oz. each black, blue, cranberry and teal
- ❏ Matching sewing thread and needle
- ❏ H and I hooks or hook sizes needed to obtain gauges

Gauges: We are not responsible for lack of materials due to project not being worked to gauge. Gauge for this pattern: **H hook,** rnds 1-7 = 4" across; 7 sc = 2"; 5 hdc = 2", 5 hdc rows = 2". **I hook,** 1 shell and 1 sc = 2"; 2 shell rows and 1 sc row = 2".

Basic Stitches: Ch, sl st, sc, hdc, dc.

Special Stitch: For **shell,** 5 dc in next st indicated in instructions.

Crown
Note: Work in continuous rnds; do not join or turn unless otherwise stated. Mark first st of each rnd.

Rnd 1: With H hook and purple, ch 2, 6 sc in second ch from hook. *(6 sc made)*

Rnd 2: 2 sc in each st around. *(12)*

Rnd 3: (Sc in next st, 2 sc in next st) around. *(18)*

Rnd 4: (Sc in next 2 sts, 2 sc in next st) around. *(24)*

Rnd 5: (Sc in next 3 sts, 2 sc in next st) around. *(30)*

Rnd 6: Sc in next 2 sts, (2 sc in next st, sc in next 4 sts) 5 times, 2 sc in next st, sc in last 2 sts. *(36)*

Rnd 7: (Sc in next 5 sts, 2 sc in next st) around. *(42)*

Rnd 8: Sc in next 3 sts, (2 sc in next st, sc in next 6 sts) 5 times, 2 sc in next st, sc in last 3 sts. *(48)*

Rnd 9: (Sc in next 7 sts, 2 sc in next st) around. *(54)*

Rnd 10: Sc in next 4 sts, (2 sc in next st, sc in next 8 sts) 5 times, 2 sc in next st, sc in last 4 sts. *(60)*

Rnd 11: (Sc in next 9 sts, 2 sc in next st) around. *(66)*

Rnd 12: Sc in next 5 sts, (2 sc in next st, sc in next 10 sts) 5 times, 2 sc in next st, sc in last 5 sts. *(72)*

Rnd 13: (Sc in next 11 sts, 2 sc in next st) around. *(78)*

Rnd 14: Sc in next 6 sts, (2 sc in next st, sc in next 12 sts) 5 times, 2 sc in next st, sc in last 6 sts. *(84)*

Rnds 15-17: Hdc in each st around. *(84 hdc)*

Rnd 18: (Hdc in next 12 sts, hdc next 2 sts tog) around. *(78)*

Rnd 19: (Hdc next 2 sts tog, hdc in next 11 sts) around. *(72)*

Rnd 20: (Hdc in next 34 sts, hdc next 2 sts tog) around. *(70)*

Rnd 21: (Hdc next 2 sts tog, hdc in next 9 sts) 5 times, hdc next 2 sts tog, hdc in last 13 sts. *(64)*

Rnd 22: (Hdc in next 14 sts, hdc next 2 sts tog) around. *(60)*

Rnd 23: (Hdc next 2 sts tog, hdc in next 8 sts) around. *(54)*

Rnd 24: Hdc in each st around.

Rnd 25: Sc in each st around.

Row 26: For **front,** working in rows, sc in next 27 sts, sl st in next st. Fasten off.

Band

Row 1: With I hook and purple, ch 70, 4 dc in fourth ch from hook, (skip next 2 chs, sc in next ch, skip next 2 chs, **shell**—*see Special Stitch*—in next st) across, turn. Fasten off. *(12 shells, 11 sc made)*

Row 2: Join black with sl st in first st, sl st in each st across, turn. Fasten off. *(71 sl sts) Front of row 2 is right side of work.*

Row 3: Working on row before last, skip first 2 dc, join teal with sl st in next dc, (skip next 2 dc, shell in next sc, skip next 2 dc, sl st in next dc) across, turn. Fasten off. *(11 shells, 12 sl sts)*

Row 4: Join black with sl st in first st, *sl st in each dc across to next sl st; working in **back lp** (see Stitch Guide) of sl st on row before last and **both lps** of last row at same time, sl st in next st; repeat from * across, turn. Fasten off.

Row 5: Working in **both lps** of row before last, join cranberry with sl st in first st, (ch 3, 4 dc) in same st, (sl st in third dc on next shell, shell in next sl st) across, turn. Fasten off. *(12 shells, 11 sl sts)*

Row 6: Join black with sl st in first dc, sl st in each dc across to next sl st; (working in **back lp** of sl st on row before last and **both lps** of last row at same time, sl st in next st; sl st in next 5 dc) across, turn. Fasten off.

Row 7: With blue, repeat row 3.

Row 8: Repeat row 4.

Row 9: With purple, repeat row 5.

Rnd 10: Working around outer edge, repeat row 6, **do not turn;** sl st in end of row 5, sl st in end of row 1; working on opposite side of starting

Continued on page 53

Teeny Tiny Snowflakes

Designed by Kathryn Clark

Snowflake Basics

Finished Sizes Range from 1¼" to 2" across.

Materials For Each:
- ❑ 25 yds. size 20 crochet cotton thread
- ❑ Fabric stiffener *(optional)*
- ❑ Cardboard *(optional)*
- ❑ Plastic wrap *(optional)*
- ❑ Rustproof straight pins *(optional)*
- ❑ White sewing thread and needle *(optional)*
- ❑ Wire earrings *(optional)*
- ❑ 10" of ⅛" satin ribbon
- ❑ No. 9 steel hook

Basic Stitches: Ch, sl st, sc, hdc, dc, tr.

Special Stitch: Front lp and left bar will be used throughout instructions *(see illustration).*

Optional Finishings

1: For **ornament,** dip Snowflake into fabric stiffener, pin flat on cardboard covered with plastic wrap and let dry. Weave strand of thread through Snowflake and tie ends in knot for hanger.

2: For **appliquè,** do not stiffen Snowflake. With sewing needle and thread, sew one or more Snowflakes on desired garment or accessory.

3: For **earrings,** stiffen Snowflake same as step 1. Insert wire earring through outer edge of each.

4: For **pencil decoration,** sew a Snowflake to each end of ribbon; tie ribbon in bow around top of pencil.

Snowflake 1

Rnd 1: Ch 6, sl st in first ch to form ring, (sc in ring, ch 4) 11 times, sc in ring, ch 1, join with dc in first sc *(counts as first ch sp). (12 ch sps made)*

Rnd 2: Sc in first ch sp, ch 3, sl st in front lp and back bar of sc just made, ch 2; *work following steps to complete rnd;*

A: Dc in next ch sp, ch 4, sc in fourth ch from hook, ch 5, sl st in front lp and left bar of sc just made, ch 4, sl st in same sc, sl st in front lp and left bar of last dc made;

B: Ch 2, sc in next ch sp, ch 3, sl st in front lp and left bar of sc just made, ch 2;

C: Dc in next ch sp, ch 4, sc in fourth ch from hook, ch 5, sl st in front lp and left bar of sc just made, ch 4, sl st in same sc, sl st in front lp and left bar of last dc made;

D: Repeat steps B and C 4 more times, ch 2, join with sl st in first sc. Fasten off.

Snowflake 2

Ch 6, sl st in first ch to form ring; *work following steps to complete rnd;*

A: Ch 2, dc in ring, ch 4, sc in fourth ch from hook, ch 4, sl st in front lp and left bar of sc just made, sl st in front lp and left bar of last dc made;

B: Ch 8, sc in fourth ch from hook, ch 5, sl st in front lp and left bar of sc just made, ch 4, sl st in same sc, sl st in next ch of ch-8, ch 3;

C: (Yo, insert hook in ring, yo, pull through ring, yo, pull through 2 lps on hook) 2 times, yo, pull through all 3 lps on hook *(cluster made);* ch 4, sc in fourth ch from hook, ch 4, sl st in front lp and left bar of sc just made, sl st in top of cluster;

D: Ch 8, sc in fourth ch from hook, ch 5, sl st in front lp and left bar of sc just made, ch 4, sl st in same sc, sl st in next ch of ch-8, ch 3;

E: Repeat steps C-D 4 more times, join with sl st in first dc. Fasten off.

Snowflake 3

Ch 6, sl st in first ch to form ring, (sc in ring, ch 3, sc in ring, ch 6, sl st in second ch from hook, sl st in next 2 chs, ch 5, sc in fourth ch from hook, ch 5, sl st in front lp and left bar of sc just made, ch 4, sl st in same sc, sl st in next ch, ch 4, sl st in second ch from hook, sl st in next 2 chs of ch-4, sl st in last 2 chs of ch-6) 6 times, join with sl st in first sc. Fasten off.

Snowflake 4

Rnd 1: Ch 6, sl st in first ch to form ring, 2 sc in ring, (ch 4, 2 sc in ring) 5 times, ch 1, join with dc in first sc *(counts as first ch sp). (6 ch sps made)*

Rnd 2: Sc in first ch sp, ch 5, sc in fourth ch from hook, ch 5, sl st in front lp and left bar of sc just made, ch 4, sl st in same sc, sl st in next ch, sl st in front lp and left bar of first sc made in first

Continued on page 48

Teeny Tiny Snowflakes

Continued from page 47

ch sp, ch 7, sl st in fourth ch from hook, ch 3; *work following steps to complete rnd;*

A: Sc in next ch sp, ch 5, sc in fourth ch from hook, ch 5, sl st in front lp and left bar of sc just made, ch 4, sl st in same sc, sl st in next ch, sl st in front lp and left bar of sc worked into ch sp on rnd 1;

B: Ch 7, sl st in fourth ch from hook, ch 3;

C: Repeat steps A and B 4 more times, join with sl st in first sc. Fasten off.

Snowflake 5

Ch 6, sl st in first ch to form ring, *(sc, ch 3, sc) in ring, (ch 5, sc in fourth ch from hook) 2 times, ch 5, sl st in front lp and left bar of sc just made, ch 4, sl st in same sc, sl st in next ch, sl st in front lp and left bar of next sc, ch 4, sl st in same sc, sl st in next ch; repeat from * 5 more times, join with sl st in first sc. Fasten off.

Snowflake 6

Rnd 1: Ch 6, sl st in first ch to form ring, ch 3, (hdc in ring, ch 1) 11 times, join with sl st in second ch of ch-3. *(12 hdc made)*

Rnd 2: (Sc in first ch sp on rnd 1, ch 4, sc in fourth ch from hook, ch 5, sl st in front lp and left bar of sc just made, ch 4, sl st in same sc, sc in same ch sp on rnd 1, sc in next ch sp on rnd

1, ch 6, sc in fourth ch from hook, ch 5, sl st in front lp and left bar of sc just made, ch 4, sl st in same sc, sl st in next 2 chs, sl st in front lp and left bar of sc worked into ch sp on rnd 1) around, join with sl st in first sc. Fasten off.

Snowflake 7

Rnd 1: Ch 6, sl st in first ch to form ring, (sc in ring, ch 4) 11 times, sc in ring, ch 1, join with dc in first sc *(counts as first ch sp). (12 ch sps made)*

Rnd 2: Sc in first ch sp; *work following steps to complete rnd;*

A: Ch 6, sc in fourth ch from hook, ch 5, sl st in front lp and left bar of sc just made, ch 4, sl st in same sc, sl st in top 2 chs of ch-6, sl st in front lp and left bar of sc worked into ch sp;

B: Ch 2, dc in next ch sp, (ch 3, sl st) 2 times in front lp and left bar of dc just made, ch 2;

C: Sc in next ch sp, ch 6, sc in fourth ch from hook, ch 5, sl st in front lp and left bar of sc just made, ch 4, sl st in same sc, sl st in next 2 chs of ch-6, sl st in front lp and left bar of sc worked into ch sp;

D: Ch 2, dc in next ch sp, (ch 3, sl st) 2 times in front lp and left bar of dc just made, ch 2;

E: Repeat steps C and D 4 more times, join with sl st in first sc. Fasten off.

No. 1   No. 2   No. 3   No. 4

No. 5   No. 6   No. 7

Snowflake 8

Ch 6, sl st in first ch to form ring; *work following steps to complete rnd;*

A: Ch 2, dc in ring, ch 6, sc in fourth ch from hook, ch 5, sl st in front lp and left bar of sc just made, ch 4, sl st in same sc, sl st in next 2 chs of ch-6, sl st in front lp and left bar of last dc made;

B: Ch 6, sl st in third ch from hook, ch 3;

C: (Yo, insert hook in ring, yo, pull through ring, yo, pull through 2 lps on hook) 2 times, yo, pull through all 3 lps on hook *(cluster made);*

D: Ch 6, sc in fourth ch from hook, ch 5, sl st in front lp and left bar of sc just made, ch 4, sl st in same sc, sl st in next 2 chs of ch-6, sl st in top of cluster;

E: Ch 6, sl st in third ch from hook, ch 3;

F: Repeat steps C-E 4 more times, join with sl st in top of first dc. Fasten off.

Snowflake 9

Rnd 1: Ch 6, sl st in first ch to form ring, ch 3, (hdc in ring, ch 1) 11 times, join with sl st in second ch of ch-3. *(12 hdc made)*

Rnd 2: *Sc in next ch-1 sp, ch 4, sl st in front lp and left bar of last sc made, ch 4, sl st in same sc, (hdc, dc) in next ch-1 sp, ch 5, sc in fourth ch from hook, ch 5, sl st in front lp and left bar of last sc made, ch 4, sl st in same sc, sl st in next ch, sl st in front lp and left bar of last dc made, hdc in same ch-1 sp; repeat from * around, join with sl st in first sc. Fasten off.

Snowflake 10

Rnd 1: Ch 6, sl st in first ch to form ring, ch 1, 12 sc in ring, join with sl st in first sc. *(12 sc made)*

Rnd 2: Ch 1, sc in first sc of rnd 1, ch 6, sc in fourth ch from hook, ch 5, sl st in front lp and left bar of sc just made, ch 4, sl st in same sc, sl st in next 2 chs, sl st in front lp and left bar of sc worked into rnd 1, ch 2, dc in next sc on rnd 1, ch 4, sl st in front lp and left bar of last dc made, ch 2, (sc in next sc of rnd 1, ch 6, sc in fourth ch from hook, ch 5, sl st in front lp and left bar of sc just made, ch 4, sl st in same sc, sl st in next 2 chs, sl st in front lp and left bar of sc worked into rnd 1, ch 2, dc in next sc of rnd 1, ch 4, sl st in front lp and left bar of dc just made, ch 2) around, join. Fasten off.

Snowflake 11

Rnd 1: Ch 6, sl st in first ch to form ring, ch 1, (2 sc in ring, ch 3, sl st in front lp and left bar of sc just made) 6 times, join with sl st in first sc. *(12 sc made)*

Rnd 2: Ch 6, sl st in fourth ch from hook, ch 7, sc in fourth ch from hook, ch 5, sl st in front lp and left bar of sc just made, ch 4, sl st in same sc, sl st in next ch of ch-7, ch 2, skip next sc and next ch sp on rnd 1, (dc in next sc on rnd 1, ch 3, sl st in front lp and left bar of dc just made, ch 7, sc in fourth ch form hook, ch 5, sl st in front lp and left bar of sc just made, ch 4, sl st in same sc, sl st in next ch of ch-7, ch 2, skip next sc and next ch sp on rnd 1) around, join with sl st in third ch of ch-6. Fasten off.

Continued on page 50

No. 8

No. 9

No. 10

No. 11

Snowflake 12

Rnd 1: Ch 6, sl st in first ch to form ring, ch 3, (hdc in ring, ch 1) 11 times, join with sl st in second ch of beginning ch-3. *(12 hdc made)*

Rnd 2: (Sc, ch 3, sc) in first ch sp; *work following steps to complete rnd;*

A: Sc in next ch sp on rnd 1, ch 5, sl st in second ch from hook, sl st in next 2 chs, ch 5, sc in fourth ch from hook, ch 5, sl st in front lp and left bar of sc just made, ch 4, sl st in same sc, sl st in next ch, ch 4, sl st in second ch from hook, sl st in next 2 chs, sl st in next ch, sc in same ch sp on rnd 1;

B: (Sc, ch 3, sc) in next ch sp;

C: Repeat steps A and B 4 more times;

D: Repeat step A, join with sl st in first sc. Fasten off.

Snowflake 13

Rnd 1: Ch 6, sl st in first ch to form ring, ch 1, 12 sc in ring, join with sl st in first sc. *(12 sc made)*

Rnd 2: Ch 1, sc in first sc, ch 3, sl st in front lp and left bar of sc just made; *work following steps to complete rnd;*

A: (Hdc, dc) in next sc on rnd 1, ch 4, sl st in second ch from hook, sl st in next 2 chs, ch 5, sc in fourth ch from hook, ch 5, sl st in front lp and left bar of sc just made, ch 4, sl st in same sc, sl st in next ch, ch 4, sl st in second ch from hook, sl st in next 2 chs, sl st in front lp and left bar of last dc made, hdc in same sc;

B: Sc in next sc on rnd 1, ch 3, sl st in front lp and left bar of sc just made;

C: Repeat steps A and B 4 more times;

D: Repeat step A, join with sl st in first sc. Fasten off.

Snowflake 14

Rnd 1: Ch 6, sl st in first ch to form ring, ch 1, 12 sc in ring, join with sl st in first sc. *(12 sc made)*

Rnd 2: ch 1, sc in first sc on rnd 1, ch 3, sl st in front lp and left bar of sc just made, (hdc dc) in next sc on rnd 1, ch 5, sc in fourth ch from hook, ch 5, sl st in front lp and left bar of sc just made, ch 4, sl st in same sc, sl st in next ch, sl st in front lp and left bar of last dc made, hdc in same sc on rnd 1, *sc in next sc on rnd 1, ch 3, sl st in front lp and left bar of sc just made, (hdc, dc) in next sc on rnd 1, ch 5, sc in fourth ch from hook, ch 5, sl st in front lp and left bar of sc just made, ch 4, sl st in same sc, sl st in next ch, sl st in front lp and left bar of last dc made, hdc in next sc on rnd 1; repeat from * around, join. Fasten off.

Snowflake 15

Rnd 1: Ch 6, sl st in first ch to form ring, ch 3, (hdc in ring, ch 1) 11 times, join with sl st in second ch of beginning ch-3. *(12 hdc made)*

Rnd 2: Skip first hdc; *work following steps to complete rnd;*

A: Sc in next ch sp on rnd 1, ch 4, sc in fourth ch from hook, ch 4, sl st in front lp and left bar of sc just made;

B: Sc in next ch sp on rnd 1, ch 6, sc in fourth ch from hook, ch 6, sl st in fifth ch from hook, sl st in next ch, sl st in front lp and left bar of last sc made, ch 4, sl st in same sc, sl st in next 2 chs, sl st in front lp and left bar of sc worked into ch sp on rnd 1;

C: Repeat steps A and B 5 more times;

D: Repeat step A, join with sl st in first sc. Fasten off.

No. 12

No. 13

No. 14

No. 15

Snowflake 16

Ch 6, sl st in first ch to form ring; *work the following steps to complete rnd;*

A: Ch 2, dc in ring, ch 4, sl st in second ch from hook, sl st in next ch, ch 3, sl st in second ch from hook, sl st in next ch, sl st in remaining ch of ch-4, sl st in top of first dc made;

B: Ch 6, sl st in third ch from hook, ch 3;

C: (Yo, insert hook in ring, yo, pull through ring, yo, pull through 2 lps on hook) 2 times, yo, pull through all 3 lps on hook *(cluster made);*

D: Ch 4, sl st in second ch from hook, sc in next ch, ch 3, sl st in second ch from hook, sl st in next ch, sl st in remaining ch of ch-4, sl st in top of cluster.

E: Ch 6, sl st in third ch from hook, ch 3;

F: Repeat steps C-E 4 more times, join with sl st in first dc.

Snowflake 17

Ch 6, sl st in first ch to form ring; *work following steps to complete rnd;*

A: Ch 10, sc in fourth ch from hook, ch 5, sl st in front lp and left bar of sc just made, ch 4, sl st in same sc, sl st in next ch;

B: Ch 2, dc in ring, ch 3, sl st in front lp and left bar of dc just made;

C: Dc in ring, ch 7, sc in fourth ch from hook, ch 5, sl st in front lp and left bar of sc just made, ch 4, sl st in same sc, sl st in next ch;

D: Ch 2, dc in ring, ch 3, sl st in front lp and left bar of dc must made;

E: Repeat steps C and D 5 more times, join with sl st in third ch of ch-10. Fasten off.

Snowflake 18

Rnd 1: Ch 6, sl st in first ch to form ring, ch 1, (2 sc in ring, ch 3, sl st in front lp and left bar of sc just made) 6 times, join with sl st in first sc. *(12 sc made)*

Rnd 2: Ch 8, sc in fourth ch from hook, ch 5, sl st in front lp and left bar of sc just made, ch 4, sl st in same sc, sl st in next ch of ch-8, ch 8, sl st in fifth ch from hook, ch 3, skip next sc and ch sp on rnd 1, (dc in next sc, ch 5, sc in fourth ch from hook, ch 5, sl st in front lp and left bar of sc just made, ch 4, sl st in front lp and left bar of last dc made, sl st in next ch, sl st in top of dc, ch 8, sl st in fifth ch from hook, ch 3) around, join with sl st in third ch of beginning ch-8. Fasten off.

Snowflake 19

Rnd 1: Ch 6, sl st in first ch to form ring, ch 1, 12 sc in ring, join with sl st in first sc. *(12 sc made)*

Rnd 2: Ch 1, sc in first sc on rnd 1, ch 3, sl st in front lp and left bar of sc just made, ch 3, tr in next sc of rnd 1, ch 4, sc in fourth ch from hook, ch 5, sl st in front lp and left bar of sc just made, ch 4, sl st in same sc, sl st in front lp and left bar of tr made, (sc in next sc on rnd 1, ch 3, sl st in front lp and left bar of sc just made, ch 3, tr in next sc on rnd 1, ch 4, sc in fourth ch from hook, ch 5, sl st in front lp and left bar of sc just made, ch 4, sl st in same sc, sl st in front lp and left bar of tr just made, ch 3) around, join. Fasten off.

Snowflake 20

Ch 6, sl st in first ch to form ring; *work following steps to complete rnd;*

A: Ch 9, sc in fourth ch from hook, ch 5, sl st in front lp and left bar of sc just made, ch 4, sl st in same sc, sl st in next 2 chs of ch-9;

Continued on page 52

No. 16 No. 17 No. 18

No. 19 No. 20

Teeny Tiny Snowflakes

Continued from page 51

B: Dc in ring, ch 5, sl st in fourth ch from hook, ch 1;

C: Dc in ring, ch 6, sc in fourth ch from hook, ch 5, sl st in front lp and left bar of sc just made, ch 4, sl st in same sc, sl st in next 2 chs;

D: Dc in ring, ch 5, sl st in fourth ch from hook, ch 1;

E: Repeat steps C and D 5 more times, join with sl st in third ch of ch-9. Fasten off.

Snowflake 21

Rnd 1: Ch 6, sl st in first ch to form ring, ch 3, (hdc in ring, ch 1) 11 times, join with sl st in second ch of beginning ch-3. *(12 hdc made)*

Rnd 2: *Sc in next ch sp, ch 5, sc in fourth ch from hook, ch 5, sl st in front lp and left bar of sc just made, ch 4, sl st in same sc, sl st in next ch, sl st in front lp and left bar of sc worked into ch sp on rnd 1, (hdc, dc, ch 3, sl st in front lp and left bar of dc just made, hdc) in next ch sp; repeat from * around, join with sl st in first sc. Fasten off.

Snowflake 22

Ch 6, sl st in first ch to form ring, (sc in ring, ch 3, sc in ring, ch 5, sc in fourth ch from hook, ch 5, sl st in front lp and left bar of last sc made, ch 4, sl st in same sc, sl st in next ch) 6 times, join with sl st in first sc. Fasten off.

Snowflake 23

Rnd 1: Ch 6, sl st in first ch to form ring, ch 3, (hdc in ring, ch 1) 11 times, join with sl st in second ch of beginning ch-3. *(12 hdc made)*

Rnd 2: (Sc, ch 3, sc) in first ch sp; *work following steps to complete rnd;*

A: Sc in next ch sp on rnd 1, ch 4, sc in fourth ch form hook, ch 5, sl st in front lp and left bar of sc just made, ch 4, sl st in same sc, sc in same ch sp on rnd 1;

B: (Sc, ch 3, sc) in next ch sp;

C: Repeat steps A and B 4 more times;

D: Repeat step A, join with sl st in first sc. Fasten off.

Snowflake 24

Rnd 1: Ch 6, sl st in first ch to from ring, 2 sc in ring, (ch 4, 2 sc in ring) 4 times, ch 1, join with dc in first sc *(counts as ch sp). (6 ch sps made)*

Rnd 2: (Sc, ch 3, sl st in front lp and left bar of sc just made, ch 8, sc in fourth ch form hook, ch 5, sl st in front lp and left bar of sc just made, ch 4, sl st in same sc, sl st in next 2 chs, ch 2) in each ch sp around, join with sl st in first sc. Fasten off. ❧

No. 21

No. 22

No. 23

No. 24

Turban Hat

Continued from page 44

ch, sl st in each ch across, sl st in end of row 5, sl st in end of row 9, join with sl st in first sl st. Fasten off.

Sew ends together, place around Crown with seam at back and with row 9 covering bottom edge.

Cut 3" strand purple, wrap around rnds 17-25 at center front of Crown and Band at same time, pull tight, secure. Tack Band in place.

Flower

Rnd 1: With I hook and purple, ch 18, sl st in first ch to form ring, ch 3, 35 dc in ring, join with sl st in top of ch-3. *(36 dc made)*

Rnd 2: Ch 1, sc in first 2 sts, **double crochet front post (fp**—*see Stitch Guide),* (sc in next 3 sts, fp around same st as last sc made, sc in next 2 sts, fp around next st) 5 times, sc in next 3 sts, fp around same st as last sc made, join with sl st in first sc. *(30 sc, 12 fp)*

Rnd 3: Ch 1, sc in first 2 sts, (2 fp around next fp, sc in next 3 sts, 2 fp around next fp, sc in next 2 sts) 5 times, 2 fp around next fp, sc in next 3 sts, 2 fp around last fp, join. *(30 sc, 24 fp)*

Rnd 4: Ch 1, sc in first 2 sts, (2 fp around next fp, fp around next fp, sc in next 3 sts, 2 fp around next fp, fp around next fp, sc in next 2 sts) 5 times, 2 fp around next fp, fp around next fp, sc in next 3 sts, 2 fp around next fp, fp around last fp, join. Fasten off. *(30 sc, 36 fp)*

With right side of rnd 4 on Flower facing you, sew Flower to ends of Band.

Bow

Row 1: With I hook and purple, ch 40, 4 dc in fourth ch from hook, (skip next 2 chs, sc in next ch, skip next 2 chs, shell) across, turn. Fasten off. *(7 shells, 6 sc made)*

Rows 2-8: Repeat rows 2-8 of Band.

Row 9: Working in ends of rows and in sts, join purple with sl st in row 1, shell in row 3, sl st in row 5, shell 2 times in row 7, (sc in third dc of next shell on row 8, shell in next sl st) across, shell in same st as last shell made, sl st in row 5, shell in row 3, sl st in row 1, turn. Fasten off.

Rnd 10: Working around entire piece, join black with sl st in first st on row 9, sl st in each st across row 9, sl st in each ch of starting ch, join with sl st in first sl st. Fasten off.

Tie knot in center of Bow; with rnd 10 on outside, sew knot to center of Flower. ❧

Beaded Floral Slippers

Designed by Mary Layfield

Finished Size: Fits 9½" to 10" sole.

Materials:
- ❑ Worsted yarn:
  - 4½ oz. black
  - 2 oz. fuchsia
  - 22 yds. green
- ❑ 16 pony beads
- ❑ Two 13" pieces black ½"-wide elastic
- ❑ Insoles for Slippers *(optional)*
- ❑ Straight pins
- ❑ Black sewing thread
- ❑ Tapestry and sewing needles
- ❑ G hook or hook size needed to obtain gauge

Gauge: We are not responsible for lack of materials due to project not being worked to gauge. Gauge for this pattern: 4 sc = 1"; 9 sc rows = 2".

Basic Stitches: Ch, sl st, sc, dc.

Slipper (make 2)
Instep
Row 1: Starting at toe end, with black, ch 6, 2 sc in second ch from hook, sc in each ch across to last ch, 2 sc in last ch, turn. *(7 sc made)*
Row 2: Ch 1, 2 sc in first st, sc in next 5 sts, 2 sc in last st, turn. *(9)*
Row 3: Ch 1, sc in each st across, turn.
Row 4: Ch 1, 2 sc in first st, sc in next 7 sts, 2 sc in last st, turn. *(11)*
Rows 5-6: Ch 1, sc in each st across, turn.
Row 7: Ch 1, 2 sc in first st, sc in next 9 sts, 2 sc in last st, turn. *(13)*
Rows 8-14: Ch 1, sc in each st across, turn. At end of last row, fasten off.

Sole
Row 1: Starting at heel, with black, ch 4, 2 sc in second ch from hook, sc in next ch, 2 sc in last ch, turn. *(5 sc made)*
Row 2: Ch 1, 2 sc in first st, sc in next 3 sts, 2 sc in last st, turn. *(7)*
Row 3: Ch 1, sc in each st across, turn.
Row 4: Ch 1, 2 sc in first st, sc in next 5 sts, 2 sc in last st, turn. *(9)*
Rows 5-26: Ch 1, sc in each st across, turn.
Row 27: Ch 1, 2 sc in first st, sc in each st across, turn. *(10)*

Row 28: Ch 1, sc in each st across, turn.
Row 29: Ch 1, 2 sc in first st, sc in each st across, turn. *(11)*
Rows 30-35: Ch 1, sc in each st across, turn.
Rows 36-37: Ch 1, sc in each st across to last 2 sts, sc last 2 sts tog, turn. *(10, 9)*
Rows 38-39: Ch 1, sc in each st across, turn.
Rows 40-44: Ch 1, sc in each st across to last 2 sts, sc last 2 sts tog, turn. At end of last row, fasten off.

Side
Rnd 1: Working around Sole, join black with sl st in center ch on row 1, ch 1, 2 sc in same ch as joining sl st, sc in next ch, sc in end of next 43 rows, 2 sc in end of next row, sc in last 4 sts, 2 sc in end of next row sc in end of last 43 rows, sc in last ch, join with sl st in first sc, **turn.** *(98 sc made)*
Rnds 2-5: Ch 1, sc in each st around, join. At end of last rnd, fasten off.
Row 6: Working in rows, skip first 32 sts on rnd 5 of Side, pin Instep to next 33 sts, with toe ends together, working through both thicknesses, with Instep facing you, join black with sc in end of row 14 on Instep, evenly space 32 more sc across Instep, skip last 3 sts on rnd 5 of Side. Fasten off.
Row 7: Working around outer edge of Side and Instep, join black with sl st in seventh st on row 14 of Instep, sc in next 6 sts, skip next st on Side, sc in next 30 sts, (2 sc in next st, sc in next st) 2 times, sc in each st across to last 7 sts, skip last st on Side, sc in last 6 sts on Instep, turn. *(77)*
Rows 8-9: Ch 1, sc in first 6 sts, skip next st, sc in each st across to last 7 sts, skip next st, sc in last 6 sts, turn. *(75, 73)*
Rows 10-11: Ch 1, sc in first 5 sts, skip next st, sc in each st across to last 6 sts, skip next st, sc in last 5 sts, turn. *(71, 69)*
Row 12: Ch 1, sc in first 4 sts, skip next st, sc in each st across to last 5 sts, skip next st, sc in last 4 sts, turn. *(67)*
Rows 13-14: Ch 1, sc in first 3 sts, skip next 2 sts, sc in each st across to last 5 sts, skip next 2 sts, sc in last 3 sts, turn. *(63, 59)*
Row 15: Ch 1, sc in first 2 sts, skip next st, sc in each st across to last 3 sts, skip next st, sc in last 2 sts, turn. *(57)*

Overlap ends of elastic ½" to form a circle, with

Continued on page 56

Beaded Floral Slippers

Continued from page 55

sewing thread and needle, tack ends together.

Row 16: Fold elastic in half and place seam at back of Slipper on top edge of row 15, working over elastic *(see illustration),* ch 1, sc loosely in each st across covering elastic as you work. Fasten off. *Elastic will go over split in front of Slipper.*

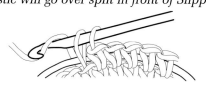

Tie & Trim

With fuchsia, for Tie, ch 50; join with sc in first st on row 16 of Side, (ch 4, sc in next st) across; for Tie, ch 50. Fasten off.

Insert one end of one Tie through one bead; tie end in knot to secure. Repeat on other Tie.

Flower

Rnd 1: With black, ch 4, sl st in first ch to form ring, ch 1, (sc in ring, ch 3) 5 times, join with sl st in first sc. Fasten off. *(5 ch sps made)*

Rnd 2: Join fuchsia with sc in any ch sp, (4 dc, sc) in same ch sp, (sc, 4 dc, sc) in each ch sp around, join. Fasten off.

Leaves

With green, ch 3, sl st in first ch to form ring, (ch 10, sc in third ch from hook, dc in next 6 chs, sc in last ch of ch-10, sc in ring) 3 times. Fasten off.

Center Flower on top of Leaves, tack in place. Sew six beads to center of Flower; sew Flower centered on top of Instep.

Optional: Place insole inside Slipper. ❧

Irish Bouquet

Continued from page 30

of Leaf, ch 1, sl st in top of st at end of row 2, ch 2, sl st in top of st at end of row 1, ch 4, sl st in same ch as 6 tr of row 1, **do not turn or fasten off.**

For **second leaf,** ch 9, repeat rows 1-3 of first leaf; sc in next 4 chs below second leaf, **do not fasten off.**

For **third leaf,** ch 5, repeat rows 1-3 of first leaf; sc in each ch across stem. Fasten off.

Bud & Leaf Spray

Beginning at bottom of stem, ch 13; for **first leaf,** [sc in second ch from hook, hdc in next ch, dc in next 3 chs, hdc in next ch, sc in next ch]; for **second leaf,** ch 9, *sc in second ch from hook, hdc in next ch, dc in next 2 chs, hdc in next ch, sc in next ch*; for **bud,** ch 8, bend ch-8 lp into small circle *(see illustration),* sl st in first ch of ch-8; working in ch lp just made, (sc, hdc, 2 dc, 2 tr) in lp, ch 3, sl st in **front lp and left bar** *(see illustration)* at top of

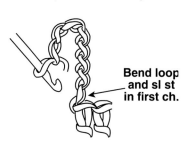

Bend loop and sl st in first ch.

last st made, (2 tr, 2 dc, hdc, sc) in remainder of lp, sl st in first ch of ch-8 lp; for **third leaf,** ch 7; repeat between * in second leaf, sl st in side of sc on second leaf, sc in next 2 chs between second and first leaves, sl st in side of sc on first leaf; for **fourth leaf,** ch 8; repeat between [ ] in first first leaf, sc in each ch across stem. Fasten off.

Assembly

Block all Sprays.

With quilting thread, sew 2" piece floral wire to back of center stem on each Spray. Tack bottom of stem on each Spray according to illustration.

Tack Rose to half of Base over ends of Leaf Sprays and Posies to other half of Base. With quilting thread, sew hair bow or clip to back of Base. ❧

Intimate Indulgences

CHAPTER THREE

Pineapple Yoke Nightgown

Designed by Dot Drake

Finished Sizes: **Girl's/lady's bust 30"-32".** Finished Measurement: 11½" across Yoke, 56"-wide skirt. **Lady's bust 34"-36".** Finished Measurement: 12½" across Yoke, 60"-wide skirt. **Lady's bust 38"-40".** Finished Measurement: 13½" across Yoke, 64"-wide skirt.

Materials:
- ❏ 225 yds. size 10 crochet cotton thread
- ❏ 3 yds. lightweight fabric
- ❏ 1 yd. double-fold bias tape to match fabric
- ❏ Sewing thread
- ❏ Sewing and tapestry needles
- ❏ No. 5 steel hook or hook size needed to obtain gauge

Gauge: We are not responsible for lack of materials due to project not being worked to gauge. Gauge for this pattern: 2 shells = 1"; 7 shell rows = 2".

Basic Stitches: Ch, sl st, sc, dc, tr.

Special Stitches: For **beginning shell (beg shell),** ch 1, sl st in first 2 sts, (sl st, ch 3, dc, ch 2, 2 dc) in first ch-2 sp.
For **shell,** (2 dc, ch 2, 2 dc) in next ch-2 sp.

Note: Instructions are for girl's/lady's bust 30"-32"; changes for 34"-36" and 38"-40" are in [ ].

Yoke
Front
Row 1: Ch 114 [124, 134], (dc, ch 2, 2 dc) in fourth ch from hook, skip next 4 chs, (2 dc, ch 2, 2 dc) in next ch, *ch 7, skip next 9 chs, (dc, ch 2, dc) in next ch, ch 7, skip next 9 chs, (2 dc in next ch, ch 2, 2 dc in same ch, skip next 4 chs) 4 [5, 6] times, (2 dc, ch 2, 2 dc) in next ch; repeat from * one time, ch 7, skip next 9 chs, (dc, ch 2, dc) in next ch, ch 7, skip next 9 chs, (2 dc, ch 2, 2 dc) in next ch, skip next 4 chs, (2 dc, ch 2, 2 dc) in last ch, turn. *(62 dc, 6 ch-7 sps made)* *[70 dc, 6 ch-7 sps made; 78 dc, 6 ch-7 sps made]*

Row 2: Beg shell *(see Special Stitches),* shell, *ch 5, 7 tr in next ch-2 sp, ch 5, shell 5 [6, 7] times; repeat from * one time, ch 5, 7 tr in next ch-2 sp, ch 5, shell 2 times, turn.

Row 3: Beg shell, shell, *ch 3, (tr in next tr, ch 1) 6 times, tr in next tr, ch 3, shell 5 [6, 7] times; repeat from * one time, ch 3, (tr in next tr, ch 1) 6 times, tr in next tr, ch 3, shell 2 times, turn.

Row 4: Beg shell, shell, *ch 3, (sc in next ch-1 sp, ch 4) 5 times, sc in next ch-1 sp, ch 3, shell 5 [6, 7] times; repeat from * one time, ch 3, (sc in next ch-1 sp, ch 4) 5 times, sc in next ch-1 sp, ch 3, shell 2 times, turn.

Row 5: Beg shell, shell, *ch 3, (sc in next ch-4 sp, ch 4) 4 times, sc in next ch-4 sp, ch 3, shell 5 [6, 7] times; repeat from * one time, ch 3, (sc in next ch-4 sp, ch 4) 4 times, sc in next ch-4 sp, ch 3, shell 2 times, turn.

Row 6: Beg shell, shell, *ch 4, (sc in next ch-4 sp, ch 4) 4 times, shell 5 [6, 7] times; repeat from * one time, ch 4, (sc in next ch-4 sp, ch 4) 4 times, shell 2 times, turn.

Row 7: Beg shell, shell, *ch 5, (sc in next ch-4 sp, ch 4) 2 times, sc in next ch-4 sp, ch 5, shell 5 [6, 7] times; repeat from * one time, ch 5, (sc in next ch-4 sp, ch 4) 2 times, sc in next ch-4 sp, ch 5, shell 2 times, turn.

Row 8: Beg shell, shell, *ch 6, sc in next ch-4 sp, ch 4, sc in next ch-4 sp, ch 6, shell 5 [6, 7] times; repeat from * one time, ch 6, sc in next ch-4 sp, ch 4, sc in next ch-4 sp, ch 6, shell 2 times, turn.

Row 9: Beg shell, shell, ch 5, 7 tr in next ch-4 sp, ch 5, shell 5 [6, 7] times, ch 7, sc in next ch-4 sp, ch 7, shell 5 [6, 7] times, ch 5, 7 tr in next ch-4 sp, ch 5, shell 2 times, turn.

Row 10: For **first strap,** beg shell, shell, ch 3, (tr in next tr, ch 1) 6 times, tr in next tr, ch 3, shell 2 times leaving remaining sts unworked, turn. *(4 shells, 7 tr)*

Continued on page 61

Hankie Edging

Designed by Dot Drake

Finished Size: 1½" wide.

Materials:
- ❑ 300 yds. white size 50 crochet cotton thread
- ❑ 10½" square handkerchief
- ❑ No. 14 steel hook or hook size needed to obtain gauge

Gauge: We are not responsible for lack of materials due to project not being worked to gauge. Gauge for this pattern: 10 sc = 1".

Basic Stitches: Ch, sl st, sc, dc, tr.

Edging

Rnd 1: Place slip knot on hook; working around hem of handkerchief starting at corner; for **sc around hem (sch), insert hook through fabric at bottom of hem, yo, pull lp through fabric, complete as sc;** 2 sch in same place; spacing 10 sch evenly across each inch, work 105 sch across each side and 3 sch in each corner, join with sl st in first sc. *(432 sch made)*

Rnd 2: Sc in first st, ch 5, skip next st, (sc in next st, ch 5, skip next st) around to last 2 sts, sc in next st, ch 3, skip last st, join with dc in first sc *(joining ch sp made). (216 ch sps)*

Rnds 3-7: Sc in joining ch sp; for **picot, ch 3, sc in**

third ch from hook; sc in same ch sp, (ch 5, sc, picot, sc) in each ch sp around, ch 3, join with dc in first sc.

Rnd 8: Sc in joining ch sp, ch 2; for **shell, (tr, picot, tr, picot, tr, picot, tr, picot, tr) in third ch of next ch-5 sp;** ch 2, (sc in next ch sp, ch 2, shell, ch 2) around, join with sl st in first sc. Fasten off.

Flower
Rnd 1: Ch 10, sl st in first ch to form ring, ch 1, 25 sc in ring, join with sl st in **front lp** *(see Stitch Guide)* of first st. *(25 sc made)*

Rnd 2: For **petals,** working in **front lps,** ch 1, sc in first st, (*ch 1, 2 dc in next st, 2 tr in next st, 2 dc in next st, ch 1*, sc in next 2 sts) 4 times; repeat between **, sc in last st, **do not join.** *(5 petals)*

Rnd 3: Working in unworked **back lps** of rnd 1, ch 1, sc in first st, (ch 3, sc in third ch from hook) 6 times, *skip next 4 sts, sc in next st, (ch 3, sc in third ch from hook) 6 times; repeat from * 3 more times, skip last 4 sts, join with sl st in first sc. Leaving 6" for sewing, fasten off.

Sew Flower centered 1" from hem in corner of handkerchief. ❧

Pineapple Yoke Nightgown
Continued from page 58

Row 11: Beg shell, shell, ch 3, (sc in next ch-1 sp, ch 4) 5 times, sc in next ch-1 sp, ch 3, shell 2 times, turn.

Row 12: Beg shell, shell, ch 3, (sc in next ch-4 sp, ch 4) 4 times, sc in next ch-4 sp, ch 3, shell 2 times, turn.

Row 13: Beg shell, shell, ch 4, (sc in next ch-4 sp, ch 4) 4 times, shell 2 times, turn.

Row 14: Beg shell, shell, ch 5, (sc in next ch-4 sp, ch 4) 2 times, sc in next ch-4 sp, ch 5, shell 2 times, turn.

Row 15: Beg shell, shell, ch 6, sc in next ch-4 sp, ch 4, sc in next ch-4 sp, ch 6, shell 2 times, turn.

Row 16: Beg shell, shell, ch 7, sc in next ch-4 sp, ch 7, shell 2 times, turn.

Row 17: For **first side,** beg shell, shell leaving remaining sts unworked, turn. *(2 shells)*

Rows 18-23: Beg shell, shell, turn. At end of last row, fasten off.

Row 17: For **second side,** join with sl st in next unworked shell on row 16, (ch 3, dc, ch 2, 2 dc) in same shell, shell, turn. *(2 shells)*

Rows 18-23: Beg shell, shell, turn. At end of last row, fasten off.

Row 10: For **second strap,** skip next 6 [8, 10] unworked shells on row 9, join with sl st in next shell, (ch3, dc, ch 2, 2 dc) in same shell, ch 3, (tr in next tr, ch 1) 6 times, tr in next tr, ch 3, shell 2 times, turn. *(4 shells, 7 tr)*

Rows 11-23: Repeat rows 11-23 of first strap and first and second sides.

Back
Rows 1-8: Repeat rows 1-8 of Front.
Rows 10-16: Repeat rows 3-9 of Front.
Rows 17-23: For **first strap,** repeat rows 10-16 of Front first strap. At end of last row, fasten off.

Row 17 : For **second strap,** repeat row 10 of Front second strap.

Rows 18-23: Repeat rows 11-16 of Front first strap. At end of last row, fasten off.

Edging
Working on opposite side of starting ch on Front, join with sl st in first ch, (ch 3, dc, ch 2, 2 dc) in same ch, *skip next 4 chs, (2 dc, ch 2, 2 dc) in next ch; repeat from * across. Fasten off.
Repeat on Back.
Sew shoulder seams.

Nightgown
1: From fabric cut two pieces each 29" [31", 33"] wide x 47" long or to desired length. With fabric folded in half lengthwise, cut armhole openings on top corners of each according to illustration.

2: Fold each armhole edge under ¼"; fold under again ½". Sew in place. Run gathering thread ¼" from top of each piece.

3: With pieces right sides tog, sew side seams.

4: Hem bottom edge.

5: For front, gather top of one gown piece to fit row 1 of Yoke Front. Leaving ¼" of bias extended at each end, sew bias to gathered edge. Press ¼" ends to inside, fold bias over raw edge, sew in place. Repeat for back.

6: Place row 1 of Yokes over bias tape on each side of gown, sew in place. ❧

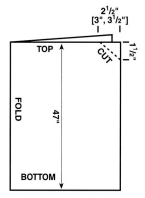

Gown & Robe

Designed by Sylvia Landman

Finished Sizes: Yoke is 15" across.

Materials:
- ❏ Cotton worsted yarn:
    - 10 oz. variegated yellow
    - 7 oz. yellow
    - 4 oz. each lt. peach, dk. peach, aqua and variegated pastels
- ❏ 6½ yds. of 45" ecru fabric
- ❏ ⅜"-wide satin ribbon:
    - 4 yds. peach
    - 2 yds. each yellow and aqua
- ❏ 2⅓ yds. of ½" seam tape
- ❏ 2 small snaps
- ❏ Tracing paper and pencil
- ❏ Ecru sewing thread
- ❏ Sewing needle
- ❏ F hook or hook size needed to obtain gauge

Gauge: We are not responsible for lack of materials due to project not being worked to gauge. Gauge for this pattern: 4 sts = 1"; Ring is 2" across.

Basic Stitches: Ch, sl st, sc, dc.

Basic Rings Band
Note: *Use the following basic instructions as specified in each individual pattern.*

First Ring: With first color, ch 15, sl st in first ch to form ring, ch 3, 29 dc in ring, join with sl st in top of ch-3. Fasten off. *(30 dc made)*

Second Ring: With second color, ch 15, with right side of sts on First Ring facing you, thread end of ch-15 through First Ring, join with sl st in first ch *(to form Second Ring)*, ch 3, 29 dc in ring, join with sl st in top of ch-3. Fasten off.

Remaining Rings: Using each remaining color, repeat Second Ring. *(Each new ring is interlocked with the one before it and always thread the ch-15 through Ring in the same direction.)*

GOWN

Yoke Rings Band
Work Basic Rings Band in color sequence of dk. peach, variegated yellow, aqua, lt. peach and variegated pastels. When each of the colors have been used, start the color sequence over and repeat the sequence until 30 Rings are made inter-

locking last Ring to First Ring *(see illustration)*.

For **Inner Edge of Band,** hold Rings with right side facing you and hide the joining of each Ring behind the next interlocking Ring as you work; join yellow with a sc in a st on any Ring, sc in next 5 sts of same Ring; for **Corner,** (working on next Ring, sc in next 3 sts) 3 times; (working on next Ring, sc in next 6 sts) 6 times, Corner, (working on next Ring, sc in next 6 sts) 4 times, Corner, (working on next Ring, sc in next 6 sts) 5 times, Corner, (working on next Ring, sc in next 6 sts) 2 times, join with sl st in first sc. Fasten off. *(144 sc made)*

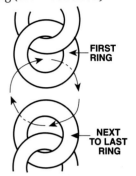

Next Rnd: Join variegated yellow with sc in first st, sc in each st around, join. Fasten off.

For **Outer Edge of Band,** with right side facing you, working on outer edge of interlocked Rings and beginning in first Ring, join yellow with sc in st directly opposite sc on other side of Ring, sc in next 5 sts of same Ring, (working on next Ring, sc in next 6 sts) around, join. Fasten off. *(180)*

Next Rnd: Join variegated yellow with sc in first st, sc in each st around, join. Fasten off.

Body
Note: *All pieces are to be sewn with right sides together allowing ½" for seams unless otherwise stated.*

1: Cut all pieces from fabric according to pattern illustrations on page 78.

2: Run gathering stitch ¼" from top edge of Front gathering to 10½" *(see red line on Gown Front/Back pattern illustrations)*. Repeat on Back.

3: Sew side seams.

4: Press each short end of one Underarm Facing under ¼"; press bottom edge under ¼" and sew ⅛" from edge. Matching center top edge of Underarm Facing with side seam of one armhole, sew top edge of Underarm Facing to armhole; tack ends in place. Clip curves. Repeat with other Underarm Facing on other armhole.

5: Cut two pieces of seam tape each 11" long;

Continued on page 64

Gown & Robe

Continued from page 63

press each short edge of each piece under ¼".

6: Place one 11" piece of seam tape over gathered edge on wrong side of Front; sewing along gathered seam, sew bottom edge of tape to Front and tack ends in place. Repeat with other 11" piece of seam tape on Back.

7: Matching center Ring at each corner of Yoke with each armhole, sew Outer Edge of Band over right side of Back covering gathered seam. Sew other edge of seam tape to wrong side of Ring Band along Outer Edge. Repeat with other side of Yoke on Front.

8: Hem bottom edge of Gown.

9: Cut 72" piece of peach ribbon and tie in 3½" bow. Tack bow to Front of Gown centered along bottom edge of Yoke.

ROBE

Back Yoke

First Rings Band

Work Basic Rings Band on page 63 in color sequence of dk. peach, variegated yellow, aqua, lt. peach and variegated pastels until 12 Rings are made. *Do not interlock the first and last Rings.*

First Row: For **Top Beading Edge of Band,** working on top edge of interlocked Rings, join yellow with sc in any st on First Ring, sc in same st, sc in next 6 sts; (working on next Ring, sc in next 6 sts) 11 times, 2 sc in next st, **do not turn.** Fasten off. *(76 sc made)*

Next Row: Skip first st, join variegated yellow with sl st in next st; for **beginning mesh, (ch 4, skip next st, dc in next st);** for **mesh, (ch 1, skip next st, dc in next st)** 36 times. Fasten off. *(37 mesh)*

Second Rings Band

Work same as First Rings Band in color sequence of aqua, lt. peach, variegated pastels, dk. peach and variegated yellow.

For **Bottom Beading Edge of Band,** working on bottom edge of interlocked Rings, join yellow with sl st in st directly opposite sc on Top Beading Edge of Band; work same as Top Beading Edge. *Do not interlock the first and last Rings.*

Third Rings Band

Work three Rings Bands in same manner as Second Rings Band in color sequence of dk. peach, variegated yellow and aqua ending with 10 mesh on each Beading Edge.

Fourth Rings Band

Work three Rings Bands in same manner as Second Rings Band in color sequence variegated pastels, dk. peach and variegated yellow ending with 10 mesh on each Beading Edge.

Assembly

Working in sts and in chs on Beading Edges, with variegated yellow, sl st First Rings Band and Second Rings Band wrong sides together *(see assembly illustration on next page).* Sl st Third and Fourth Rings to Second Rings Band in same manner.

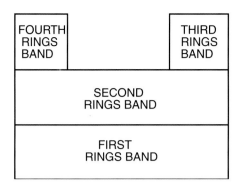

Left Front Yoke
First Rings Band

Work Basic Rings Band on page 63 in color sequence of dk. peach, variegated yellow, aqua, lt. peach and variegated pastels until six Rings are made.

First Row: For **Top Beading Edge of Band,** working on top edge of interlocked Rings, join yellow with sc in any st on First Ring, sc in same st, sc in next 6 sts; (working on next Ring, sc in next 6 sts) 5 times, 2 sc in next st, **do not turn.** Fasten off. *(40 sc made)*

Next Row: Join variegated yellow sl st in first st, beginning mesh, mesh 17 times. Fasten off. *(18 mesh)*

Second Rings Band

Work same as First Rings Band in color sequence of aqua, lt. peach, variegated pastels, dk. peach and variegated yellow.

For **Bottom Beading Edge of Band,** working on bottom edge of interlocked Rings, join yellow with sl st in st directly opposite sc on Top Beading Edge of Band; work same as Top Beading Edge.

Third Rings Band

Work three Rings Bands in same manner as Second Rings Band in color sequence of dk. peach, variegated yellow and aqua ending with 10 mesh on each Beading Edge.

Assembly

Working in sts and in chs on Beading Edges, with variegated yellow, sl st First and Second Rings wrong sides together *(see assembly illustration).* Sl st Third Rings Band to Second

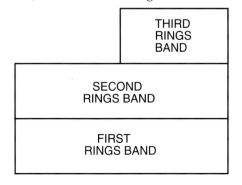

Rings Band in same manner.

Right Front Yoke
First Rings Band

Work Basic Rings Band on page 63 in color sequence of variegated yellow, aqua, lt. peach, variegated pastels and dk. peach until six Rings are made.

Work Top Beading Edge same as Left Front Yoke Beading Edge.

Second Rings Band

Work same as First Rings Band in color sequence of lt. peach, variegated pastels, dk. peach, variegated yellow and aqua.

For **Bottom Beading Edge of Band,** working on bottom edge of interlocked Rings, join yellow with sl st in st directly opposite sc on Top Beading Edge of Band; work same as Top Beading Edge.

Third Rings Band

Work three Rings Bands in same manner as Second Rings Bands in color sequence of variegated pastels, dk. peach and variegated yellow ending with 10 mesh on each Beading Edge.

Assembly

Working in sts and in chs on Beading Edges, with variegated yellow, sl st First and Second Rings Bands wrong sides together *(see assembly illustration).* Sl st Third Rings Band to Second Rings Band in same manner; sl st shoulders of Front Yokes to Back Yoke wrong sides together.

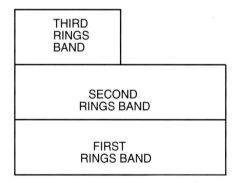

Yoke Edging

First Rnd: With right side of assembled Yoke facing you, beginning at Top Beading Edge on Fourth Rings Band, join yellow with sc in end of row at Neck Edge, sc in end of same row; working around entire outer edge of assembled Yoke, 2 sc in end of each dc row, sc in end of each sc row, sc in each unworked st on each Rings Band and sc in each unworked st and ch across Top Edge of Second Rings Band, join with sl st in first sc. Fasten off.

Next Rnd: With right side of Yoke facing you, join

Continued on page 69

Lacy Camisole

Designed by Sharon Maruch

Finished Sizes: Lady's one size fits all.

Materials:
- ❏ 500 yds. size 30 crochet cotton thread
- ❏ 1 yd. fabric
- ❏ 5 yds. of ¼" satin ribbon
- ❏ 2⅓ yds. of ½" seam tape
- ❏ Sewing needle and matching thread
- ❏ No. 12 steel hook or hook size needed to obtain gauge

Gauge: We are not responsible for lack of materials due to project not being worked to gauge. Gauge for this pattern: 12 sts or chs = 1".

Basic Stitches: Ch, sl st, sc, dc, tr.

Body

1: Cut all pieces from fabric according to pattern illustrations on page 68. With right sides together, sew ½" side seams.

2: Clip top corners of front, hem ¼" on all remaining edges.

Trim
Front

Row 1: Ch 331, dc in fifth ch from hook *(counts as first dc and ch-1),* (ch 1, skip next ch, dc in next ch) across, turn. *(165 dc made)*

Row 2: Ch 1, sc in first st, (ch 7, skip next st, sc in next st) across to last ch sp, ch 4, skip next ch sp, dc in fourth ch of beginning ch-5. *(82 ch sps)*

Row 3: (Ch 7, sc in next ch sp) across to last ch sp, ch 4, dc in last ch sp, turn. *(81 ch sps)*

Row 4: (Ch 7, sc in next ch sp) across, turn. Fasten off. *(80 ch sps)*

Row 5: Skip first 11 ch sps, join with sc in next ch sp, (ch 7, sc in next ch sp) 56 times, ch 4, dc in next ch sp leaving remaining ch sps unworked, turn. *(57 ch sps)*

Rows 6-8: (Ch 7, sc in next ch sp) across to last ch sp, ch 4, dc in last ch sp, turn. At end of last row *(54 ch sps).*

Row 9: (Ch 7, sc in next ch sp) across, turn. Fasten off.

Row 10: Skip first 11 ch sps, join with sc in next ch sp, (ch 7, sc in next ch sp) 29 times, ch 4, dc in next ch sp leaving remaining ch sps

unworked, turn. *(30 ch sps)*

Rows 11-13: (Ch 7, sc in next ch sp) across to last ch sp, ch 4, dc in last ch sp, turn. At end of last row *(27 ch sps).*

Row 14: For **base of leaves,** ch 1, sc in first st, *ch 3, (7 tr, ch 3, 7 tr) in next ch sp, ch 3, sc in next ch sp; repeat from * across, turn. *(13 leaves)*

Row 15: Ch 1, sc in first st, *ch 3, tr in each tr across to ch-3 sp, (3 tr, ch 3, 3 tr) in ch-3 sp, tr in each tr across leaf, ch 3, sc in next sc; repeat from * across, turn.

Row 16: Ch 1, sc in first st, *ch 7, skip first 5 tr, tr in next 5 tr, (3 tr, ch 3, 3 tr) in next ch-3 sp, tr in next 5 tr, ch 7, sc in next sc; repeat from * across, turn.

Row 17: Ch 8, *[sc in first tr, ch 4, skip each of next 3 tr, sc in next tr, ch 3, (3 dc, ch 2, 3 dc) in next ch-3 sp, ch 3, skip next 3 tr, sc in next tr, ch 4, skip next 3 tr, sc in next tr], ch 5, dc in next sc, ch 5; repeat from * 11 more times; repeat between [ ], ch 8, sl st in last sc. Fasten off.

Sew remaining ch sps of rows 4 and 9, and ends of rows 5-13, and row 13 to top of Body Front as shown on pattern illustration.

Row 18: With right side facing you, top nearest you and Body away from you, working around post of sc on row 2, join with sc around first sc, (ch 8, skip next sc, sc around next sc) across to last 2 sc, ch 4, skip next sc, dc around last sc, turn. *(41 ch sps)*

Rows 19-22: Repeat rows 14-17. *(20 leaves).*

Row 23: For **left side,** with right side of work facing you and top nearest you, working in ch sps of row 9, join with sc in first ch sp, (ch 8, skip next ch sp, sc in next ch sp) 6 times, ch 4, skip next ch sp, dc in next ch sp, turn. *(7 ch sps)*

Rows 24-27: Repeat rows 14-17. *(3 leaves)*

Row 23: For **right side,** skip next 24 sc across row 9, join with sc in next sc, (ch 8, skip next sc, sc around next sc) 6 times, ch 4, skip next sc, dc in next ch sp, turn. *(7 ch sps)*

Rows 24-27: Repeat rows 14-17. *(3 leaves)*

Right Armhole

Rnd 1: With right side facing you, working through fabric, join with sc at right side seam, evenly space 49 more sc across armhole to back top

Continued on page 68

Lacy Camisole

Continued from page 66

corner, ch 114, 2 sc in end of row 1 of front, sc in each of rows 2-4, evenly space 50 sc across front of armhole to seam, join with sl st in first sc. *(106 sc, 114 chs made)*

Rnd 2: Ch 6, skip next 2 sts, (tr in next 2 sts or chs, ch 2, skip next 2 sts or chs) around to last st, tr in last st, join with sl st in fourth ch of ch-6. *(110 tr)*

Rnd 3: Ch 1, sc in each st and each ch around, join with sl st in first sc. *(220 sc)*

Rnd 4: Ch 3, [skip next 2 sts, (dc, ch 6, dc in top of last dc made, dc) in next st] around, join with sl st in top of ch-3. Fasten off.

Left Armhole

Rnd 1: With right side facing you, working through fabric, join with sc at left side seam, evenly space 49 more sc across armhole to front top corner, sc in each of rows 4-2, 2 sc in end of row 1, ch 114, evenly space 50 sc across back of armhole to seam, join with sl st in first sc. *(106 sc, 114 chs made)*

Rnds 2-4: Repeat rnds 2-4 of Right Armhole.

Neck

Rnd 1: With right side facing you, working through fabric, join with sc at right back corner, evenly space 196 more sc across back; working on opposite side of left armhole ch, sc in each ch across, sc in each ch across starting ch of Front, sc in each ch across right armhole ch, join with sl st in first sc.

Rnds 2-4: Repeat rnds 2-4 of Right Armhole.

Bottom

Rnd 1: Working through fabric, join with sc at side seam, ch 1, (sc, ch 1) 8 times per inch around bottom, join with sl st in first sc. *(392 sc made)*

Rnd 2: Sl st in next ch sp, ch 7, skip next 3 ch sps, (sc in next ch sp, ch 7, skip next 3 ch sps) around, join with sl st in first ch. *(98 ch-7 sps)*

Rnd 3: Sl st in next 3 chs, *ch 3, (7 tr, ch 3, 7 tr) in next ch sp, ch 3, sc in next ch sp; repeat from * around, join with sl st in first ch. Fasten off.

Belt

For **belt loop,** working through fabric, join with sl st in side seam at waist, ch 8, sl st in seam ½" below first sl st. Fasten off. Repeat for other side.

Cut ribbon to fit waist plus 20", slip ribbon through belt loops, tie in bow at front.

Finishing

Cut piece ribbon 28" long; starting at shoulder, weave through rnd 2 of armhole trim, tie in bow at shoulder. Repeat for other armhole.

Starting at center front, weave remaining ribbon through rnd 2 of Neck Trim, tie in bow. Trim to desired length. &

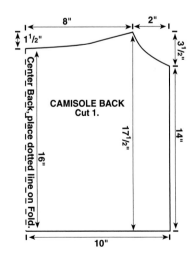

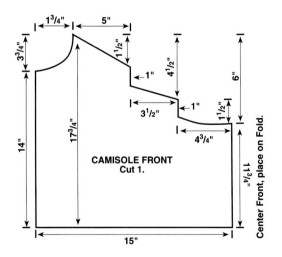

Gown & Robe

Continued from page 65

variegated yellow with sc in first st, sc in each st around, join. Fasten off.

Sleeve Rings Band (make 2)

Work Basic Rings Band in color sequence of dk. peach, variegated yellow, aqua, lt. peach and variegated pastels until 10 Rings are made, interlocking last Ring to First Ring.

First Rnd: For **Top Outer Edge of Band,** with right side facing you, working on outer edge of interlocked Rings, join yellow with sc in any st on any Ring, sc in next 6 sts of same ring; (working on next Ring, sc in next 5 sts) around, join with sl st in first sc. Fasten off. *(60 sc made)*

Next Rnd: Join variegated yellow with sc in first st, sc in each st around, join. Fasten off.

For **Bottom Outer Edge of Band,** join yellow with sc in st directly opposite sc on other side of Ring; work same as Top Outer Edge of Band.

Body

Note: All pieces are to be sewn with right sides together allowing ½" for seams unless otherwise stated.

1: Cut all pieces from fabric according to pattern illustrations.

2: Sew side seams.

3: Sew Sleeve seams.

4: Matching Sleeve seams with side seams, sew Sleeves in armholes. Clip curves.

5: Turn bottom edge of one Sleeve under ½" and sew ⅛" from edge. Turn under again ½" and hem. Repeat on other Sleeve.

6: Hem bottom edge of Body.

7: For **each Front piece,** run gathering stitch ¼" from top edge gathering to 6¾" across leaving 4½" ungathered from center front edge *(see red line on Robe Front pattern illustration).* Turn front edge under ½" and sew ⅛" from edge. Turn under again 2" and hem.

8: Run gathering stitch ¼" from top edge of Back piece gathering to 15" across *(see red line on Robe Back pattern illustration).*

9: Gathering Sleeves to fit, sew Top Edge of Sleeve Rings Bands to bottom edge of Sleeves.

10: Sew bottom edge of Yoke Fronts to right side of Body Fronts covering gathered edge; sew bottom edge of Yoke Back to right side of Body Back covering gathered edge.

11: Sew sides of Yoke to Sleeves covering Sleeve seam.

12: Cut one piece of seam tape 15½" long, two pieces each 16½" long and two pieces each 7" long; press each short edge of each piece under ¼".

13: Place 15½" piece of seam tape over gathered edge on wrong side of Back; sewing along gathered seam, sew bottom edge of tape to Back and tack ends in place. Sew other edge of seam tape to wrong side of Yoke.

14: Place one 7" piece of seam tape over gathered edge on wrong side of one Front; sewing along gathered seam, sew bottom edge of tape to Front and tack ends in place. Sew other edge of seam tape to wrong side of Yoke. Repeat on other Front.

15: Place one 16½" piece of seam tape evenly across wrong side of upper armhole along Yoke edge; sew bottom edge of tape to armhole and tack ends in place. Sew other edge of seam tape to wrong side of Yoke. Repeat on other armhole.

16: Sew snaps to front at top and bottom of Yoke.

17: Cut 72" piece each peach, aqua and yellow ribbon; hold all ribbon pieces together and tie in 5" bow. Tack bow to center front neck edge on Right Front. ❧

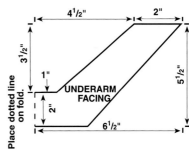

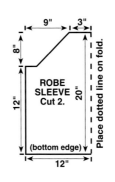

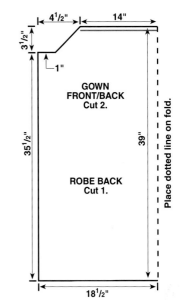

Lady's Bed Jacket & Slippers

An Original by Annie

BED JACKET
Finished Size: One size fits all.

Materials:
- Worsted yarn:
  - 16 oz. pink
  - 12 oz. white
- 2¼" square piece cardboard
- Tapestry needle
- G hook or hook size needed to obtain gauge

Gauge: We are not responsible for lack of materials due to project not being worked to gauge. Gauge for this pattern: 4 sc = 1", 4 sc rows = 1". Each cluster and ch-1 of Center = 1". Strip is 4¼" wide.

Basic Stitches: Ch, sl st, sc, hdc, dc.

Special Stitch: For **double crochet cluster (dc cluster),** *yo, insert hook in st, yo, pull through st, yo, pull lp through 2 lps on hook, leaving last lp on hook; working in same st, repeat from * for each dc of cluster, yo, pull through all lps on hook.

Strip A (make 8)
Note: Strip is 19½" long.
For **Center of Strip,** with pink, *ch 4, **3-dc cluster** *(see Special Stitch)* in third ch from hook; repeat from * 14 more times, ch 2. Fasten off. *(This will make a long chain of clusters.)*

Border
Rnd 1: Join white with sc in first ch-1 between clusters, ch 3, (sc in next ch-1 between clusters, ch 3) across side of Center to ch-1 at end; 3 sc in end ch-1, (ch 3, sc in opposite side of ch-1 on other side of Center) across side to ch-2 at other end, ch 3, 3 sc in end of ch-2, ch 3, join with sl st in first sc.

Rnd 2: Ch 1, sc in first st, *(3 sc in next ch-3 sp, sc in next st) down side to 3-sc group at end, (2 sc in next st, 3 sc in next st, 2 sc in next st; repeat from * one time, 3 sc in remaining ch-3 sp, join. Fasten off.

Rnd 3: Working in **back lps** *(see Stitch Guide),* join pink with sc in first st, sc in each st around sides with (2 sc in each of next 3 sts, sc in next st, 2 sc in each of next 3 sts) in center 7 sts at each end of Strip, join. Fasten off.

Rnd 4: Working in **back lps,** join white with sc in first st, *skip next st, (dc, ch 1, dc, ch 1, dc) in next st, skip next st, sc in next st; repeat from * around to last st, skip last st, join. Fasten off.

Rnd 5: Join with pink sc in first st, *(ch 4, sc in next st) down side to center 3 ch-1 sps at end, (ch 5, sc in next ch sp) 3 times; repeat from * one time, ch 4, join.

Rnd 6: (Sc, ch 1, hdc) in next ch-4 sp, *5 hdc in each ch-4 sp down side, 9 hdc in next ch-5 sp, 12 hdc in next ch-5 sp, 9 hdc in next ch-5 sp; repeat from * one time, 5 hdc in last ch-4 sp, join. Fasten off.

Strip B (make 8)
Note: Strip is 15½" long.
For **Center of Strip,** with pink, (ch 4, 3-dc cluster in third ch from hook) 11 times, ch 2. Fasten off.

Border
Work same as Strip A Border.

Strip C (make 4)
Note: Strip is 9½" long.
For **Center of Strip,** with pink, (ch 4, 3-dc cluster in third ch from hook) 5 times, ch 2. Fasten off.

Border
Work same as Strip A Border.

Continued on page 72

Lady's Bed Jacket & Slippers

Continued from page 71

Drawstring

With two strands pink held together as one, ch until piece measures 60" long. Fasten off.

For each pom-pom *(make 2),* wrap pink yarn around cardboard 100 times. Slip loops off cardboard, tie separate piece yarn tightly around center of all loops. Cut ends and trim to shape a 2¼" ball.

Finishing

Arrange Strips according to illustration, leaving the center 28 sts around each end free, with pink, whipstitch edges of Strips together through **back lps.**

Weave Drawstring through Strips across top of Bed Jacket *(see photo);* tack pom-poms to each end of Drawstring.

SLIPPERS

Finished Sizes: Small 7½"-8" sole. Medium 8½"-9" sole. Large 9½"-10" sole.

Materials:

❑ Worsted yarn:
    7 oz. pink
    1 oz. white
❑ G, I and J hooks or hook size needed to obtain gauges

Gauges: We are not responsible for lack of materials due to project not being worked to gauge. Gauge for this pattern: **G hook and single strand,** 4 sc = 1". Each cluster and ch-1 of Center = 1". Strip is 4¼" wide. **J hook and two strands held tog,** 7 sc = 2"; 7 sc **back lp** rows = 2".

Basic Stitches: Ch, sl st, sc, hdc, dc.

Special Stitch: For **double crochet cluster (dc cluster),** *yo, insert hook in st, yo, pull through st, yo, pull lp through 2 lps on hook, leaving last lp on hook; working in same st, repeat from * for each dc of cluster, yo, pull through all lps on hook.

Note: Instructions are for small; changes for medium and large are in [ ].

Slipper (make 2)

Note: Work entire Slipper in **back lps** *(see Stitch Guide).*

Row 1: With J hook and two strands pink held tog as one, ch 15 [18, 21], sc in second ch from hook, sc in each ch across, turn. *(14 sc made)* *[17 sc made, 20 sc made]*

Rows 2-3: Ch 1, sc in each st across, turn.

Row 4: Ch 1, sc in each st across, ch 13, turn.

Row 5: Sc in second ch from hook, sc in each ch across, sc in each st across row 4, turn. *(26 sc)* *[29 sc, 32 sc]*

Rows 6-21: Ch 1, sc in each st across, turn.

Row 22: Ch 1, sc in first 14 [17, 20] sts leaving remaining sts unworked, turn.

Rows 23-25: Ch 1, sc in each st across, turn. At end of last row *(end of toe),* leave 8" end and weave it through the end of every other row. Pull to end tightly and tie off.

Sl st top of Slipper together and back of heel together *(see illustration on page 78).*

Cuff

Rnd 1: With I hook and single strand pink, join with sc at center back seam, ch 2 *(counts as first dc),* dc in each st around top opening and across instep, join with sl st in top of ch-2.

Rnds 2-3: Ch 1, **sc front post** *(see Stitch Guide)* around first st, ch 2, **dc front post** in each st around, join. At end of last rnd, fasten off.

Strip (make 2)

Note: Strip is 8½" long.

For **Center of Strip,** with G hook and pink, (ch 4, 3-dc cluster in third ch from hook) 4 times, ch 2. Fasten off.

Continued on page 78

Eyelet Lace Slip-Ons

An Original by Annie

Finished Sizes: **Lady's small** (4-5) sole is 8½" long; **medium** (6-7) sole is 9½" long; **large** (8-9) sole is 10½" long.
Girl's small (6-8) sole is 7½" long; **medium** (10-13) sole is 8" long; **large** (1-3) sole is 10½" long.

Materials:
❏ For **lady's sizes:**
    5 oz. blue cotton worsted yarn
    1 oz. white woven acrylic sport yarn
❏ For **girl's sizes:**
    3 oz. blue cotton worsted yarn
    ½ oz. white woven acrylic sport yarn
❏ 1 pair of size large foam insoles
❏ 10½" x 13½" sheet plastic canvas
❏ Quilting thread

❏ Thread elastic
❏ Sewing and tapestry needles
❏ D and G hooks or hook sizes needed to obtain gauges

Gauges: We are not responsible for lack of materials due to project not being worked to gauge. Gauge for this pattern: **D hook and sport yarn,** 7 sts = 1"; 2 dc rows = ⅞"; eyelet is 2½" wide. **G hook and worsted yarn,** 4 sc = 1", 4 sc rows = 1"; 4 dc = 1", 2 dc rows = 1".

Basic Stitches: Ch, sl st, sc, hdc, dc.

Note: Instructions are for small; changes for
Continued on page 76

Ballerina Slippers

An Original by Annie

Finished Sizes: **Lady's small** (4-5) sole is 8½" long; **medium** (6-7) sole is 9½" long; **large** (8-9) sole is 10½" long.
Girl's small (6-8) sole is 7½" long; **medium** (10-13) sole is 8" long; **large** (1-3) sole is 8½" long.

Materials:
- Woven acrylic sport yarn for **lady's sizes:**
  - 4 oz. pink
  - 2 oz. tan
  - ½ oz. natural
- Woven acrylic sport yarn for **girl's sizes:**
  - 3 oz. pink
  - 1½ oz. tan
  - ¼ oz. natural
- 25 yds. ecru size 10 crochet cotton thread for all sizes
- Tapestry needle
- No. 7 steel hook, D and G hooks or hook sizes needed to obtain gauges

Gauges: We are not responsible for lack of materials due to project not being worked to gauge. Gauge for this pattern: **G hook and two strands sport yarn held tog,** 4 sc = 1", 4 sc rows = 1"; 4 dc rows = 1", 2 dc rows = 1". **No. 7 hook and size 10 cotton thread,** 10 chs = 1". **D hook and single strand sport yarn,** 5 dc = 1".

Basic Stitches: Ch, sl st, sc, hdc, dc, tr.

Notes: Instructions are for small; changes for medium and large are in [ ].
Use two strands held together unless otherwise stated.

Lady's Slipper (make 2)

Rnd 1: With tan and G hook, ch 24 [27, 30], 2 sc in second ch from hook, sc in next 10 [13, 16] chs, hdc in next ch, dc in next 9 chs, 2 dc in next ch, 5 dc in last ch; working on opposite side of starting ch, 2 dc in next ch, dc in next 9 chs, hdc in next ch, sc in last 11 [14, 17] chs, join with sl st in first sc. *(52 sts made) [58 sts made, 64 sts made]*

Rnd 2: Ch 1, sc in first st, 2 sc in next st, sc in next 13 [14, 15] sts, hdc in next 10 [12, 14] sts, 2 hdc in next st, 3 hdc in next st, 2 hdc in next st, hdc in next 10 [12, 14] sts, sc in next 13 [14, 15] sts, 2 sc in last st, join. *(58) [64, 70]*

Rnd 3: For **small and medium sizes only**, ch 1, sc in first st, 2 sc in next st, sc in next 12 [13] sts, skip next st, sc in next 10 [12] sts, (2 sc in next st, sc in next 3 sts) 2 times, 2 sc in next st, sc in next 10, [12] sts, skip next st, sc in next 12 [13] sts, 2 sc in last st, join. Fasten off. *(61) [67]*

Rnd [3]: For **large size only**, ch 2, 2 hdc in next st, hdc in next 15 sts, skip next st, hdc in next 13 sts, (2 hdc in next st, hdc in next 3 sts) 2 times, 2 hdc in next st, hdc in next 13 sts, skip next st, hdc in next 15 sts, 2 hdc in last st, join with sl st in top of ch-2. Fasten off. *[73]*

Rnd 4: For **all sizes**, join pink with sc in first st, 2 sc in next st, sc in next 27 [30, 33] sts, 2 sc in next st, sc in next 3 sts, 2 sc in next st, sc in next 26 [29, 32] sts, 2 sc in last st, join. *(65) [71, 77]*

Rnd 5: Ch 1, sc in first st, sc in next 2 sts, 2 sc in next st, sc in next 26 [29, 32] sts, 2 sc in next st, sc in next 7 sts, 2 sc in next st, sc in next 25 [28, 31] sts, 2 sc in last st, join. *(69) [75, 81]*

Rnds 6-8: Ch 1, sc in each st around, join.

Rnd 9: Ch 1, sc in first st, sc in next 24 [26, 30] sts, (skip next st, sc in next 2 sts) 4 times, (sc in next 2 sts, skip next st) 4 times, sc in last 20 [24, 26] sts, join. *(61) [67, 73]*

Rnd 10: Ch 1, sc in first st, sc in next 26 [28, 32] sts, (skip next st, sc in next st) 3 times, (sc in next st, skip next st) 3 times, sc in last 22 [26, 28] sts, join. *(55) [61, 67]*

Rnd 11: Ch 1, sc in first st, sc in next 27 [29, 34] sts, (skip next st, sc in next st) 3 times, sc in last 21 [25, 26] sts, join. *(52) [58, 64]*

Rnd 12: Working this rnd in **back lps** *(see Stitch Guide)*, with D hook, join single strand natural with sc in first st, sc in next 27 [29, 34] sts, sc next 3 sts tog, sc in last 21 [25, 26] sts, join with sl st in **back lp** of first sc. *(50) [56, 62]*

Rnd 13: Working this rnd in **back lps**, ch 3, dc in each st around, join with sl st in top ch-3.

Rnd 14: Working this rnd in **front lps**, ch 1, sc in first st, ch 3; for **picot, sl st in front lp and left bar of last sc made** *(see illustration)*; (sc in each of next 2 sts, ch 3, picot) around to last st, sc in

last st, join with sl st in first sc. Fasten off.

For **picot edging**, hold slipper upside down; working in front lps of rnd 12, with D hook, join single strand natural with sc in last st, picot, (sc in each of next 2 sts, picot) 8 [10, 12] times, (2 sc in each of next 2 sts, picot) 10 [11, 12] times, sc in last st, join. Fasten off.

Drawstring

With G hook and pink, ch 100 [100, 110]. Fasten off. Beginning at center front, weave through sts of rnd 13. Tie knot at each end of Drawstring.

Rose

Row 1: With D hook and single strand pink, ch 24, sc in second ch from hook, 2 sc in next ch, (hdc in next ch, 2 hdc in next ch) 2 times, (dc in next ch, 2 dc in next ch) 3 times, (tr in next ch, 2 tr in next ch) 5 times, 3 tr in last ch, turn. *(36 sts)*

Row 2: Skip first st, 5 dc in next st, skip next st, sc in next st, (skip next st, 5 dc in next st, skip next st, sc in next st) across. Fasten off.

To form rose, starting at first st of row 1, roll up piece, tacking bottom edge together as you work.

Doily Motif

Rnd 1: With No. 7 steel hook and single strand ecru crochet cotton, ch 10, sl st in first ch to form ring, (ch 7, sc in ring) 10 times. **Do not join rnds.** *(10 ch lps).*

Rnd 2: (Ch 7, sc in next ch lp) 10 times.

Rnds 3-4: (Ch 7, sc, ch 7, sc) in each ch lp around.

Rnd 5: (Ch 5; for **picot, sl st in second ch from hook;** ch 3, sc in next ch lp) around. Fasten off.

Tack bottom of Rose to center of Doily. Tack center of Doily to rnds 12 and 14 at center front of Slipper.

Girl's Slipper (make 2)

Rnd 1: With G hook and tan, ch 21 [25, 29] 2 sc in second ch from hook, sc in next 9 [11, 13] chs, hdc in next ch, dc in next 7 [9, 10] chs, 2 dc in next ch, 5 dc in last ch; working on opposite side of starting ch, 2 dc in next ch, dc in next 7 [9, 11] chs, hdc in next ch, sc in next 9 [11, 13] chs, 2 sc in last ch, join with sl st in first sc. *(47 sts made) [55 sts made, 63 sts made]*

Rnd 2: Ch 1, sc in first st, 2 sc in next st, sc in next 12 [14, 16] sts, hdc in next 8 [10, 12] sts, 2 hdc in next st, 3 hdc in next st, 2 hdc in next st, hdc in next 8 [10, 12] sts, sc in next 13 [15, 17] sts, 2 sc in last st, join. Fasten off. *(53) [61, 69]*

Rnd 3: Join pink with sc in first st, 2 sc in next st, sc in next 10 [12, 14] sts, skip next st, sc in next

Continued on page 76

Ballerina Slippers

Continued from page 75

11 [13, 15] sts, 2 sc in next st, sc in next 5 sts, 2 sc in next st, sc in next 11 [13, 15] sts, skip next st, sc in next 9 [11, 13] sts, 2 sc in last st, join. *(55) [63, 71]*

Rnds 4-5: Ch 1, sc in each st around, join.

Rnd 6: Ch 1, sc in first st, sc in next 19 [23, 27] sts, (skip next st, sc in next 2 sts) 3 times, (sc in next 2 sts, skip next st) 3 times, sc in last 17 [21, 25] sts, join. *(49) [57, 65]*

Rnd 7: Ch 1, sc in first st, sc in next 19 [23, 27] sts, (skip next st, sc in next st) 3 times, (sc in next st, skip next st) 3 times, sc in last 17 [21, 25] sts, join. *(43) [51, 59]*

Rnd 8: Ch 1, sc in first st, sc in next 19 [23, 27] sts, (skip next st, sc in next st) 3 times, sc in last 17 [21, 25] sts, join. Fasten off. *(40) [48, 56]*

Rnd 9: Working this rnd in **back lps** *(see Stitch Guide)*, with D hook, join single strand natural with sc in first st, sc in each st around, join with sl st in **back lp** of first sc.

Rnds 10-11: Repeat rnds 13-14 of Lady's Slipper.

For **picot edging,** hold slipper upside down; working in **front lps** of rnd 9, with D hook, join single strand natural with sc in last st, picot, (sc in next 2 sts, picot) 7 [8, 11] times, (2 dc in next st, picot) 10 times, (sc in next 2 sts, picot) 7 [10, 11] times, sc in last st, join. Fasten off.

Drawstring

With ch 75 [75, 80], work same as Lady's Drawstring.

Rose

Row 1: With D hook and single strand pink, ch 19, sc in second ch from hook, sc in next ch, 2 sc in next ch, (hdc in next ch, 2 hdc in next ch) 2 times, (dc in next ch, 2 dc in next ch) 2 times, (tr in next ch, 2 tr in next ch) 3 times, 3 tr in last st, turn. *(28 sts made)*

Row 2: Skip first st, 5 dc in next st, skip next st, sc in next st, (skip next st, 5 dc in next st, skip next st, sc in next st) across. Fasten off.

To form Rose, starting at first st of row 1, roll up piece, tacking bottom edge tog as you work.

Doily Motif

Rnds 1-3: Repeat rnds 1-3 of Lady's Doily Motif.

Rnd 4: Repeat rnd 5 of Lady's Doily Motif.

Tack bottom of Rose to center of Doily. Tack center of Doily to rnds 9 and 11 at center front of Slipper. ❧

Eyelet Lace Slip-Ons

Continued from page 73

medium and large are in [ ].

Lady's Slip-Ons
Sole (make 4)

Rnd 1: With G hook and blue, ch 24 [27, 30], 2 sc in second ch from hook, sc in next 10 [13, 16] chs, hdc in next ch, dc in next 9 chs, 2 dc in next ch, 5 dc in last ch; working on opposite side of starting ch, 2 dc in next ch, dc in next 9 chs, hdc in next ch, sc in last 11 [14, 17] chs, join with sl st in first sc. *(52 sts made) [58 sts made, 64 sts made]*

Rnd 2: Ch 1, sc in first st, 2 sc in next st, sc in next 13 [14, 15] sts, hdc in next 10 [12, 14] sts, 2 hdc in next st, 3 hdc in next st, 2 hdc in next st, hdc in next 10 [12, 14] sts, sc in next 13 [14, 15] sts, 2 sc in last st, join. *(58) [64, 70]*

Rnd 3: Ch 1, sc in first st, 2 sc in next st, sc in next 12 [13, 15] sts, skip next st, sc in next 10 [12, 13] sts, (2 sc in next st, sc in next 3 sts) 2 times, 2 sc in next st, sc in next 10 [12, 13] sts, skip next st, sc in next 12 [13, 15] sts, 2 sc in last st, join. *(61) [67, 73]*

Rnd 4: For **small and medium sizes only,** ch 1, sc in first st, 2 sc in next st, sc in next 27 [30] sts, 2 sc in next st, sc in next 3 sts, 2 sc in next st, sc in next 26 [29] sts, 2 sc in last st, join. *(65) [71]*

Rnd [4]: For **large size only,** ch 2, 2 hdc in next st, hdc in next 33 sts, 2 hdc in next st, hdc in next 3 sts, 2 hdc in next st, hdc in next 32 sts, 2 hdc in last st, join with sl st in top of ch-2. *(77)*

Rnd 5: For **all sizes,** ch 1, sc in first 3 sts, 2 sc in next st, sc in next 26 [29, 32] sts, 2 sc in next st, sc in next 7 sts, 2 sc in next st, sc in next 25 [38, 31] sts, 2 sc in last st, join with sl st in first sc. Fasten off.

Sole Assembly

For **padding and lining,** using crocheted piece as

pattern, cut one piece from each insole and two pieces from plastic canvas each ⅛" smaller than Sole on all edges. With quilting thread, sew each insole to each plastic canvas piece.

For each **Sole**, matching sts, hold two crocheted pieces with wrong sides tog; working through both thicknesses, insert hook under **both lps** of first st at heel, pull lp through, sl st in each st around to toe end; with padding next to layer of Sole facing you, insert padding and lining piece insides; sl st in each st around. Fasten off.

Vamp (make 2)
Row 1: With G hook and blue, ch 21 [22, 23], dc in fourth ch from hook, dc in each ch across, turn. *(19 dc made) [20 dc made, 21 dc made]*

Row 2: Ch 3, dc in each st across, turn.

Rows 3-5: Ch 3, dc in each st across leaving last st unworked, turn. At end of last row *(16) [17, 18]*.

Row 6: Ch 3, dc next 2 sts tog, dc in each st across to last 3 sts, dc next 2 sts tog leaving last st unworked. Fasten off. *(13) [14, 15]*

Weave thread elastic across each long edge of Vamp and secure ends.

Placing last row of Vamp 1½" from toe end of Sole, sew ends of rows to side edges of Sole.

Eyelet Lace (make 4)
Row 1: With D hook and white, ch 38, hdc in third ch from hook, hdc in each ch across, turn. *(37 hdc made)*

Row 2: (Ch 3, dc) in first st, (ch 1, skip next 2 sts, 2 dc in next st) across, turn. *(12 ch sps)*

Row 3: Ch 1, sc in sp between first 2 sts, sc in next ch-1 sp, (ch 2, skip next 2 sts, sc in next ch-1 sp) across, sc in sp between last 2 sts, turn. *(14 sc, 11 ch sps)*

Row 4: Ch 3, skip next st, 5 dc in each ch-2 sp across to last 2 sts, skip next st, dc in last st, turn. *(57 dc)*

Row 5: Ch 3, dc in each st across, turn.

Row 6: Ch 1, sc in first st, ch 2, skip next 3 sts, (dc, ch 4, dc) in next st, *ch 2, skip next 2 sts, sc in next st, ch 2, skip next 2 sts, (dc, ch 4, dc) in next st; repeat from * across to last 4 sts, ch 2, skip next 3 sts, sc in last st, turn.

Row 7: Ch 1, sc in first st, (skip next ch-2 sp, 9 dc in next ch-4 sp, skip next ch-2 sp, sc in next sc) across. Fasten off.

Run gathering thread across bottom edge of row 1 on one Lace piece; pull tight, gathering piece into a U-shape. Position ends of rows on gathered Lace

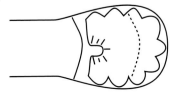

across top of sts on row 2 of Vamp *(see illustration)*, tack in place. Sew row 1 of second Lace piece across top of sts on row 1 of Vamp. Repeat with other two Lace pieces on other Vamp.

Bow (make 2)
With G hook and blue, ch 40; working in **back bar of ch** *(see Stitch Guide)*, sc in second ch from hook, sc in each ch across. Fasten off.

Fold piece in Bow according to diagram. Wrap separate piece blue tightly around center of Bow 2 times, tie ends in knot to secure. Tack to center top of second Lace piece.

Girl's Slip-Ons
Sole (make 4)
Rnd 1: With blue, ch 21 [25, 29], 2 sc in second ch from hook, sc in next 9 [11, 13] chs, hdc in next ch, dc in next 7 [9, 11] chs, 2 dc in next ch, 5 dc in last ch; working on opposite side of starting ch, 2 dc in next ch, dc in next 7 [9, 11] chs, hdc in next ch, sc in next 9 [11, 13] chs, 2 sc in last ch, join with sl st in first sc. *(47 sts made) [55 sts made, 63 sts made]*

Rnd 2: Ch 1, sc in first st, 2 sc in next st, sc in next 12 [14, 16] sts, hdc in next 8 [10, 12] sts, 2 hdc in next st, 3 hdc in next st, 2 hdc in next st, hdc in next 8 [10, 12] sts, sc in next 13 [15, 17] sts, 2 sc in last st, join. *(53) [61, 69]*

Rnd 3: Ch 2, 2 hdc in next st, hdc in next 10 [12, 14] sts, skip next st, hdc in next 11 [13, 15] sts, 2 hdc in next st, hdc in next 5 sts, 2 hdc in next st, hdc in next 11 [13, 15] sts, skip next st, hdc in next 9 [11, 13] sts, 2 hdc in last st, join with sl st in top of ch-2. Fasten off. *(55) [63, 71]*

Sole Assembly
Work same as Lady's Sole Assembly.

Vamp (make 2)
Row 1: With G hook and blue, ch 17 [18, 19], dc in fourth ch from hook, dc in each ch across, turn. *(15 dc made) [16 dc made, 17 dc made]*

Rows 2-3: Ch 3, dc in each st across leaving last st unworked, turn. At end of last row *(13) [14, 15]*.

Row 4: Ch 3, dc next 2 sts tog, dc in each st across to last 3 sts, dc next 2 sts tog leaving last st unworked. Fasten off. *(10) [11, 12]*

Weave thread elastic across each long edge of Vamp and secure ends.

Continued on page 78

Eyelet Lace Slip-Ons

Continued from page 77

Placing last row of Vamp 1" from toe end of Sole, sew ends of rows to side edges of Sole.

Eyelet Lace (make 4)
Row 1: With D hook and white, ch 26, sc in second ch from hook, sc in each ch across, turn. *(25 sc made)*
Row 2: (Ch 3, dc) in first st, (ch 1, skip next 2 sts, 2 dc in next st) across, turn.
Row 3: Ch 1, sc in sp between first 2 sts, sc in next ch-1 sp, (ch 2, skip next 2 sts, sc in next ch-1 sp) across, sc in sp between last 2 sts, turn.

Row 4: Ch 3, skip next st, 5 dc in each ch-2 sp across to last 2 sts, skip next st, dc in last st, turn.
Row 5: Ch 1, sc in first st, *ch 2, skip next 2 sts, (dc, ch 4, dc) in next st, ch 2, skip next 2 sts, sc in next st; repeat from * across, turn.
Row 6: Ch 1, sc in first st, (skip next ch-2 sp, 9 dc in next ch-4 sp, skip next ch-2 sp, sc in next sc) across. Fasten off.

Bow (make 2)
With ch 30, work same as Lady's Bow. ❧

Lady's Bed Jacket & Slippers

Continued from page 72

Border
With G hook, work same as Bed Jacket Strip A Border using white yarn on rnds 1-2, pink yarn on rnd 3, white yarn on rnd 4 and pink yarn on rnds 5-6.
Tack Center and rnd 4 of Strip to top of Slipper. ❧

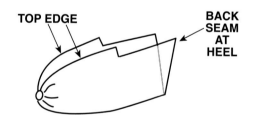

Leave 28 stitches around ends free.

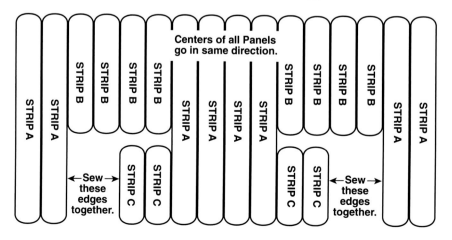

Summer Sensations

CHAPTER FOUR

Butterfly Dress

Designed by Angelina Varona

Finished Sizes: **Lady's bust (small)** 30"-32". Finished measurement: 34". **Lady's bust (medium)** 34"-36". Finished measurement: 36½". **Lady's bust (large)** 38"-40". Finished measurements: 42".

Materials:
- ❑ Size 20 crochet cotton amount needed for size:
    - 3,500 yds. for small
    - 3,900 yds. for medium
    - 4,300 yds. for large
- ❑ 3 yds. of ⅜" satin ribbon *(optional)*
- ❑ Small cluster of silk flowers *(optional)*
- ❑ Tapestry needle
- ❑ No. 10 steel hook or hook size needed to obtain gauge

Gauge: We are not responsible for lack of materials due to project not being worked to gauge. Gauge for this pattern: 3 mesh = 1"; 15 mesh rows = 4".

Basic Stitches: Ch, sl st, sc, dc, tr.

Special Stitches: For **beginning sc mesh (beg sc mesh)**, ch 5, sc in next ch-3 sp, ch 2, dc in next dc.
For **dc mesh**, ch 3, skip next sc, dc in next dc.
For **sc mesh**, ch 2, sc in next ch-3 sp, ch 2, dc in next dc.
For **ending sc mesh (end sc mesh)**, ch 2, sc inch-6 sp, ch 2, dc in third ch of ch-6.
For **beginning dc mesh (beg dc mesh)**, ch 6, skip next sc, dc in next dc.
For **ending dc mesh (end dc mesh)**, ch 3, skip next sc, dc in third ch of ch-5.

Note: Instructions are for lady's bust 30"-32": changes for 34"-36" and 38"-40" are in [ ].

Dress
Bodice
Row 1: Beginning at waist, ch 208 [224, 256], dc in sixth ch from hook, (ch 1, skip next ch, dc in next ch) across, turn. *(103 dc, 102 ch-1 sps made) [111 dc, 110 ch-1 sps made; 127 dc, 126 ch-1 sps made]*

Row 2: Ch 6, skip next dc, (dc in next dc, ch 2, sc in next dc, ch 2, dc in next dc, ch 3, skip next dc) across to ch-6, dc in third ch of ch-6, turn. *(52 dc, 25 sc) [56 dc, 27 sc; 64 dc, 31 sc] Front of row 2 is right side of work.*

Row 3: Beg sc mesh *(see Special Stitches)*, **dc mesh, sc mesh,** dc mesh, (sc mesh, dc mesh) across to ch-6 sp, **end sc mesh,** turn. *(51 mesh) [55 mesh, 63 mesh]*

Row 4: Beg dc mesh, sc mesh, (dc mesh, sc mesh) across to last mesh, **end dc mesh,** turn.

Pattern is established in rows 3 and 4. Be sure to work correct beg and end mesh on each row.

Rows [5-6, 5-6]: For sizes 34"-36" and 38"-40" only, work in pattern.

For **all sizes,** for **natural waistline,** work in pattern for 4" more, ending on even-numbered row.

Row 5 [7, 7]: For all sizes, work in pattern across first 21 [23, 27] mesh; for row 1 of bodice graph *(see bodice graph on page 83)*, work in pattern across next 4 mesh, ch 1, 3 dc evenly spaced in next mesh, ch 1, dc in next dc, work in pattern across next 4 mesh; work in pattern across, turn.

Rows 6-15 [8-17, 8-17]: Work in pattern across first 21 [23, 27] mesh, work next row of bodice graph, work in pattern across, turn. At end of last row, fasten off.

Row 16 [18, 18]: For sleeve, ch 56 [56, 64]; with wrong side of last row facing you, dc in first dc, ch 3, dc in next dc, work in pattern across next 20 [22, 26] mesh, work next row of bodice graph, work in pattern across; for **sleeve,** ch 60 [60, 68], turn.

Row 17 [19, 19]: Sc in seventh ch from hook, ch 2, skip next ch, dc in next ch, ch 3, skip next 3 chs, (dc in next ch, ch 2, skip next ch, sc in next ch, ch 2, skip next ch, dc in next ch, ch 3, skip next 3 chs) 6 [6, 7] times, work in pattern across next 21 [23, 27] mesh, work next row of bodice graph, work in pattern across to sleeve, (ch 3, skip next 3 chs, dc in next ch, ch 2, skip next ch, sc in next ch, ch 2, skip next ch, dc in next ch) 7 [7, 8] times, turn. *(79 mesh) [83 mesh, 95 mesh]*

Rows 18-21 [20-23, 20-23]: Work in pattern.

Row 22 [24, 24]: For first side, work in pattern across first 39 [41, 47] mesh, dc in second ch of next ch-3 sp leaving remaining mesh

Continued on page 82

Butterfly Dress

Continued from page 80

unworked, turn. *(39 mesh) [41 mesh, 47 mesh]*

Row 23 [25, 25]: Work in pattern.

Row 24 [26, 26]: Work in pattern across to last mesh, dc in last sc leaving ch-5 unworked, turn. *(38 mesh) [40 mesh, 46 mesh]*

Row 25 [27, 27]: Work in pattern.

Row 26 [28, 28]: Work in pattern across to last mesh, dc in fifth ch of ch-6, turn. *(37 mesh) [39 mesh , 45 mesh]*

Rows 27-38 [29-40, 29-44]: Repeat row 23-26 [25-28, 25-28] consecutively. At end of last row *(31 mesh) [33 mesh, 37 mesh].*

Rows 39-60 [41-62, 45-66]: Work in pattern.

Row 61 [63, 67]: Ch 4, dc in first dc, work in pattern across, turn.

Row 62 [64, 68]: Work in pattern across to ch-4, ch 2, sc in ch-4 sp, ch 2, dc in third ch ch-4, turn. *(32 mesh) [34 mesh, 38 mesh]*

Row 63 [65, 69]: Ch 4, dc in first dc, work in pattern across, turn. Fasten off.

Row 22 [24, 24]: For **second side,** join with sl st in same ch on row 21 [23, 23] as last st worked, ch 3, dc in next dc, work in pattern across, turn. *(39 mesh) [41 mesh, 47 mesh]*

Row 23 [25, 25]: Work in pattern across to last mesh, dc in second ch of ch-3 sp, turn. *(38 mesh) [40 mesh, 46 mesh]*

Row 24 [26, 26]: Work in pattern.

Row 25 [27, 27]: Work in pattern across to last sc, dc in last sc, turn. *(37 mesh) [39 mesh, 45 mesh]*

Row 26 [28, 28]: Work in pattern.

Rows 27-38 [29-40, 29-44]: Repeat rows 23-26 [25-28, 25-28] consecutively. At end of last row *(31mesh) [33 mesh, 37 mesh].*

Rows 39-60 [41-62, 45-66]: Work in pattern.

Row 61 [63, 67]: Work in pattern across, ch 1, dc in same st as last st, turn.

Row 62 [64, 68]: Ch 5, sc in next ch-1 sp, ch 2, dc in next dc, work in pattern across, turn. *(32 mesh) [34 mesh, 38 mesh]*

Row 63 [65, 69]: Work in pattern across, ch 1, dc in same st as last st; for back neck edge, ch 51 [51, 67], join with sl st in third ch ch-4 on last row of first side, turn. Fasten off.

Row 64 [66, 70]: For **back,** working across both sides of front and across **back neck edge,** join with sl st in first st, work in pattern across first 32 [34, 38] mesh, ch 3, skip next ch-1 sp, dc in next dc, (ch 2, skip next ch, sc in next ch, ch 2, skip next ch, dc in next ch, ch 3, skip next 3 chs, dc in next ch) 6 [6, 8] times, ch 2, skip next ch, sc in next ch, ch 2, skip next ch, dc in next dc, ch 3, skip next ch-1 sp, dc in next dc, work in pattern across, turn. *(79 mesh) [83 mesh, 95 mesh]*

Rows 65-80 [67-82, 71-86]: Work in pattern. At end of last row, fasten off.

Row 81 [83,87]: For **sleeves,** skip first 14 [14, 16] dc, join with sl st in next dc, work in pattern across next 51 [55, 63] mesh leaving last 14 [14, 16] mesh unworked turn. *(51 mesh) [55 mesh, 63 mesh]*

Rows 82- 95 [84-99, 88-103]: Work in pattern.

Row 96 [100, 104]: Ch 4, dc in next sc, ch 1, dc in next dc, (ch 1, dc in next ch-3 sp or next sc, ch 1, dc in next dc) across. Fasten off. *(103 dc, 102 ch-1 sps) [111dc, 110 ch-1 sps; 127 dc, 126 ch-1 sps]*

Sew side and sleeve seams.

Skirt

Rnd 1: Working around bottom of Bodice, using each seam as one st, with right side of back facing you, join with sl st in sixth dc from right seam on back, ch 4, tr in next ch sp, tr in next dc, ch 3, skip next dc, (tr in next dc, tr in next ch sp, tr in next dc, ch 3, skip next dc) around to last 0 [1, 0] dc, skip last 0 [1, 0] dc , join with sl st in top of ch-4. *(204 tr, 68 ch-3 sps made) [219 tr, 73 ch-3 sps made; 252 tr, 84 ch-3 sps made]*

Rnd 2: Ch 4, skip next tr, dc in next tr, ch 1, dc in next ch-3 sp, ch 1, (dc in next tr, ch 1, skip next tr, dc in next tr, ch 1, dc in next ch-3 sp, ch 1) around, join with sl st in third ch of ch-4. *(204 dc, 204 ch sps) [219 dc, 219 ch sps; 252 dc, 252 ch sps]*

Rnd 3: For **size 30"-32" only,** ch 5, sc in next ch sp, *[ch 2, (dc in next dc, ch 3, dc in next dc, ch 2, sc in next ch sp, ch 2) 16 times, dc in next dc, (ch 3, dc, ch 2, sc, ch 2) in next ch sp, (dc in next dc, ch 3, dc in next dc, ch 2, sc in next ch sp, ch 2) 16 times, dc in next dc, ch 3, dc in next dc, (ch 2, sc, ch 2, dc, ch 3) in next ch sp], dc in next dc, ch 2, sc in next ch sp; repeat from * one time; repeat between [ ]; join with sl st in third ch of ch-5. *(210 mesh)*

Rnd [3]: For **size 34"-36"only,** ch 5, sc in next ch sp, ch 2, *[dc in next dc, (ch 3, dc in next dc, ch 2, sc in next ch sp, ch 2, dc in next dc) 11 times, ch 3, skip next dc, dc in next dc], (ch 2, sc in next ch sp, ch 2, dc in next dc, ch 3, dc in next dc) 11 times, ch 2, sc in next ch sp, ch 2, repeat from * 3 more times; repeat between [ ], ch 2, sc in next ch sp, ch 2, dc in last dc, ch 3, join with sl st in third ch of ch-5. *[210 mesh]*

Rnd [3] : For **size 38"-40" only,** ch 5, sc in next ch sp, *[ch 2, (dc in next dc, ch 3, dc in next dc, ch 2, sc in next ch sp, ch 2) 30 times, dc in next dc, ch 3, skip next dc], dc in next dc, ch 2, sc in next ch sp, ch 2; repeat from * 2 more times; repeat between [ ], join with sl st in third ch of ch-5. *[248 mesh]*

Rnd 4: For **all sizes,** beg dc mesh, (sc mesh, dc mesh) around to last mesh, ch 2, sc in last mesh, ch 2, join with sl st in third ch of ch-6.

Rnd 5: Beg sc mesh, (dc mesh, sc mesh) around to last mesh, ch 3, join with sl st in third ch of ch-5.

Rnds 6-85 [6-89, 6-93]: Or to 9" about desired hemline, repeat rnds 4 and 5 alternately.

Rnds 86 [90, 94]: Beg dc mesh; for row 1 of skirt graph *(see graph on page 91),* *work in pattern across next 3 mesh, 2 dc evenly spaced in next mesh, ch 1, (dc in next dc, ch 1, dc in next mesh, ch 1) 2 times, dc in next dc, 2 dc evenly spaced in next mesh, ch 1, dc in next dc, work in pattern across next 12 mesh; repeat from * around, join.

Rnds 87-113 [91-117, 95-121]: Working in pattern, beg mesh; repeat next row of skirt graph around, join.

Rnd 114 [118, 122]: Beg sc mesh; repeat row 29 of skirt graph around, join.

Rnds 115-120 [119-124, 123-128]: Work in pattern.

Rnd 121[125, 129]: For **edging,** sl st in next 2 chs, (sc in next sc, ch 3, 3 dc in next ch-3 sp; for **picot, ch 3, sl st in second ch from hook, ch 1;** 3 dc in same ch-3 sp, ch 3) around, join with sl st in first sc. Fasten off.

Sleeve Edging

Working in ends of rows around armhole, join with sl st in first row at underarm, ch 3, (2 dc, picot, 3 dc) in same row; *for **shell, ch 3, skip next row, sc in next row, ch 3, skip next row, (3 dc, picot, 3 dc) in next row;** repeat from * around to 3 rows before seam, ch 3, skip next row, sc in next row, ch 3, join with sl st in third ch of ch-5.

Repeat on other sleeve.

Neck Edging

Working in ends or rows, in sts and in ch sps around neck opening, join with sl st in ch sp at center back, ch 3, (2 dc, picot, 3 dc) in same ch sp; spacing sts so edging lays flat, work 11 [11,15] shells evenly spaced around to 2 rows before center front, 6 dc in next row, ch 3, skip next row, sc between 2 dc at center front, ch 3, skip next row, 3 dc in next row; sl st between center 2 dc of last 6 dc worked, 3 dc in same row, work 11 [11,15] shells evenly spaced around to 2 sps before joining, ch 3, skip next sp, sc in next sp, ch 3, join with sl st in top of ch-3. Fasten off.

If desired weave ribbon though ch sps of row 1 on skirt. Tie around flowers in bow at front. 🦋

KEY:
⬜ = SC MESH OR DC MESH
│ = DOUBLE CROCHET
● = CHAIN

BODICE GRAPH

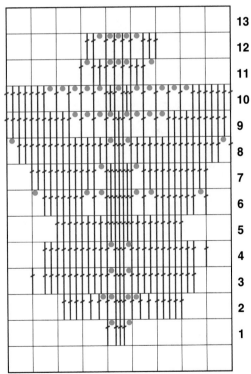

Rose Trellis Scarf/Stole

Designed by Angelina Varona

Finished Size: 13½" x 63".

Materials:
- ❏ Lightweight baby yarn:
    - 50 oz. pink
    - 3½ oz. green
- ❏ F hook or hook size needed to obtain gauge

Gauge: We are not responsible for lack of materials due to project not being worked to gauge. Gauge for this pattern: 23 sts and chs = 4"; rows 3-11= 2".

Basic Stitches: Ch, sl st, sc, hdc, dc, tr.

Scarf/Stole

Row 1: With green, ch 240 or to desired length in multiples of 16 chs, sc in second ch from hook, *[ch 1, skip next ch, hdc in next ch, ch 1, skip next ch, dc in next ch, ch 1, skip next ch, tr in next ch, ch 1, skip next ch, tr in next ch, ch 1, skip next ch, dc in next ch, ch 1, skip next ch, hdc in next ch], (ch 1, skip next ch, sc in next ch) 2 times; repeat from * 13 more times; repeat between [ ], ch 1, skip next ch, sc in last ch, turn. *(239 sts and chs made)*

Row 2: Ch 1, sc in each st and in each ch across, turn. Fasten off. *(239 sc) Front of row 2 is right side of work.*

Row 3: Join pink with sc in first st, sc in each st across, turn.

Row 4: Ch 5, skip next st, *[dc in next st, ch 1, skip next st, hdc in next st, (ch 1, skip next st, sc in next st) 2 times, ch 1, skip next st, hdc in next st, ch 1, skip next st, dc in next st], (ch 1, skip next st, tr in next st) 2 times, ch 1, skip next st; repeat from * 13 more times; repeat between [ ], ch 1, skip next st, tr in last st, turn.

Row 5: Ch 1, sc in each st and in each ch across, turn. Fasten off.

Row 6: Join green with sc in first st, sc in each st across, turn.

Row 7: Ch 1, sc in first st, *[ch 1, skip next st, hdc in next st, ch 1, skip next st, dc in next st, ch 1, skip next st, (tr in next st, ch 1, skip next st) 2 times, dc in next st, ch 1, skip next st, hdc in next st], (ch 1, skip next st , sc in next st) 2 times; repeat from * 13 more times; repeat between [ ], ch 1, skip next st, sc in last st, turn.

Rows 8-67: Repeat rows 2-7 consecutively.

Rnd 68: Working around outer edge, ch 1, (sc in each st across to next corner, 3 sc in corner, evenly space 76 sc across ends of rows to next corner, 3 sc in corner) 2 times, join with sl st in first sc. *(80 sts across each end)*

Rnd 69: Ch 1, sc in each st around with 3 sc in each center corner st, join. Fasten off. *(82 sts across each end)*

First Flower Row
First Rose

Rnd 1: With pink, ch 4, sl st in first ch to form ring, ch 4, (dc in ring, ch 1) 7 times, join with sl st in third ch of ch-4. *(8 dc, 8 ch-1 sps)*

Rnd 2: For **petals**, ch 1, (sc, hdc, dc, hdc, sc) in each ch-1 sp around. *(8 petals)*

Rnd 3: Working around ch on rnd 1, between sts of petals, working behind petals, sl st around ch before first hdc, ch 1, sl st around ch before first dc, ch 3, (sl st around ch before dc on next petal, ch 3) 7 times, skip first sl st and ch 1, join with sl st in next sl st. *(8 ch-3 sps)*

Notes: *For **petal**, (sc, hdc, 3 dc, hdc, sc) in next ch-3 sp.*

*For **joining petal**, (sc, hdc, dc, join with sl st where stated, 2 dc, hdc, sc) in next ch-3 sp.*

Rnd 4: With right side of Scarf facing you, ch 1, joining in third st from left corner st, work joining petal; joining in fourth st from last joining, work joining petal; work petal in each ch-3 sp around, join with sl st in first sc. Fasten off.

Second Rose

Rnds 1-3: Repeat rnds 1-3 of First Rose.

Rnd 4: Ch 1, joining in 14th st from last joining, work joining petal; joining in fourth st from last joining, work joining petal; work petal in each of next 4 ch-3 sps on Rose, (joining in center st of

Continued on page 102

Waves Barrette

Designed by Deborah Levy-Hamburg

Finished Size: 3¾" long.

Materials:
- ❑ Small amount each red and white worsted yarn
- ❑ 3¾" metal barrette
- ❑ Tapestry needle
- ❑ H hook or hook size needed to obtain gauge

Gauge: We are not responsible for lack of materials due to project not being worked to gauge. Gauge for this pattern: Tr are 1" tall.

Basic Stitches: Ch, sl st, tr.

Barrette

Row 1: With white, ch 17, tr in fifth ch from hook, tr in each ch across, turn. Fasten off. *(14 tr made)*

Row 2: Join red with sl st around post of first tr, ch 4, 6 tr around same st, **turn,** (skip next st on row 1, 7 tr around next st, **turn)** across leaving last tr unworked. Fasten off.

Row 3: Working around skipped tr sts on row 1 between red groups, join white with sl st around first skipped st, ch 4, 6 tr around same st, **turn,** (7 tr around next skipped st, **turn)** across. Fasten off.

Tack on Barrette. ❧

Waves Headban

Designed by Deborah Levy-Hamburg

Finished Size: One size fits all.

Materials:
- ❏ 1 oz. each navy and red worsted yarn
- ❏ 1½ yds. elastic cord
- ❏ Tapestry needle
- ❏ H hook or hook size needed to obtain gauge

Gauge: We are not responsible for lack of materials due to project not being worked to gauge. Gauge for this pattern: Tr are 1" tall.

Basic Stitches: Ch, sl st, tr.

Waves

Row 1: With red, ch 75 loosely or to fit around head plus 1", ending with an odd number; tr in fifth ch from hook, tr in each ch across, turn. Fasten off.

Row 2: Join navy with sl st around post of second tr, ch 4, 6 tr around same st, **turn,** (skip next st on row 1, 7 tr around next st, **turn)** across leaving last 2 sts on row 1 unworked. Fasten off.

Row 3: Working around skipped tr sts on row 1 between navy groups, join red with sl st around post of first st, ch 4, 6 tr around same st, **turn,** (7 tr around next st on row 1, **turn)** across. Fasten off.

Sew ends tog.

Cut two pieces elastic cord to fit around head. Weave one piece of cord through top of sts and one piece of cord through bottom of sts on row 1. Tie knot, leaving 1½" ends, secure ends. 🍂

Sailor Bow Hat

Designed by Deborah Levy-Hamburg

Finished Size: One size fits all.

Materials:
- ❑ Worsted yarn:
    2½ oz. white
    1 oz. navy
    Small amount red
- ❑ F and H hooks or hook sizes needed to obtain gauges

Gauges: We are not responsible for lack of materials due to project not being worked to gauge. Gauge for this pattern: H hook, 7 sc = 2"; 7 sc rows = 2". F hook, 9 sc = 2"; 9 sc rows = 2".

Basic Stitches: Ch, sl st, tr.

Note: Work in continuous rnds; do not join or turn unless otherwise stated. Mark first st of each rnd.

Crown
Rnd 1: Starting at top, with white, ch 2, 6 sc in second ch from hook. *(6 sc made)*
Rnd 2: 2 sc in each st around. *(12)*
Rnd 3: (Sc in next st, 2 sc in next st) around. *(18)*
Rnd 4: (Sc in next 2 sts, 2 sc in next st) around. *(24)*
Rnd 5: (Sc in next 3 sts, 2 sc in next st) around. *(30)*
Rnd 6: Sc in next 2 sts, (2 sc in next st, sc in next 4 sts) 5 times, 2 sc in next st, sc in last 2 sts. *(36)*
Rnd 7: (Sc in next 5 sts, 2 sc in next st) around. *(42)*
Rnd 8: Sc in next 3 sts, (2 sc in next st, sc in next 6 sts) 5 times, 2 sc in next st, sc in last 3 sts. *(48)*
Rnd 9: (Sc in next 7 sts, 2 sc in next st) around. *(54)*
Rnd 10: Sc in next 4 sts, (2 sc in next st, sc in next 8 sts) 5 times, 2 sc in next st, sc in last 4 sts. *(60)*

Rnd 11: (Sc in next 9 sts, 2 sc in next st) around. *(66)*
Rnd 12: Sc in next 5 sts, (2 sc in next st, sc in next 10 sts) 5 times, 2 sc in next st, sc in last 5 sts. *(72)*
Rnds 13-28: Sc in each st around. At end of last rnd, join with sl st in first sc. Fasten off.

Brim
Rnd 1: With wrong side of rnd 28 facing you, join navy with sc in first st, sc in next 16 sts, 2 sc in next st, (sc in next 17 sts, 2 sc in next st) around. *(76 sc made)*
Rnds 2-7: Sc in each st around.
Rnd 8: (Sc in next 18 sts, 2 sc in next st) around. *(80)*
Rnd 9: Sc in each st around.
Rnd 10: (Sc in next 19 sts, 2 sc in next st) around. *(84)*
Rnd 11: Sc in each st around.
Rnd 12: (Sc in next 20 sts, 2 sc in next st) around. At end of last rnd, join with sl st in first sc. Fasten off. *(88)*
Turn Brim up.

Bow
Row 1: With red, ch 11, sc in second ch from hook, sc in each ch across, turn. *(10 sc)*
Rows 2-8: Ch 1, sc first 2 sts tog, sc in each st across, turn. At end of last row *(3)*.
Rows 9-18: Ch 1, sc in each st across, turn.
Rows 19-25: Ch 1, 2 sc in first st, sc in each st across, turn. At end of last row *(10)*. **Do not turn.**
Rnd 26: Working around outer edge, ch 1, sc in end of each row and in each st around with 3 sc in each other corner, join with sl st in first sc. Fasten off.
Tie knot in center of Bow.
Pin or tack Bow to Brim. ❧

Waves Ponytail Holder

Designed by Deborah Levy-Hamburg

Finished Size: One size fits all.

Materials:
- ❑ Small amount each white and navy worsted yarn
- ❑ ⅓ yd. elastic cord
- ❑ Tapestry needle
- ❑ H hook or hook size needed to obtain gauge

Gauge: We are not responsible for lack of materials due to project not being worked to gauge. Gauge for this pattern: Tr are 1" tall.

Basic Stitches: Ch, sl st, tr.

Ponytail Holder
Row 1: With white, ch 25, tr in fifth ch from hook, tr in each ch across, turn. Fasten off. *(22 tr made)*

Row 2: Join navy with sl st around post of second tr, ch 4, 6 tr around same st, **turn,** (skip next st on row 1, 7 tr around next st, **turn)** across leaving last 2 sts on row 1 unworked. Fasten off.

Row 3: Working around skipped tr sts on row 1 between navy groups, join white with sl st around post of first st, ch 4, 6 tr around same st, **turn,** (7 tr around next st on row 1, **turn)** across. Fasten off.

Sew ends together with last 2 unworked sts sewn to first 2 worked sts.

Cut two 6" pieces elastic cord. Weave one piece of cord through top of sts and one piece of cord through bottom of sts on row 1. Tie in knot, leaving 1½" ends, secure ends. ❧

Butterfly Dress

Continued from page 80

SKIRT GRAPH

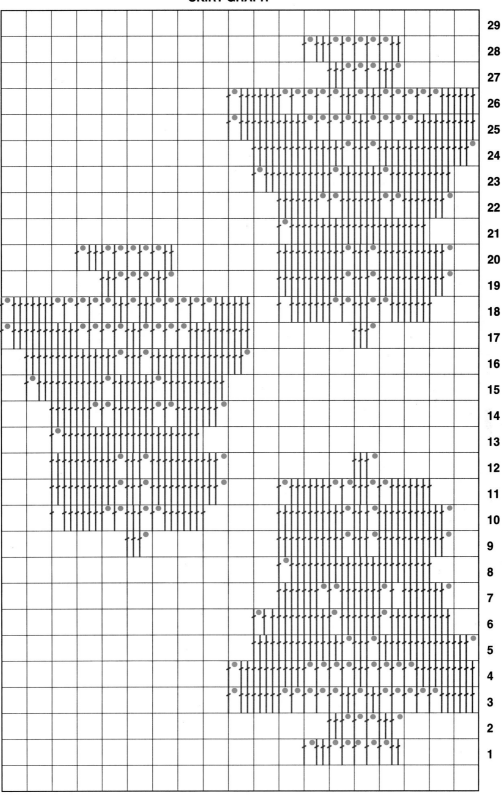

Butterfly Shawl

Designed by Teri Dusenbury

Finished Size: 46" wide x 26" long.

Materials:
- ❑ 785 yds. ecru size 10 crochet cotton thread
- ❑ Tapestry needle
- ❑ No. 2 steel hook or hook size needed to obtain gauge

Gauge: We are not responsible for lack of materials due to project not being worked to gauge. Gauge for this pattern: 4 ch sps = 2"; 5 ch lp rows = 1" 1 shell = 5/8"; 3 shell rows = 1".

Basic Stitches: Ch, sl st, sc, dc.

Butterfly

Rnd 1: Starting at center of body, ch 10, sl st in first ch to form ring, ch 1, 23 sc in ring, join with sl st in first sc. *(23 sc made)*

Row 2: Working in rows, ch 5, skip next st, dc in next st, (ch 2, skip next st, dc in next st) 6 times leaving last 8 sts unworked, turn. *(8 dc, 7 ch sps)*

Row 3: Ch 3, 2 dc in first ch sp, (ch 3, 2 dc in next ch sp) 6 times, dc in third ch of ch-5, turn.

Row 4: Ch 3; for **shell**, **(3 dc, ch 3, 3 dc) in first ch sp;** shell in each ch sp across, dc in top of ch-3, turn.

Row 5: Ch 3, shell in ch sp of each of first 3 shells, (sl st, ch 4, sl st, ch 6, sl st, ch 4, sl st) in next sp between shells, shell in each of last 3 shells, dc in top of ch-3, turn.

Row 6: For **first top wing**, ch 3, shell in first shell, ch 2, 10 dc in next shell, ch 2, shell in next shell leaving last shells unworked, turn.

Row 7: Ch 3, shell in first shell, ch 2, (sc in next dc, ch 3) 9 times, sc in next dc, ch 2, shell in last shell, turn.

Rows 8-13: Ch 3, shell in first shell, ch 2, skip next ch sp, sc in next ch sp, (ch 3, sc in next ch sp) across to ch-2, skip ch 2, ch 2, shell in last shell, turn.

Row 14: Ch 3, shell in first shell, ch 2, skip next ch sp, (sc in next ch sp, ch 3) 2 times, sc in next ch lp, ch 2, shell in last shell, turn.

Row 15: Ch 3, shell in first shell, ch 2, skip next ch sp, sc in next ch sp, ch 3, sc in next ch sp, ch 2, shell in last shell, turn.

Row 16: Ch 3, shell in first shell, ch 2, skip next ch sp, sc in next ch sp, ch 2, shell in last shell, turn.

Row 17: Ch 3, sc first and last shells tog, sc in top of ch-3, turn.

Row 18: Ch 3, (sl st, ch 4, sl st, ch 6, sl st, ch 4, sl st) in next sc. Fasten off.

Row 6: For **Second top wing**, with wrong side of rnd 1 facing you, join with sl st in top of ch-3 on row 5; repeat row 6 of first top wing.

Rows 7-18: Repeat rows 7-18 of first top wing.

Row 19: For **bottom section**, with right side of rnd 1 facing you, join with sl st in ch-3 sp at end of row 6, (ch 3, 2 dc, ch 3, 3 dc) in same sp, shell in ch sp at end of row 4, shell in end of row 2, next 3 unworked sts on rnd 1, sc in next 2 sts, shell in other end of row 2, shell in end of row 4, shell in end of row 6, turn.

Row 20: Ch 3, shell in first shell, ch 2, 6 dc in next shell, ch 2, shell in each of next 2 shells, ch 2, 6 dc in next shell, ch 2, shell in last shell, turn.

Row 21: Ch 3, shell in first shell, *ch 2, skip next ch sp, (sc in next st, ch 3) 5 times, sc in next st, ch 2, shell in next shell*, shell in next shell; repeat between **, turn.

Row 22: Ch 3, shell in first shell, *ch 2, skip next ch sp (sc in next ch sp, ch 3) 4 times, sc in next ch sp, ch 2, shell in next shell*, ch 1, sc in next sp between shells, ch 1, shell in next shell; repeat between **, turn.

Row 23: For **first wing**, ch 3, shell in first shell, ch 2, skip next ch sp, (sc in next ch sp , ch 3) 3 times, sc in next ch sp, ch 2, shell in next shell leaving last 2 shells and 4 ch sps unworked, turn.

Rows 24-27: Repeat rows 14-17 of first top wing.

Row 28: Ch 3, (sl, st, ch 6, sl st) in next sc, turn. Fasten off.

Row 23: For **second wing**, join with sl st in first unworked shell on row 22, (ch 3, 2 dc, ch 2, 3 dc) in same shell, ch 2, skip next ch sp, (sc in next ch sp, ch 3) 3 times, sc in next ch sp, ch 2, shell in last shell, turn.

Rows 24-27: Repeat rows 14-17 of first top wing.

Row 28: Ch 3, (sl st, ch 6, sl st) in next sc. Fasten off.

Shawl

Row 1: Starting at center top, ch 6, sl st in first ch to form ring, (ch 5, sc in ring) 4 times, ch 2, dc in ring, turn. *(5 ch sps)*

Row 2: For **beginning increase (beg inc)**, ch 1, (sc,

Continued on page 103

Beach Bag

Designed by Teri Dusenbury

Finished Size: 22" circumference.

Materials:
- ❏ 375 yds. size 10 crochet cotton thread
- ❏ No. 6 steel hook or hook size needed to obtain gauge

Gauge: We are not responsible for lack of materials due to project not being worked to gauge. Gauge for this pattern: Rnds 1 and 2 = 1¼" diameter; 6 dc and 10 ch =2", 7 dc rows = 2".

Basic Stitches: Ch, sl st, sc, dc, tr.

Bag

Rnd 1: Starting at bottom, ch 4, 15 dc in fourth ch from hook, join with sl st in top of ch-3. *(16 dc made)*

Rnd 2: Ch 5, (dc in next st, ch 2) around, join with sl st in third ch of ch-5.

Rnd 3: St st in first ch-2 sp, (ch 3, dc, ch 3, 2 dc) in same sp; *for **single loop (s lp), (sc, ch 3, sc) in next ch -2 sp;** for **shell, (2 dc, ch 3, 2 dc) in next ch-2 sp;** repeat from * around to last ch-2 sp, s lp in last ch-2 sp, join with sl st in top of ch-3. *(8 shells, 8 s lps)*

Rnd 4: Sl st in first dc, (sl st, ch 3, 7 dc) in next ch sp, skip next s lp, (8 dc in next ch sp, skip next s lp) around, join. *(64 dc)*

Rnd 5: Ch 4, (dc, ch 1) in each st around, join with sl st in third ch of ch-4.

Rnd 6: Ch 1, *(sc in next ch sp, ch 3) 6 times, sc in next 2 ch sps; repeat from * around, join with sl st in first sc. *(64 sc, 48 ch-3 sps)*

Rnd 7: Ch 1, *(sc in next ch sp, ch 3) 2 times; for **slanted shell, (sc, ch 2, 1 dc) in next ch sp;** (sc in next ch sp, ch 3) 2 times; sc in next ch sp, ch 2, skip next 3 sc; repeat from * around, join.

Rnd 8: Ch 1, *(sc in next ch-3 sp, ch 3) 2 times, skip next sc, sc in top of ch-3, ch 3, (sc in next ch-3 sp, ch 3) 2 times, skip next ch-2 sp; repeat from * around, join.

Rnd 9: Ch 1, *sc in next ch sp, ch 3, slanted shell, (sc in next ch sp, ch 3) 2 times, (dc, ch 3, dc, ch 3) in next ch sp; repeat from * around, join.

Rnd 10: Ch 1, (sc in next ch sp, ch 3, skip next sc, sc in top of ch-3, ch 3, sc in next ch sp, ch 3, skip next ch sp, shell in next ch sp, ch 3, skip next ch sp) around, join.

Rnd 11: Ch 1, slanted shell, sc in next ch sp, ch 3, skip next ch sp, 10 dc in ch-3 sp of next shell, ch 3, skip next ch-3 sp) around, join.

Rnd 12: Ch 1, skip first 2 chs, *sc in top of ch-3, ch 3, skip next ch sp, (dc in next dc, ch 1) 9 times, dc in next dc, ch 3, skip next ch 3-sp, skip next sc; repeat from * around, join.

Rnd 13: Sl st in next 3 chs, sl st in next st, *(sc in next ch-1 sp, ch 3) 8 times, sc in next ch-1 sp, ch 6, skip next 2 ch sps; repeat from * around, join.

Rnd 14: Ch 1, *(sc in next ch-3 sp, ch 3) 3 times, slanted shell, (sc in next ch-3 sp, ch 3) 4 times, (dc, ch 3, dc) in next ch-6 sp, ch 3; repeat from * around, join.

Rnd 15: Ch 1, *(sc in next ch sp, ch 3) 3 times, skip next sc, sc in top of ch-3, ch 3, (sc in next ch sp, ch 3) 3 times, skip next ch sp, shell in next ch sp, ch 3, skip next ch sp; repeat from * around, join.

Rnd 16: Ch 1, *(sc in next ch sp, ch 3) 2 times, slanted shell, (sc in next ch sp, ch 3) 3 times, skip next ch sp, (3 dc, ch 3, 3 dc, ch 3) in next shell, skip next ch sp; repeat from * around, join.

Rnd 17: Ch 1, *(sc in next ch sp, ch 3) 2 times, skip next sc, sc in top of ch-3, ch 3, (sc in next ch sp, ch 3) 2 times, skip next ch sp, 12 dc in next ch sp, ch 3, skip next ch sp; repeat from * around, join.

Rnd 18: Ch 1, *sc in next ch sp, ch 3, slanted shell, (sc in next ch sp, ch 3) 2 times, (dc in next dc, ch 1) 11 times, dc in next dc, ch 3, skip next ch sp; repeat from * around, join.

Rnd 19: Ch 1, *sc in next ch sp, ch 3, skip next sc, sc in top of ch-3, ch 3, sc in next ch sp, ch 3, (sc in next ch-1 sp, ch 3) 11 times, skip next ch sp; repeat from * around, join.

Rnd 20: Ch 1, *slanted shell, sc in next ch sp, ch 3, skip next ch sp, (sc in next ch sp, ch 3) 4 times, slanted shell, (sc in next ch sp, ch 3) 5 times, skip next ch sp; repeat from * around, join.

Rnd 21: Ch 1, skip first 2 chs, *sc in top of ch-3, ch 3, skip next ch-3 sp, (sc in next ch-3 sp, ch 3) 4 times, skip next sc, sc in top of next ch, ch 3, (sc in next ch-3 sp, ch 3) 4 times, skip next ch-3 sp; repeat from * around, join.

Rnd 22: Ch 3, skip first ch sp, *(sc in next ch sp,

Continued on page 102

Snood

Designed by Teri Dusenbury

Finished Size: 9¼" diameter.

Materials:
- ❑ 150 yds. size 10 crochet cotton thread
- ❑ 1¼ yds. of ¼" ribbon
- ❑ No. 6 steel hook or hook size needed to obtain gauge

Gauge: We are not responsible for lack of materials due to project not being worked to gauge. Gauge for this pattern: 8 sts = 1"; rnds 1-7 = 2".

Basic Stitches: Ch, sl st, sc, dc, tr.

Snood

Rnd 1: Ch 4, 15 dc in fourth ch from hook, join with sl st in top of ch-3. *(16 dc made)*

Rnd 2: Ch 5, (dc in next st, ch 2) around, join with sl st in third ch of ch-5. *(16 dc, 16 ch sps)*

Rnd 3: (Sl st, ch 3, dc, ch 3, 2 dc) in first ch sp, *(sc, ch 3, sc) in next ch sp; for **shell, (2 dc, ch 3, 2 dc) in next ch sp;** repeat from * around to last ch sp, (sc, ch 3, sc) in last ch sp, join with sl st in top ch-3. *(8 shells, 8 ch-3 sps)*

Rnd 4: Sl st in next st, (sl st, ch 3, 7 dc) in ch-3 sp of next shell, skip next ch-3 sp, (8 dc in ch-3 sp of next shell, skip next ch-3 sp) around, join. *(64 dc)*

Rnd 5: Ch 4, (dc in next st, ch 1) around, join with sl st in third ch of ch-4.

Rnd 6: Ch 1, *(sc in next ch sp, ch 3) 6 times, sc in next 2 ch sps; repeat from * around, join with sl st in first sc. *(64 sc, 48 ch-3 sps)*

Rnd 7: Ch 1, *(sc in next ch sp, ch 3) 2 times, (sc, ch 3, 2 dc) in next ch sp, (sc in next ch sp, ch 3) 2 times, sc in next ch sp, ch 2, skip next 3 sts; repeat from * around, join.

Rnd 8: Ch 1, *(sc in next ch-3 sp, ch 3) 2 times, skip next sc, sc in top of ch-3, (ch 3, sc in next ch-3 sp) 2 times, ch 6, sc in next ch-2 sp, ch 6; repeat from * around, join.

Rnd 9: Ch 1, *sc in next ch-3 sp, ch 3, (sc, ch 3, 2 dc) in next ch-3 sp, sc in next ch-3 sp, ch 3, sc in next ch 3 sp, ch-6, (sc in next ch-6 sp, ch 6) 2 times; repeat from * around, join.

Rnd 10: Ch 1, *sc in next ch-3 sp, ch 3, skip next sc, sc in top of ch-3, ch 3, sc in next ch-3 sp, ch 6, (sc in next ch-6 sp, ch 6) 3 times; repeat from * around, join.

Rnd 11: Ch 1, *(sc, ch 3, 2 dc) in next ch-3 sp, sc in next ch-3 sp, ch 6, (sc in next ch-6 sp, ch 6) 4 times; repeat from * around, join.

Rnd 12: Sl st in first 2 chs, sc in next ch, *ch 6, (sc in next ch-6 sp, ch 6) 5 times, skip next sc, sc in top of ch-3; repeat from * 6 times, (ch 6, sc in next ch-6 sp) 5 times; for **joining loop,** ch 3, join with dc in first sc.

Rnd 13: Ch 1, sc in joining lp, ch 6, sc in first ch-6 sp, (ch 6, sc in next ch-6 sp) around, ch 3, join.

Rnd 14: Ch 1, sc in joining lp, ch 8, sc in first ch-6 sp, (ch 8, sc in next ch-6 sp) around, ch 4, join with tr in first sc.

Rnd 15: Ch 1, sc in joining sp, ch 10, sc in first ch-8 lp, (ch 10, sc in next ch-8 sp) around, ch 5, join.

Rnds 16-20: Ch 1, sc in joining sp, ch 10, sc in first ch-10 sp, (ch 10, sc in next ch-10 sp) around, ch 5, join.

Rnd 21: Ch 1, sc in joining sp, ch 5, sc in first ch-10 sp, (ch 5, sc in next ch-10 sp) around, ch 2, join with dc in first sc.

Rnd 22: Ch 1, sc in joining sp, ch 5 , sc in first ch-5 sp, (ch 5, sc in next ch-5 sp) around, ch 2, join.

Rnd 23: Ch 1, 2 sc in joining lp, *[2 sc in next ch-5 lp, ch 3, sl st in **front lp and left bar** *(see Stitch Guide)* of last sc worked, ch 5, sl st in same place as last sl st, ch 3, sl st in same place as last sl st], 2 sc in same ch-5 sp; repeat from * 45 more times; repeat between [ ], join with sl st in first sc. Fasten off.

Weave ribbon through rnd 22. ❧

Tennis Cardigan

Designed by Helene Rush

Finished Sizes: **Girl's/lady's bust 30"-32".** Finished measurement: 37¼". **Lady's bust 34"-36".** Finished measurement: 40¾". **Lady's bust 38"-40".** Finished measurement: 44½". **Lady's bust 42"-44".** Finished measurement: 48". **Lady's bust 46"-48":** Finished measurement: 51½".

Materials:
❏ Amount sport yarn needed for size:
  16 oz. white, 4 oz. green for 30"-32"
  18 oz. white, 4 oz. green for 34"-36"
  21 oz. white, 5 oz. green for 38"-40"
  23 oz. white, 5 oz. green for 42"-44"
  25 oz. white, 5 oz. green for 46"-48"
❏ ⅝" buttons needed for size:
  6 for small for 30"-32" and 34"-36"
  7 for large for 38"-40", 42"-44" and 46"-48"
❏ Tapestry needle
❏ E and F hooks or hook sizes needed to obtain gauges

Gauges: We are not responsible for lack of materials due to project not being worked to gauge. Gauge for this pattern: **E hook,** 5 post sts = 1"; 10 post st rows = 3". **F hook,** 5 pattern sts = 1"; 8 rows in pattern = 2".

Basic Stitches: Ch, sl st, dc.

Note: Instructions are for lady's bust 30"-32"; changes for 34"-36", 38"-40", 42"-44", 46"-48" are in [ ].

Back

Row 1: For **ribbing,** with E hook and white, ch 84 [94, 102, 110, 120], dc in third ch from hook, dc in each ch across, turn. *(83 dc made) [91 dc, 101 dc, 109 dc, 119 dc made]*

Row 2: Ch 3, *dc front post *(fp—see Stitch Guide)* around next st, dc in next st; repeat from * across, turn. *Front of row 2 is right side of work.*

*Note: For **post st (ps),** work fp on right side rows, work bp on wrong side of rows. Work ps around next st unless otherwise stated.*

Rows 3-9: Ch 3, ps around each ps and dc in each dc across, turn.

Row 10: Ch 3, (ps, dc in next st) 2 [3, 4, 2, 6] times ps; for **inc, 2 dc in next dc;** *(ps, dc in next

dc) 6 [5, 7, 7, 8] times, ps, inc; repeat from * 4 [5, 4, 5, 4] more times, (ps, dc in next dc) across, turn. *(89 sts) [98 sts, 107 sts, 116 sts, 125 sts]*

Row 11: For **body,** with F hook, ch 3, dc in each st across, turn.

Row 12: Ch 3, dc in next st, (*fp 4 times, dc in next 2 sts*, fp, dc in next 2 sts) across to last 6 sts; repeat between **, turn.

Row 13: Ch 3, dc in each dc and ps around each ps across, turn.

Row 14: Ch 3, dc in next st; (*to **cross cable, skip next 2 sts, fp 2 times, fp around each of 2 skipped sts;** dc in next 2 sts*, fp, dc in next 2 sts) across to last 6 sts; repeat **, turn.

Row 15: Repeat row 13.

Row 16: Repeat row 12 changing to green *(see Stitch Guide)* in last st made. **Do not** fasten off white.

Row 17: Ch 1, sc in each st across, turn.

Row 18: Working this row in **back lps** *(see Stitch Guide),* ch 1, sc in each st across changing to white in last st made, turn. Fasten off green.

Row 19: Working in **both lps,** sl st in first st, ch 3, dc in each st across, turn.

Rows 20-88 [20-88, 20-96, 20-96, 20-96]: Repeat rows 12-19 consecutively, ending with row 16. At end of last row, **do not** change to green. Fasten off white.

Left Front

Row 1: With E hook and white, ch 38 [44, 48, 52, 56], dc in third ch from hook, dc in each ch across, turn. *(37 dc made [43 dc, 47 dc, 51 dc, 55 dc made]*

Rows 2-9: Repeat rows 2-9 of Back.

Row 10: Ch 3, (ps, dc in next st) 1 [2, 3, 1, 2] time, ps inc, *(ps, dc in next st) 4 [7, 7, 6, 6,] times, ps, inc; repeat from * 2 [1, 1, 2, 2] times, (ps, dc in next st) across, turn. *(41 sts) [46 sts, 50 sts, 55 sts, 59 sts]*

Row 11: Repeat row 11 of Back.

Row 12: Ch 3, dc in next st, (*fp, dc in next 2 sts*, fp 4 times, dc in next 2 sts) 4 [4, 5, 5, 6] times; repeat between **; for **sizes 34"-36" and 42"-44" only,** fp 4 times, dc in last st; for **all sizes,** turn.

Row 13: Ch 3, dc in each dc and ps around each ps across, turn.

Row 14: Ch 3, dc in next st, (*fp, dc in each of

Continued on page 100

Tennis Cardigan

Continued from page 99

next 2 sts*, cross cable, dc in each of next 2 sts) 4 [4, 5, 5, 6] times; repeat between **, for **sizes 34"-36" and 42"-44" only**, cross cable, dc in last st; for **all sizes**, turn.

Row 15: Repeat row 13.

Row 16: Repeat row 12 changing to green in last st made. **Do not** fasten off white.

Rows 17-19: Repeat rows 17-19 of Back.

Left Front pattern is established in rows 12-19.

Rows 20-50 [20-50, 20-58, 20-58, 20-58]: Work in left front pattern.

Row 51 [51, 59. 59, 59]: For **neck shaping**, with white, sl st in first st, ch 2, work in Left Front pattern across, turn. *(40) [45, 49, 54, 58]*

Notes: Ch 2 is not used or counted as a st.

Do not work ps at end of row; if last st is ps work dc instead.

Row 52 [52, 60, 60, 60]: Work in Left Front pattern across to last 2 sts, dc last 2 sts tog, turn. *(39) [44, 48, 53, 57]*

Row 53 [53, 61, 61, 61]: Ch 2, work in Left Front pattern across, turn. *(38) [43, 47, 52, 56]*

Rows 54-55[54-55, 62-63, 62-63, 62-63]: Repeat rows 52-53 [52-53, 60-61, 60-61, 60-61]. At end of last row *(36) [41, 45, 50, 54]*.

Row 56 [56, 64, 64, 64]: Repeat row 52 [52, 60, 60, 60] changing to green in last st made. *(35) [40, 44, 49, 53]*

Rows 57-58 [57-58, 65-66, 65-66, 65-66]: Work in Left Front pattern.

Rows 59-63 [59-64, 67-72, 67-72, 67-72]: Repeat rows 51-55 [51-56, 59-64, 59-64, 59-64]. At end of last row *(30) [34, 38, 43, 47]*.

Rows 64-66 [65-66, 73-74, 73-74, 73-74]: Work in Left Front pattern.

Row [75, 75]: For **sizes 42"-44" and 46"-48" only**, repeat row [59, 59], ending with *[42,46] sts*.

Rows 67-88 [67-88, 75-96, 75-96, 75-96]: For all sizes, work in left front pattern. At end of last row, fasten off.

Right Front

Rows 1-11: Repeat rows 1-11 of Left Front.

Row 12: Ch 3; for **sizes 30"-32", 38"-40", and 46"-48" only**, dc in next st, fp, dc in next 2 sts; for all sizes, (fp 4 times, dc in next 2 sts, fp, dc in next 2 sts) across, turn.

Row 13: Ch 3, dc in each dc and ps around each ps across, turn.

Row 14: Ch 3; for **sizes 30"-32", 38"-40" and 46"-48" only**, dc in next st, fp, dc in next 2 sts; for **all sizes,** (cross cable, dc in next 2 sts, fp, dc,

in next 2 sts) across, turn.

Row 15: Repeat row 13.

Row 16: Repeat row 12 changing to green in last st made. **Do not** fasten off white.

Row 17-19: Repeat rows 17-19 of back.

Right Front pattern is established in rows 12-19.

Rows 20-50 [20-50, 20-58, 20-58, 20-58]: Work in Right Front pattern.

Row 51 [51, 59, 59, 59]: For **neck shaping,** with white, sl st in first st, ch 3, work in Right Front pattern across to last 2 sts, dc last 2 sts tog, turn. *(40) [45, 49, 54, 58]*

Row 52 [52, 60, 60, 60]: Ch 2, work in Right Front pattern across, turn. *(39) [44, 48, 53, 57]*

Row 53 [53, 61, 61, 61]: Ch 3, work in Right Front pattern across to last 2 sts, dc last 2 sts tog, turn. *(38) [43, 47, 52, 56]*

Rows 54-55 [54-55, 62-63, 62-63, 62-63]: Repeat rows 52-53 [52-53, 60-61, 60-61, 60-61]. At end of last row *(36) [41, 45, 50, 54]*.

Row 56 [56, 64, 64, 64]: Repeat row 52 [52, 60, 60, 60] changing to green in last st made. *(35) [40, 44, 49, 53]*

Rows 57-58 [57-58, 65-66, 65-66, 65-66]: Work in Right Front pattern.

Rows 59-63 [59-64, 67-72, 67-72, 67-72]: Repeat rows 51-55 [51-56, 59-64, 59-64, 59-64]. At end of last row *(30) [34, 38, 43, 47]*.

Rows 64-66 [65-66, 73-74, 73-74, 73-74]: Work in Right Front pattern.

Row [75, 75]: For **sizes 42"-44" and 46"-48" only,** repeat row [59, 59]. *[42, 46]*

Rows 67-88 [67-88, 75-96, 76-96, 76-96]: For **all sizes,** work in Right Front pattern. At end of last row, fasten off.

Sleeve (make 2)

Row 1: For **ribbing**, with E hook and white, ch 40, [42, 42, 44, 44], dc in third ch from hook, dc in each ch across, turn. *(39 dc made) [41 dc, 41 dc, 43 dc, 43 dc made]*

Rows 2-9: Repeat rows 2-9 of Back.

Row 10: For **size 30"-32" only**, (ch 3, dc) in first st, fp, 2 dc in next st, * fp, dc in next st, (fp, 2 dc in next st) 2 times; repeat from * across, turn. *(53 sts)*

Row [10, 10]: For **sizes 34"-36" and 38"-40" only**, (ch 3, dc) in first st, (fp, 2 dc in next st) across, turn. *[62, 62]*

Row [10, 10]: For **sizes 42"-44" and 46"-48" only,** (ch 3, dc) in first st, fp, 3 dc in next st, *fp, (2 dc in next st, fp) 3 times, 3 dc in next st; repeat from * across, turn. *[71, 71]*

Row 11: For **all sizes;** for **arm,** with F hook, ch 3, dc in each st across, turn.

Row 12: Ch 3, dc in next st, fp 4 times, dc in next 2 sts, (fp, dc in next 2 sts, fp 4 times, dc in next 2 sts) across, turn.

Row 13: Ch 3, dc in each dc and ps around each ps across, turn.

Row 14: Ch 3, dc in next st, cross cable, dc in next 2 sts, (fp, dc in next 2 sts, cross cable, dc in next 2 sts) across, turn.

Row 15: Repeat row 13.

Row 16: Repeat row 12 changing to green in last st made. **Do not** fasten off white.

Rows 17-19: Repeat rows 17-19 of Back.

Sleeve pattern is established in rows 12-19.

Row 20: (Ch 3, dc) in first st, work in sleeve pattern across to last st, 2 dc in last st, turn. *(55) [64, 64, 73, 73]*

Rows 21-23: Work in Sleeve pattern.

Rows 24-67: Repeat rows 20-23 consecutively. At end of last row *(77) [86, 86, 95, 95].* Fasten off.

Matching center of last row on Sleeve to shoulder seam, stretching each side of Sleeve ½", sew Sleeve to Front and Back.

Sew sleeve and side seams.

Front & Neck Band

Row 1: With right side of work facing you, with E hook and white, join with sl st in bottom right corner, ch 3; spacing sts evenly, 65 [65, 78, 78, 78] dc across Front to first row of neck shaping, 3 dc next row, 54 dc across to shoulder seam, 29 [29, 31, 31, 33] dc across back neck, 54 dc across to last neck shaping row, 3 dc in next row, 66 [66, 79, 79, 79] dc across Front to bottom left corner, turn. *(275 dc made) [275 dc, 303 dc, 303 dc, 305 dc made]*

Row 2: Ch 3, bp, (dc in next st, bp) across to last 65 [65, 77, 77, 77] sts; for **buttonhole, ch 1, skip next st, bp;** *(dc in next st, bp) 5 times, buttonhole; repeat from * 4 [4, 5, 5, 5] more times, dc in next st, bp, dc in last st, turn. *(6 [6, 7, 7, 7] buttonholes)*

Row 3: Ch 3, (fp, dc in next st or ch) across. Fasten off.

Sew buttons on Left Front band matching buttonholes. ❧

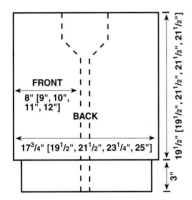

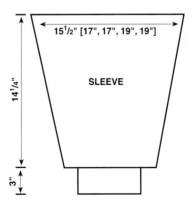

Rose Trellis Scarf/Stole

Continued from page 85

next petal on last Rose worked, work joining petal) 2 times, join with sl st in first sc. Fasten off. Repeat Second Rose for next three Roses leaving last 3 sts on Stole unworked.

Second Flower Row

Joining first 2 petals of each Rose in center dc of next 2 unjoined petals on bottom of corresponding Rose on First Flower Row, work Second Flower Row same as first flower row.

Border

Row 1: With right side of work facing you, join green with sl st in center st at corner of Scarf, (ch 6, sc in center dc of next petal, ch 3, sc in center dc of next petal) 2 times; for **corner,** ch 8; *[sc in center dc of next petal, ch 3, sc in center dc of next petal], ch 12; repeat from * 3 more times; repeat between [ ]; for **corner,** ch 8; (sc in center dc of next petal, ch 6) 2 times, join with sl st in center st at corner. Fasten off.

Row 2: With right side of work facing you, join green with sc in fifth ch of corner, sc in each st, 3 sc in each ch-3 sp and 12 sc in each ch-12 sp across to next corner, 3 sc in corner ch-8 sp, sc in fourth ch of ch-8, turn. *(81 sc)*

Row 3-6: Ch 1, sc in each st across, turn. At end of last row, fasten off.

Repeat First Flower Row, Second Flower Row and Border on other end of Scarf.

Fringe

For each **Fringe,** cut one strand 12" long, fold in half, insert hook around st, pull fold through st, pull ends through fold, tighten. Fringe in each st across row 6 on each end of border, alternating two pink and two green. 🦋

Beach Bag

Continued from page 95

ch 3) 3 times, slanted shell, (sc in next ch sp, ch 3) 3 times, sc in next ch sp, ch 4, skip next 2 ch sps; repeat from * around, join.

Rnd 23: Ch 1, *(sc in next ch-3 sp, ch 3) 3 times, skip next sc, sc in top of ch-3, ch 3, (sc in next ch-3 sp, ch 3) 3 times, (dc, ch 3, dc, ch 3) in next ch-4 sp; repeat from * around, join.

Rnd 24: Ch 1, *(sc in next ch sp, ch 3) 2 times, slanted shell, (sc in next ch sp, ch 3) 3 times, skip next ch sp, shell in next ch sp, ch 3, skip next ch sp; repeat from * around, join.

Rnd 25: Sl st in next ch sp, ch 6, *[dc in next ch sp, ch 3, skip next sc, sc in top of ch-3, ch 3, (dc in next ch sp, ch 3) 2 times, dc in next ch sp, ch 3, dc in next shell, ch 3, dc in next ch sp, ch 3], dc in next ch sp, ch 3; repeat from *6 more times; repeat between [ ], join with sl st in third ch of ch-6. *(56 dc, 8 sc)*

Rnds 26-44: Ch 6, (dc in next st, ch 3) around, join. *(64 dc)*

Row 45: For **first side of first strap,** working in rows, ch 4, (dc in next dc, ch 3) 12 times, dc in next dc, tr in next dc, turn. *(13 dc, 2 tr)*

Rows 46-50: Ch 4, skip first dc, (dc in next dc, ch 3) across to last 2 dc, dc in next dc, tr in last dc, turn. At end of last row *(3 dc, 2 tr)*.

Row 51: Ch 4, skip first dc, dc in next dc, tr in last dc, turn. *(1 dc, 2 tr)*

Row 52: Ch 1, skip next dc, sc in next ch-4 sp, turn. Fasten off.

Row 45: For **second side of first strap,** skip next dc on rnd 44, join with sl st in next dc, ch 4, (dc in next dc, ch 3) 12 times, dc in next dc, tr in next dc, turn. *(13 dc, 2 tr)*

Rows 46-52: Repeat rows 46-52 of first side of first strap. At end of last row, **do not fasten off.**

Row 53: (Ch 3, dc) in first st, (ch 3, dc between last dc an ch-3 made) 51 times, join with sc in last sc worked on first side of strap.

Row 54: Working around strap in ends of rows and in ch sps, (4 sc in next row or sp, sc in next dc) 15 times, 4 sc in last row, 3 sc in each ch-3 sp across, join with sl st in first sc.

Rnd 55: Ch 1, sc in each st around, join. Fasten off.

Row 45: For **first side of second strap,** skip next dc on rnd 44, join with sl st in next dc, ch 4, (dc in next dc, ch 3) 12 times, dc in next dc, tr in next dc, turn. *(13 dc, 2 tr)*

Rows 46-52: Repeat rows 46-52 of first side of first strap.

Rows 45-53: For **second side of second strap,** repeat rows 45-53 of second side of first strap.

Rnds 54-55: Repeat rnds 54-55 of first strap.

Repeat rnds 54-55 on opposite side of straps. 🦋

Butterfly Shawl

Continued from page 92

ch 5, sc) in first ch sp; ch 5, sc in next ch sp; for **center increase (center inc), (sc, ch 5, sc) in next ch sp;** ch 5, sc in next ch sp; for **ending decrease (end dec) (sc, ch 2, dc) in last ch sp;** turn. *(7 ch sps)*

Note: *Add 3 rows for each additional inch of length desired.*

Rows 3-60: Or to desired length; beg inc, ch 5, (sc, ch 5) in each ch sp across to center inc, center inc in next ch sp, ch 5, (sc, ch 5) in each ch sp across to last sp, end inc, turn.

Row 61: Beg inc, ch 5, (sc, ch 5) in each ch sp across to center inc, sc in center inc, ch 2, sc in ch-3 sp at end of row 7 on second top wing of Butterfly, ch 2, sc in ch-3 sp at end of row 7 on first top wing ch 2, sc in center inc; for **first side,** (ch 5, sc in next ch sp on Shawl, ch 2, sc in next ch-3 sp on first top wing, ch 2, sc in next ch sp on Shawl) 2 times, ch 5, (sc, ch 5) in each ch sp across to last ch sp, end inc, turn.

Row 62: Beg inc, (ch 5, sc) in each ch-5 sp across, turn.

Row 63: Ch 2, sc in next ch-3 sp of first top wing, ch 2, sc in next ch sp on Shawl, ch 5, (sc, ch 5) in each ch sp across to last ch sp, end inc, turn.

Rows 64-68: Repeat rows 62 and 63 alternately, ending with row 62.

Row 69: Ch 2, sc in ch-6 at tip of first wing, ch 2, sc in next ch sp on Shawl, ch 5, (sc, ch 5) in each ch sp across to last ch sp, end inc, **do not turn.** Fasten off.

Row 70: Join with sc in first ch-5 sp of row 69, 6 sc in same sp, 7 sc in each ch sp across to last ch sp, (sc, ch 5, sl st) in last ch sp. Fasten off.

Row 61: For **second side,** with wrong side facing you, join with sl st in first sc on center inc, (ch 5, sc in next ch sp on Shawl, ch 2, sc in next ch-3 sp on second top wing, ch 2, sc in next ch sp on Shawl) 2 times, ch 5, (sc, ch 5) in each ch sp across to last sp, end inc, turn.

Rows 62-69: Repeat rows 62-69 of first side.

Row 70: Join with sc in end inc on row 69, ch 5, sl st in same end inc, 7 sc in each ch sp across to last ch-5 sp. Fasten off.

Flower (make 64)

Ch 5, sl st in first ch to form ring, [ch 4, *yo 2 times, insert hook in ring, yo, pull through ring, (yo, pull through 2 lps on hook) 2 times; repeat from * one time, yo, pull through all 3 lps on hook, ch 4, sl st in ring]; repeat between [ ] 5 times. Fasten off. *(6 petals made)*

Sew Flowers to every other sc on next to last row and evenly space 10 Flowers above top of wings on Butterfly. ❧

Cleaning Tips for Needlework

We know that our finished needlework pieces are likely to become soiled with time and use, but sometimes a beautiful piece of needlework gets spotted or stained just from daily use or wear. It's especially annoying if it happens before it's completed just from handling the piece as we work. It is a good preventive measure to wash our hands each time we get ready to work on our projects. Pets can also leave stains and odors, as well as hairs, on our handmade clothing when they affectionately jump up into our laps for attention or napping. Tobacco smoke also leaves an unpleasant odor in some fibers. We can protect our work from stains, spills and other soil by keeping it in a plastic bag or special tote when we aren't working on it. Some pieces need to be washed as the final step of completion. But, if you simply need to remove dust, lint, pet hairs or odors, most pieces can be tumbled in the dryer with a fabric-softener sheet to restore freshness.

Before washing or attempting any spot removal, check the fiber content of the needlework to determine which cleaning procedure can be sued safely, and check the dyes to see if they are colorfast. If you don't have the manufacturer's label with this information, use a small swatch of fabric, thread, yarn, etc., to test the cleaning procedure. Some pieces with dyes that bleed can be soaked in cold water; change the water as many times as needed until it is completely clear of dye. Pieces with nonwashable fibers or colors that bleed may need professional cleaning. If you decide to use dry cleaning fluids or color remover, follow the label instructions and precautions carefully.

Cleaning and washing can deteriorate fibers and colors because of the scrubbing, tamping, and harsh compounds sometimes needed to remover stubborn stains. So, a good rule to follow to preserve the life of your needlework is to use the minimum amount necessary to keep your projects fresh. With this in mind, use the following cleaning suggestions to the minimum degree, apply the harsh cleaners only to the stained areas and avoid scrubbing or tamping if possible.

Blood: Soak in cold water, warm soapy water wash, rinse.

Candy: Soak in cold water, laundry spot remover, rinse.

Coffee/tea: Soak in warm soapy water, boiling water over stain.

Grass: Apply ammonia and hydrogen peroxide alternately, cold water rinse.

Grease: Warm soapy water wash, rinse, alcohol sponge if needed.

Ink on whites: Dampen, apply table salt and lemon juice, place in sun one-two hours, warm soapy water wash, rinse. Or apply hydrogen peroxide, rinse.

Ink on colors: Soak in milk (change often), cold water rinse, warm soapy water wash, rinse.

Lipstick: Petroleum jelly, warm soapy water wash, rinse.

Wax: Apply ice, scrape off wax; press (low heat) between white paper towels with waxside down, warm water wash, rinse. For colored wax, also alcohol sponge if needed.

Wine: Dampen and apply table salt, wait one-two hours, flush with boiling water; soak in lemon juice and hot water, rinse.

Open Shell Jacket

Designed by Ann Parnell

Finished Size: Lady's bust 34"-42". Finished measurement fits approximately 42" bust.

Materials:
- ❑ 36 oz. cotton sport yarn
- ❑ Tapestry needle
- ❑ G hook or hook size needed to obtain gauge

Gauge: We are not responsible for lack of materials due to project not being worked to gauge. Gauge for this pattern: Four 7-dc groups, 4 dc= 6"; three 7-dc group rows, 2 V st rows and 5 dc rows = 4".

Basic Stitches: Ch, sl st, sc, dc.

Jacket
Back

Row 1: Starting at bottom, ch 116, 7 dc in eighth ch from hook *(counts as dc and ch-1)*, (ch 1, skip next 3 chs, dc in next ch, ch 1, skip next 3 chs, 7 dc in next ch) 13 times, ch 1, skip next 3 chs, dc in last ch, turn. *(Fourteen 7-dc groups, 15 dc made) Front of row 1 is right side of work.*

Row 2: Skip ch-1 sps throughout; for **beg V st (ch 6, dc) in first st;** *(ch 6 counts as dc and ch-3),* ch 1, skip first 2 sts of first 7-dc group, dc in next 3 sts of same group, ch 1, skip last 2 sts of same group; for **V st, (dc, ch 3, dc) in next st;** (ch 1, skip first 2 sts of next 7-dc group, dc in next 3 sts of same group, ch 1, skip last 2 sts of same group, V st) across, turn.

Row 3: Ch 3, 3 dc in ch sp of first V st, ch 1, dc in center st of next 3-dc group, (ch 1, 7 dc in ch sp of next V st, ch 1, dc in center st of next 3-dc group) across to last V st, 4 dc in ch sp of last V st, turn.

Row 4: Ch 3, dc in next st of first 4-dc group, ch 1, skip last 2 sts of same group, V st, (ch 1, skip first 2 sts of next 7-dc group, dc in next 3 sts of same group, ch 1, skip last 2 dc of same group, V st) across to last 4-dc group, ch 1, skip first 2 sts on last 4-dc group, dc in last 2 sts, turn.

Row 5: Ch 4, skip next st, 7 dc in ch sp of first V st, (ch 1, dc in center st of next 3-dc group, ch 1, 7 dc in ch sp of next V st) across to last 2-dc group, skip next st of last 2-dc group, dc in last st, turn.

Rows 6-70: Repeat rows 2-5 consecutively ending with row 2. At end of last row, fasten off.

Left Front

Row 1: Starting at bottom, ch 60, 7 dc in eighth ch from hook, *(counts as dc and ch-1),* (ch 1, skip next 3 chs, dc in next ch, ch 1, skip next 3 chs, 7dc in next ch) 6 times, ch 1, skip next 3 chs, dc in last ch, turn. *(Seven 7-dc groups, 8 dc made) Front of row 1 is right side work.*

Rows 2-49: Repeat rows 2-5 of Back consecutively.

Row 50: For **neck shaping,** ch 3, skip first 2 sts of first 7-dc group, dc in next 3 sts of same group, ch 1, skip last 2 sts of same group, V st, (ch 1, skip first 2 sts of next 7-dc group, dc in next 3 sts of same group, ch 1, skip last 2 sts of same group, V st) across, turn.

Row 51: Ch 3, 3 dc in ch sp of first V st, (ch 1, dc in center of st of next 3-dc group, ch 1, 7 dc in ch sp of next V st) across to last 3-dc group, ch 1, dc in center st of last 3-dc group, dc in last st, turn.

Row 52: Ch 3, skip first 2 sts of first 7-dc group, dc in next 3 sts of same group, ch 1, skip last 2 sts of same group, V st, (ch 1, skip first 2 sts of next 7-dc group, dc in next 3 sts of same group, ch 1, skip last 2 sts of same group, V st) across to last 4-dc group, ch 1, skip first 2 sts of last 4-dc group, dc in last 2 sts, turn.

Row 53: Ch 4, skip next st, 7 dc in ch sp of first V st, (ch 1, dc in center st of next 3-dc group, ch 1, 7 dc in ch sp of next V st) across to last 3-dc group, ch 1, dc in center st of last 3-dc group, dc in last st, turn.

Rows 54-57: Repeat rows 50-53.

Rows 58-70: Repeat rows 2-5 of Back consecutively ending with row 2. At end of last row, fasten off.

Right Front

Row 1 Starting at bottom, ch 60, 7 dc in eighth ch from hook *(counts as dc and ch-1),* (ch 1, skip next 3 chs, dc in next ch, ch 1 skip next

Continued on page 128

Classic Cardigan

Designed by Marie Jones

Finished Sizes: Lady's 34-36 *(small)*, 38-40 *(medium)* and 42-44 *(large)*.

Materials:
- ❑ Amount sport yarn needed for size:
  - 28 oz. for small
  - 30 oz. for medium
  - 32 oz. for large
- ❑ Hook stated for size or hook size needed to obtain gauge

Gauge: We are not responsible for lack of materials due to project not being worked to gauge. Gauge for this pattern: **C hook for small,** 11 dc = 2"; 5 dc rows = 1". **D hook for medium,** 5 dc = 1"; 9 dc rows = 2". **E hook for large,** 9 dc =2"; 4 dc rows = 1".

Basic Stitches: Ch, sl st, sc, hdc, dc.

Special Stitch: For **popcorn (pc),** 5 dc in next sp, drop lp from hook, insert hook in first dc of group and pull dropped lp through, ch 1.

Ribbing
Row 1: Ch 7, sc in second ch from hook, sc in each ch across, turn. *(6 sc made)*

Row 2-197: Working these rows in **back lps** *(see Stitch Guide),* ch 1, sc in each st across, turn. At end of last row, **do not turn or fasten off.**

Body
Row 1: Ch 3; working in ends of rows across Ribbing, dc in each row across, turn. *(197 dc made)*

Rows 2-54: Ch 3; working in sps between sts, dc in each sp across, turn.

Row 55: For **right front,** ch 3, dc in first sp, **pc** *(see Special Stitch),* dc in next 35 sps, dc next 2 sps tog leaving last 157 sps unworked, turn. *(38 dc, 1 pc)*

Row 56: Ch 3, skip first sp, dc in each sp across, turn. *(38)*

Row 57: Ch 3, dc in first sp, pc in next sp, dc in next 2 sps, pc in next sp, dc in each sp across to last 2 sps, dc last 2 sps tog, turn. *(35 dc, 2 pc)*

Row 58: Ch 3, skip first sp, dc in each sp across, turn. *(36)*

Row 59: Ch 3, dc in first sp, pc in next sp, (dc in next 2 sps, pc in next sp) 2 times, dc in each sp across to last 2 sps, dc last 2 sps tog, turn. *(32 dc, 3 pc)*

Row 60: Ch 3, dc in each sp across turn. *(35)*

Row 61: Ch 3, dc in first sp, pc in next sp, (dc in next 2 sps, pc in next sp) 3 times, dc in each sp across, turn. *(31 dc, 4 pc)*

Row 62: Ch 3, dc in each sp across turn.

Row 63: Ch 3, dc in first sp, pc in next sp, (dc in next 2 sps, pc in next sp) 4 times, dc in each sp across, turn. *(30 dc, 5 pc)* *Mark first st of row.*

Row 64: Ch 3, dc in each sp across to last 2 sps, dc last 2 sps tog, turn. *(34)*

Note: Ch-2 is used as a decrease. Do not count it as a stitch.

Row 65: Ch 2, pc in first sp, (dc in next 2 sps, pc in next sp) 5 times, dc in each sp across, turn. *(27 dc, 6 pc)*

Row 66: Ch 3, dc in each sp across to last 2 sps, dc last 2 sps tog, turn. *(32)*

Row 67: Sl st in first sp, ch 2, pc in next sp, (dc in next 2 sps, pc in next sp) 5 times, dc in each sp across, turn. *(24 dc, 6 pc)*

Row 68: Ch 3, dc in each sp across to last 3 sps, dc next 2 sps tog leaving last sp and ch-2 unworked, turn. *(28)*

Row 69: Ch 2, pc in next sp, (dc in next 2 sps, pc in next sp) 5 times, dc in each sp across, turn. *(21 dc, 6 pc)*

Row 70: Ch 3, dc in each sp across to last 2 sps, dc last 2 sps tog leaving ch-2 unworked, turn. *(26)*

Row 71: Sl st in first sp, ch 2, pc in next sp, (dc in next 2 sps, pc in next sp) 5 times, dc in each sp across, turn. *(18 dc, 6 pc)*

Row 72: Ch 3, dc in each sp across to last 2 sps, dc last 2 sps tog leaving ch-2 unworked, turn. *(23)*

Row 73: Ch 3, skip first sp, pc in next sp, (dc in next 2 sps, pc in next sp) 5 times, dc in each sp across, turn. *(16 dc, 6 pc)*

Row 74: Ch 3, dc in each sp across, turn. *(22)*

Row 75: Ch 2, (pc in next sp, dc in next 2 sps) 7 times, turn. *(14 dc, 7 pc)*

Row 76: Ch 3, dc in each sp across leaving ch-2 unworked, turn. *(21)*

Row 77: Ch 3, dc in first 2 sps, (pc in next sp, dc in next 2 sps) 6 times, turn. *(15 dc, 6 pc)*

Row 78: Ch 3, dc in each sp across, turn.

Continued on page 110

Classic Cardigan

Continued from page 109

Rows 79-83: Repeat rows 77 and 78 alternately. At end of last row, fasten off.

Row 84: Join with sl st in eighth sp, ch 1, hdc in next sp, dc in each sp across. Fasten off. *(11 dc, 1 hdc)*

Row 55: For **back**, skip next 18 sps on row 54, join with sl st in next sp, ch 2, dc in next 39 sps, pc in next sp, dc in next 38 sps, dc next 2 sps tog leaving last 58 sps unworked, turn. *(78 dc, 1 pc)*

Row 56: Ch 2, dc in each sp across to last 2 sps, dc last 2 sps tog leaving ch-2 unworked, turn. *(77 dc)*

Row 57: Ch 2, dc in first 34 sps, pc in next sp, (dc in next 2 sps, pc in next sp) 2 times, dc in each sp across to last 2 sps, dc last 2 sps tog leaving ch-2 unworked, turn. *(72 dc, 3 pc)*

Row 58: Ch 2, dc in each sp across to last 2 sps, dc last 2 sps tog leaving ch-2 unworked, turn. *(73)*

Row 59: Ch 2, dc in first 29 sps, pc in next sp, (dc in next 2 sps, pc in next sp) 4 times, dc in each sp across to last 2 sps, dc last 2 sps tog leaving ch-2 unworked, turn. *(66 dc, 5 pc)*

Row 60: Ch 3, dc in each sp across leaving ch-2 unworked, turn. *(71)*

Row 61: Ch 3, dc in first 25 sps, pc in next sp, (dc in next 2 sps, pc in next sp) 6 times, dc in each sp across, turn.

Row 62: Ch 3, dc in each sp across, turn.

Row 63: Ch 3, dc in first 22 sps, pc in next sp, (dc in next 2 sps, pc in next sp) 8 times, dc in each sp across, turn.

Row 64: Ch 3, dc in each sp across, turn.

Row 65: Ch 3, dc in first 19 sps, pc in next sp, (dc in next 2 sps, pc in next sp) 10 times, dc in each sp across, turn.

Row 66: Ch 3, dc in each sp across, turn.

Row 67: Ch 3, dc in first 16 sps pc in next sp, (dc in next 2 sps, pc in next sp) 12 times, dc in each sp across, turn.

Row 68: Ch 3, dc in each sp across, turn.

Row 69: Ch 3, dc in first 13 sps, pc in next sp, (dc in next 2 sps, pc in next sp) 14 times, dc in each sp across, turn.

Row 70: Ch 3, dc in each sp across, turn.

Row 71: Ch 3, dc in first 10 sps, pc in next sp, (dc in next 2 sps, pc in next sp) 16 times, dc in each sp across, turn.

Row 72: Ch 3, dc in each sp across, turn.

Row 73: Ch 3, dc in first 7 sps, pc in next sp, (dc in next 2 sps, pc in next sp) 18 times, dc in each sp across, turn.

Row 74: Ch 3, dc in each sp across, turn.

Row 75: Ch 3, dc in first 4 sps, pc in next sp, (dc in next 2 sps, pc in next sp) 20 times, dc in each sp across, turn.

Row 76: Ch 3, dc in each sp across, turn.

Row 77: Ch 3, dc in next sp, (pc in next sp, dc in next 2 sps) across, turn.

Row 78: Ch 3, dc in each sp across turn.

Row 79-85: Repeat rows 77 and 78 alternately.

Row 86: For **left shoulder**, ch 1, sc in first 5 sps, hdc in next sp, dc in next 15 sps. Fasten off. *(21 sts)*

Row 86: For **right shoulder**, skip next 28 sps, join with sl st in next sp, ch 3, dc in next 14 sps, hdc in next sp, sc in last 5 sps. Fasten off. *(21 sts)*

Row 55: For **left front**, skip next 18 sps on row 54, join with sl st in next sp, ch 2, dc in next 36 sps, pc in next sp, dc in last 2 sps, turn. *(38 dc, 1 pc)*

Row 56: Ch 3, dc in each sp across to last 2 sps, dc last 2 sps tog, turn. *(38)*

Row 57: Ch 2, dc in next 31 sps, (pc in next sp, dc in next 2 sps) across, turn. *(35 dc, 2 pc)*

Row 58: Ch 3, dc in each sp across to last 2 sps, dc last 2 sps tog, turn. *(36)*

Row 59: Ch 2, dc in next 26 sps, (pc in next sp, dc in next 2 sps) across, turn. *(32 dc, 3 pc)*

Row 60: Ch 3, dc in each sp across, turn. *(35)*

Row 61: Ch 3, dc in first 22 sps, (pc in next sp, dc in next 2 sps) across, turn. *(31 dc, 4 pc)*

Row 62: Ch 3, dc in each sp across, turn.

Row 63: Ch 3, dc in first 19 sps, (pc in next sp, dc in next 2 sps) across, turn. *(30 dc, 5 pc)* Mark last st of row.

Row 64: Sl st in first sp, ch 3, dc in each sp across, turn. *(34)*

Row 65: Ch 3, dc in first 16 sps, pc in next sp, (dc in next 2 sps, pc in next sp) 5 times, dc in last sp, turn. *(28 dc, 6 pc)*

Row 66: Sl st in first sp, ch 2, dc in each sp across, turn. *(32)*

Row 67: Ch 3, dc in first 13 sps, (pc in next sp, dc in next 2 sps) 5 times, pc in next sp, dc in next sp leaving last sp unworked, turn. *(25 dc, 6 pc)*

Row 68: Sl st in first 3 sps, ch 2, dc in next sp, dc in each sp across, turn. *(27)*

Row 69: Ch 3, dc in first 10 sps (pc in next sp, dc in next 2 sps) 5 times, pc in next sp, dc in ch-2, turn. *(22 dc, 6 pc)*

Row 70: Sl st in first 3 sps, ch 2, dc in next sp, dc in each sp across, turn. *(24)*

Row 71: Ch 3, dc in first 7 sps, (pc in next sp, dc in next 2 sps) 5 times, pc in next sp, dc in ch-2, turn. *(19 dc, 6 pc)*

Row 72: Sl st in first 3 sps, ch 2, dc in next sp, dc

in each sp across, turn. *(21)*

Row 73: Ch 3, dc in first 4 sps, (pc in n next sp, dc in next 2 sps) 5 times, pc in next sp, dc in ch-2, turn. *(16 dc, 6 pc)*

Row 74: Ch 3, dc in each sp across, turn. *(22)*

Row 75: Ch 3, dc in next sp, (pc in next sp, dc in next 2 sps) 6 times, pc in next sp, dc in last sp, turn. *(15 dc, 7 pc)*

Row 76: Ch 3, dc in each sp across, turn. *(22)*

Row 77: Ch 3, dc in first sp, (pc in next sp, dc in next 2 sps) 6 times, dc last 2 sps tog, turn. *(15 dc, 6 pc)*

Row 78: Ch 3, dc in each sp across, turn. *(21)*

Row 79: Ch 3, dc in first sp, (pc in next 2 sps, dc in next 2 sps) across with dc in last sp, turn. *(15 dc, 6 pc)*

Rows 80-83: Repeat rows 76 and 79 alternately.

Row 84: Ch 3, dc in first 9 sps, hdc in next sp, sc in next sp, ch 1, sl st in next sp leaving last 8 sps unworked. Fasten off. *(12 sts)*

Matching sts, sew shoulder seams.

Trim

Row 1: With wrong side of work facing you, join with sl st in lower left front corner, ch 2, hdc in each st across Ribbing and in ends of rows across to marker, space 23 hdc evenly across to shoulder seam, hdc next row and next sp tog, sc in next 26 sps across back, hdc next sp and next row tog, space 23 hdc evenly across to marker, hdc in each row and in each ribbing st across turn. *(212 sts made)*

Row 2: Ch 2, hdc in first 67 sps, 3 hdc in each of next 3 sps, hdc in next 5 sps, hdc next 2 sps tog, hdc in next 15 sps, hdc next 2 sps tog, *hdc in next 4 sps, hdc next 2 sps tog*, hdc in next 10 sps, hdc next 2 sps tog; repeat between **, hdc in next 15 sps, hdc next 2 sps tog, hdc in next 5 sps, 3 hdc in each of next 3 sps, hdc in last 68 sps, turn. *(218)*

Row 3: Ch 2, hdc in first 68 sps, (2 hdc in next sp, hdc in next sp) 3 times, 2 hdc in next sp, hdc in next 6 sps, hdc next 2 sps tog, hdc in next 51 sps, hdc next 2 sps tog, hdc in next 6 sps, (2 hdc in next sp, hdc in next sp) 4 times, hdc in last 67 sps, turn. *(224)*

Row 4: Ch 2, hdc in each sp across. Fasten off.

Sleeve (make 2)
Ribbing

Row 1: Ch 13, sc in second ch from hook, sc in each ch across, turn. *(12 sc made)*

Rows 2-38: Working these rows in **back lps**, ch 1, sc in each st across, turn.

Row 39: Hold rows 1 and 38 tog; working through both thicknesses, sl st in each st across. **Do not turn or fasten off.**

Arm

Rnd 1: Ch 3, dc in end of each ribbing row around, join with sl st in top of ch-3, **turn.** *(39 dc made)*

Rnds 2-3: Sl st in next sp, ch 3, dc in each sp around with 2 dc in last sp, join, **turn.** *(40, 41)*

Rnd 4: Sl st in next sp, ch 2, hdc in each sp around, join, turn.

Rnds 5-63: Repeat rnds 2-4 consecutively, ending with 81 sts in last rnd.

Rnds 64-66: Or to desired length; repeat rnd 4.

Row 67: Working in rows across cap of Sleeve, sl st in first 9 sps, ch 2, dc in next 30 sps, pc in next sp, dc in next 29 sps, dc next 2 sps tog leaving last 9 sps unworked, turn. *(60 dc, 1 pc)*

Row 68: Sl st in first sp, ch 2, dc in each sp across to last 3 sps, dc in next 2 sps tog leaving last sp and ch-2 unworked, turn. *(57)*

Row 69: Sl st in first sp, ch 2, dc in next 23 sps, pc in next sp, (dc in next 2 sps, pc in next sp) 2 times, dc in next 22 sps, dc next 2 sps tog leaving last sp and ch-2 unworked, turn. *(50 dc, 3 pc)*

Row 70: Sl st in first sp, ch 2, dc in each sp across to last 3 sps, dc in next 2 sps tog leaving last sp and ch-2 unworked, turn. *(49)*

Row 71: Ch 2, dc in next 17 sps, (pc in next sp, dc in next 2 sps) 4 times, pc in next sp, dc in next 16 sps, dc last 2 sps tog leaving ch-2 unworked, turn. *(42 dc, 5 pc)*

Row 72: Ch 2, dc in each sp across to last 2 sps, dc last 2 sps tog leaving ch-2 unworked, turn. *(45)*

Row 73: Ch 2, dc in next 12 sps, pc in next sp, (dc in next 2 sps, pc in next sp) 6 times, dc in next 11 sps, dc last 2 sps tog, turn. *(36 dc, 7 pc)*

Row 74: Ch 2, dc in each sp across leaving ch-2 unworked, turn.

Row 75: Ch 3, dc in first 8 sps, pc in next sp, (dc in next 2 sps, pc in next sp) 8 times, dc in last 9 sps, turn. *(34 dc, 9 pc)*

Row 76: Ch 3, skip first sp, dc in each sp across to last 2 sps, dc last 2 sps tog, turn. *(41)*

Row 77: Ch 3, dc in first 4 sps, pc in next sp, (dc in next 2 sps, pc in next sp) 10 times, dc in last 5 sps turn. *(30 dc, 11 pc)*

Row 78: Ch 3, dc in each sp across, turn. *(41)*

Row 79: Ch 3, dc in first sp, (pc in next sp, dc in next 2 sps) across, turn. *(28 dc, 13 pc)*

Row 80: Ch 3, dc in each sp across, turn.

Row 81: Ch 2, dc in next sp, pc in next sp, (dc in next 2 sps, pc in next sp) 12 times, dc last 2 sps tog, turn. *(26 dc, 13 pc)*

Row 82: Sl st in first sp, ch 2, dc in each sp across to last 2 sps, dc last 2 sps tog leaving ch-2 unworked, turn. *(36)*

Row 83: Sl st in first sp, ch 2, dc in next sp, pc in next sp, (dc in next 2 sps, pc in next sp) 10 times,

Continued on page 115

Antique Lace Shawl

Designed by Ann Parnell

Finished Size: 70" x 40" excluding fringe.

Materials:
- ❏ 2600 yds. cream size 10 crochet cotton thread
- ❏ No. 4 steel hook or hook size needed to obtain gauge

Gauge: We are not responsible for lack of materials due to project not being worked to gauge. Gauge for this pattern: 1 shell = ¾"; 3 shell rows = 1".

Basic Stitches: Ch, sl, st, sc, hdc, dc.

Special Stitch: For **cluster (cl)**, yo 2 times insert hook in next ch sp, yo, pull through sp, (yo, pull through 2 lps on hook) 2 times, *yo 2 times, insert hook in same sp, yo, pull through sp, (yo pull through 2 lps on hook) 2 times; repeat from * 2 more times, yo, pull through all 5 lps on hook.

Note: Work into center of dc *(see illustration)* throughout.

First Motif

Rnd 1: Ch 5, sl st in first ch to form ring, ch 4, (dc in ring, ch 1) 11 times, join with sl st in third ch of ch-4. *(12 dc, 12 ch sps made) First 3 ch count as first dc.*

Rnd 2: Ch 1, (sc in next ch sp, ch 4) around, join with sl st in first sc.

Rnd 3: Working behind rnd 2 into sts of rnd 1, sl st in next dc, ch 4, yo 2 times, insert hook in same st, yo, pull through st, (yo, pull through 2 lps on hook) 2 times, yo 2 times, insert hook in next dc, yo, pull through st, (yo, pull through 2 lps on hook) 2 times, yo 2 times, insert hook in same st, yo, pull through st, (yo, pull through 2 lps on hook) 2 times, yo, pull through all 4 lps on hook, ch 8, *[yo 2 times, insert hook in next dc, yo, pull through st, (yo, pull through 2 lps on hook) 2 times, yo 2 times, insert hook in same st, yo, pull through st, (yo, pull through 2 lps on hook) 2 times; repeat from * one time, yo, pull through all 5 lps on hook, ch 8], repeat between [ ] 4 more times, join with sl st in top of first st.

Rnd 4: (Sl st, ch 3, 5 dc, ch 8, dc in sixth ch from hook, dc in last 2 chs, 6 dc) in first ch sp, (6 dc in next ch sp, ch 8, dc in sixth ch from hook, dc in last 2 chs, 6 dc) in each ch sp around, join with sl st in top of ch-3.

Rnd 5: Ch 1, sc in first 4 sts, *[hdc in next 2 sts, dc in base of next 3 sts, (4 dc, ch 4, 4 dc) in next ch sp, dc in next 3 sts, hdc in next 2 sts, sc in next 4 sts, ch 12, sc in next 4 sts, hdc in next 2 sts, dc in base of next 3 sts, (4 dc, ch 4, 4 dc) in next ch sp, dc in next 3 sts, hdc in next 2 sts, sc in next 4 sts], ch 4, sc in next 4 sts; repeat from * one time, repeat between [ ], ch 2, join with dc in first sc.

Rnd 6: Ch 3, 2 dc around post of joining dc, *[ch 3, skip next 10 sts, sc in next 3 sts, ch 3, sc in next ch sp, ch 3, sc in next 3 sts, ch 3; for **shell, (3 dc, ch 3, 3 dc)** in next ch-12 sp; ch 3, skip next 10 sts, sc in next 3 sts, ch 3, sc in next ch sp, ch 3, sc in next 3 sts, ch 3], shell in next ch-4 sp; repeat from * one time; repeat between [ ], 3 dc in beginning ch sp; for **beginning ch sp on next rnd,** ch 1, join with dc in top of first ch-3.

Rnd 7: Ch 3, 2 dc around post of joining dc, *[ch 4, skip next ch sp and next 2 sts, sc in next st, (3 sc, hdc) in next ch sp, ch 3, (hdc, 3 sc) in next ch sp, sc in next st, ch 4, 3 dc in ch sp of next shell, ch 12, dc in tenth ch from hook, dc in next 2 chs, 3 dc in same ch sp, ch 4, skip next ch sp and next 2 sts, sc in next st, (3 sc, hdc) in next ch sp, ch 3, (hdc, 3 sc) in next ch sp, sc in next st, ch 4], shell in ch sp of next shell; repeat from * one time; repeat between [ ], 3 dc in beginning ch sp, ch 1, join.

Rnd 8: Ch 3, 2 dc around post of joining dc, *[ch 4, skip next ch sp, (3 dc, ch 3, 3 dc, ch 3, 3 dc) in next ch sp, ch 4, skip next ch sp, dc in next 3 dc, dc in base of next 3 dc, (6 dc, ch 4, 6 dc) in next ch sp, dc in next 6 dc, ch 4, skip next ch sp, (3 dc, ch 3, 3 dc, ch 3, 3 dc) in next ch sp, ch 4, shell in next shell; repeat from * one time, ch 5, skip next ch sp, (sc, ch 3, sc) in next ch sp, ch 5, skip next ch sp, dc in next 3 dc, dc in base of next 3 dc, (3 dc, ch 4, 3 dc) in next ch sp, dc in next 6 dc, ch 5, skip next ch sp, (sc, ch 3, sc) in next ch sp, ch 5, 3 dc in beginning ch sp, ch 1, join.

Rnd 9: Ch 3, 2 dc around post of joining dc, * ch 5, skip next ch sp, shell in next ch sp, ch 3, **cl shell (see Special Stitch) in next ch sp, ch 5, cl in same ch sp, ch 7;** skip next ch sp and next 9 sts, sc in next st, skip next st, 3 dc in next st, ch

Continued on page 114

Antique Lace Shawl

Continued from page 112

3, shell in next ch sp ch 3, 3 dc in next st, skip next st, sc in next st, ch 7, skip next ch sp, cl shell in next ch sp, ch 3, shell in next ch sp, ch 3, shell in next shell; repeat from * one time, ch 5, skip next ch sp, shell in next ch sp, ch 5, skip next ch sp and next 6 sts, sc in next st, skip next st, 3 dc in next st, ch 3, shell in next ch sp, ch 3, 3 dc in next st, skip next st, sc in next st, ch 7, skip next ch sp, shell in next ch sp, ch 5, 3 dc in beginning ch sp, ch 1, join.

Rnd 10: Ch 3, 2 dc around post of joining dc, ch 5, shell in next shell, *ch 5, cl shell in next cl shell, ch 3, skip next ch sp, (cl, ch 7, cl) in next ch sp, ch 3, (cl, ch 9, cl) in next ch sp, ch 3, (cl, ch 7, cl) in next ch sp, ch 3, cl shell in next cl shell, (ch 5, shell in next shell) 3 times; repeat from * one time, ch 5, skip next ch sp, shell in each of next 3 ch sps, ch 5, shell in next shell, ch 5, 3 dc in beginning ch sp, ch 1, join.

Rnd 11: Ch 3, 2 dc around post of joining dc, ch 5, shell in next shell, * ch 5, cl shell in next cl shell, ch 3, skip next ch sp, (cl, ch 7, cl) in next ch sp, ch 3, skip next ch sp, (cl, ch 9, cl, ch 11, cl, ch 9, cl) in next ch sp, ch 3, skip next ch sp, (cl, ch 7, cl) in next ch sp, ch 3, cl shell in next cl shell, (ch 5, shell in next shell) 3 times; repeat from * one time, ch 5, shell in next shell, (ch 3, shell in next shell) 2 times, ch 5, shell in next shell, ch 5, 3 dc in beginning ch sp, ch 1, join.

Rnd 12: Ch 3, 2 dc around post of joining dc, ch 5, shell in next shell, *ch 5, cl shell in next cl shell, ch 3, skip next ch sp, (cl, ch 7, cl) in next ch sp, ch 3, (cl, ch 9, cl) in next ch sp, ch 3, (cl, ch 11, cl, ch 13, cl, ch 11, cl) in next ch sp ch 3, (cl, ch 9, cl) in next ch sp ch 3, (cl, ch 7, cl) in next ch sp, ch 3, cl shell in next cl shell, (ch 5, shell in next shell) 3 times; repeat from * one time, ch 5, shell in next shell, ch 5, (3 dc, ch 7, 3 dc) in next shell, (ch 5, shell in next shell) 2 times, ch 5, 3 dc in beginning ch sp, ch 1, join.

Rnd 13: Ch 3, 2 dc around post of joining dc, ch 5, shell in next shell *ch 5, cl shell in next cl shell, ch 3, skip next ch sp, (c , ch 7, cl) in next ch sp, ch 3, skip next ch sp, (cl, ch 7, cl) in next ch sp, ch 3, skip next ch sp, (cl, ch 7, cl) in next ch sp, ch 3, skip next ch sp, (cl, ch 9, cl) in next ch sp, ch 3, (cl, ch 11, cl; for **Corner,** ch 15; cl, ch 11, cl) in next ch sp, ch 3, (cl, ch 9, cl) in next ch sp, ch 3, skip next ch sp, (cl, ch 7, cl) in next ch sp, ch 3, skip next ch sp, (cl, ch 7, cl) in next ch sp, ch 3, cl shell in next cl shell, (ch 5, shell in next shell) 3 times; repeat from * one time, ch 5, shell in next shell, ch 5, skip next ch sp, (cl, ch 5, cl;

for **Corner,** ch 5; cl, ch 5, cl) in next ch sp, (ch 5 shell in next shell) 2 times, ch 5, 3 dc in beginning ch sp, ch 1, join.

Rnd 14: Ch 3, 2 dc around post of joining dc, *(ch 4, skip next ch sp, shell in next shell or next ch sp) across to Corner ch sp, ch 3, (cl, ch 5, cl ; for **Corner,** ch 15; (cl, ch 5, cl) in next ch sp, ch 3, shell in next ch sp; repeat from * 2 more times, (ch 4, skip next ch sp, shell in next ch sp or next shell) across, ch 4, 3 dc in beginning ch sp, ch 3, join with sl st in top of ch-3. Fasten off.

Second Motif

Rnd 1-13: Repeat rnds 1-13 of First Motif.

Rnd 14: Ch 3, 2 dc around post of joining dc, (ch 4, skip next ch sp, shell in next shell or next ch sp) across to next Corner ch sp, ch 3, (cl, ch 5, cl) in next ch sp, working on long edge of last Motif, ch 7, sc in Corner ch sp on last Motif, ch 7, cl in same ch sp on this Motif, ch 2, sc in next ch sp on last Motif, ch 2, cl in same ch sp on this Motif, ch 3, 3 dc in next ch sp, ch 1, sc in next shell on last Motif, ch 1, 3 dc in same ch sp on this Motif, *ch 4, skip next ch sp 3 dc in next ch sp or next shell, ch 1, sc in next shell on last Motif, ch 1, 3 dc in same ch sp or same shell on this Motif; repeat from * across to next Corner ch sp, ch 3, cl in next ch sp, ch 1, skip next ch sp on last Motif, sc in next ch sp, ch 1, cl in same ch sp on this Motif, ch 7, sc in Corner ch sp on last Motif, ch 7, (cl, ch 5, cl) in same ch sp on this Motif, ch 3 shell in next ch sp, (ch 4, skip next ch sp, shell in next ch sp or next shell) across to Corner ch sp, (cl, ch 5, cl; for **Corner,** ch 15; cl, ch 5, cl) in next ch sp, ch 3, shell in next ch sp, (ch 4, skip next ch sp, shell in next ch sp or next shell) across, ch 4, 3 dc in beginning ch sp, ch 3, join with sl st in top of ch-3. Fasten off.

Next Motif (make 13)

Work same as Second Motif, joining rnd 14 to short edges or long edges of other Motifs according to joining illustration.

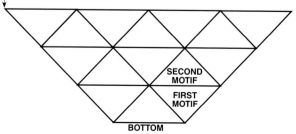

Border

Rnd 1: With right side facing you, join with sc in left-hand Corner ch sp; working around sides and bottom, ch 7, sc in same ch sp, ch 7, sc in next ch sp, *(ch 7, sc in next shell) across to next 2 cls, ch 7, sc in ch sp between cls, (ch 7, sc in next ch sp) 3 times*; repeat between ** 5 more times, (ch 7, sc in next shell) across to next 2 cls, ch 7, sc in ch sp between 2 cls, (ch 7, sc) 2 times in next Corner ch sp, ch 7, sc in next ch sp; repeat between ** 3 times, (ch 7, sc in next shell) across to next 2 cls, ch 7, sc in ch sp between cls, ch 7, join with sl st in first sc.

Rnd 2: Sl st in next 3 chs, ch 1, sc in same ch sp, (ch 7, sc in center ch of next ch sp) around to right- hand Corner ch sp on top long edge, ch 7, sc in next ch sp, ch 7, (hdc, 6 dc) in next ch sp, (7 dc in each ch sp across to last ch sp, (7 dc in each ch sp across to last ch sp, (6 dc, hdc) in last ch sp, join with sl st in first sl st. Fasten off.

Fringe

For each Fringe, cut ten strands each 10" long. With all strands held together, fold in half, insert hook in ch sp, pull fold through sp, pull ends through fold, tighten.

Fringe in each ch sp on each side an bottom edge of Shawl. ❧

Classic Cardigan

Continued from page 111

dc last 2 sps tog leaving ch-2 unworked, turn. *(22 dc, 11 pc)*

Row 84: Sl st in first sp, ch 2, dc in each sp across to last 2 sps, dc last 2 sps tog leaving ch-2 unworked, turn. *(30)*

Row 85: Sl st in first sp, ch 2, dc in next sp, pc in next sp, (dc in next 2 sps, pc in next sp) 8 times, dc next 2 sps tog leaving ch-2 unworked, turn. *(18 dc, 9 pc)*

Row 86: Sl st in first sp, ch 2, dc in each sp across to last 2 sps, dc last 2 sps tog leaving ch-2 unworked, turn. *(24)*

Row 87: Sl st in first sp, ch 2, dc in next sp, pc in next sp, (dc in next 2 sps, pc in next sp) 6 times, dc in next sp, ch 2, sl st in last sp. Fasten off. *(14 dc, 7 pc)*

Matching rows 66-81 of Sleeve to rows 55-75 of Back and Front, gathering rows 81-87 of Sleeve to fit, sew Sleeve in armhole. Repeat for other Sleeve.

Pocket

Row 1: Ch 23, dc in fourth ch from hook, dc in each ch across, turn. *(21 sc made)*

Row 2: Ch 3, dc in first 9 sps, pc in next sp, dc in last 10 sps, turn. *(20 dc, 1 pc)*

Row 3: Ch 3, dc in each sp across, turn.

Row 4: Ch 3, dc in first 6 sps, (pc in next sp, dc in next 2 sps) 2 times, pc in next sp, dc in last 7 sps, turn. *(18 dc, 3 pc)*

Row 5: Ch 3, dc in each sp across, turn.

Row 6: Ch 3, dc in first 3 sps, pc in next sp, (dc in next 2 sps, pc in next sp) 4 times, dc in last 4 sps, turn. *(16 dc, 5 pc)*

Row 7: Ch 3, dc in each sp across, turn.

Row 8: Ch 3, pc in first sp, (dc in next 2 sps, pc in next sp) across with dc in last sp, turn. *(14 dc, 7 pc)*

Row 9: Ch 3, dc in each sp across turn.

Row 10: Ch 3, pc in first sp, (dc in next 2 sps, pc in next sp) across with dc in last sp, turn.

Row 11: Ch 3, dc in each sp across, turn.

Row 12: Ch 3, dc in first 3 sps, pc in next sp, (dc in next 2 sps, pc in next sp) 4 times, dc in last 4 sps, turn.

Row 13: Ch 3, dc in each sp across, turn.

Row 14: Ch 3, dc in first 6 sps, (pc in next sp, dc in next 2 sps) 2 times, pc in next sp, dc in last 7 sps, turn.

Row 15: Ch 3, dc in each sp across, turn.

Row 16: Ch 3, dc in first 9 sps, pc in next sp, dc in last 10 sps, turn.

Row 17: Ch 3, dc in each sp across, turn.

Row 18: Ch 1, sc in each sp across. Fasten off.

Center Pocket on second row above ribbing on right front, sew in place. ❧

Lacy V-Neck Vest

Designed by Donna Jones

Finished Sizes: Lady's bust 32"-34". Finished measurements: 34½". Lady's bust 36"-38". Finished measurement: 38½". Lady's bust 40"-42". Finished measurements: 42".

Materials:
- ❑ Size 10 crochet cotton thread needed for size:
    - 1,450 yds. Lady's bust 32"-34"
    - 1,600 yds. Lady's bust 36"-38"
    - 1, 775 yds. Lady's bust 40"-42"
- ❑ 6 bobby pins for stitch markers
- ❑ Embroidery needle
- ❑ No.4 steel hook or hook size needed to obtain gauge

Gauge: We are not responsible for lack of materials due to project not being worked to gauge. Gauge for this pattern: 8 sc = 1", 9 sc **back lp** rows = 1"; 5 diamonds = 3", 7 diamond rows = 3".

Basic Stitches: Ch, sl st, sc, hdc, dc, tr.

Note: Instructions are for lady's bust 32"-34"; changes for 36"-38" and 40"-42" are in [ ].

Ribbing
Row 1: Leaving 8" end, ch 31, sc in second ch from hook, sc in each ch across, turn. *(30 sc made)*
Rows 2-232 [2-256, 2-280]: Working these rows in **back lps** *(see Stitch Guide)*, ch 1, sc in each st across, turn. At end of last row, **do not turn of fasten off.**
Overlap first and last rows to form rib; using 8" end, sew together.

Body
Rnd 1: Working in ends of ribbing rows, ch 1, (sc, ch 1) 2 times in first row, skip next row, *(sc, ch 1) 2 times in next row, repeat from * around, join with sl st in first sc. *(232 sc made) [256 sc made, 280 sc made] Front of rnd 1 is right side of work.*
Rnd 2: Sl st in first ch-1 sp, skip next 4 sc, 3 tr in next ch-1 sp, ch 4, sl st in same ch-1 sp, *skip next 4 sc, (3 tr, ch 4, sl st) in next ch-1 sp; repeat from * around to last 3 sc, skip last 3 sc, (3 tr, ch 4, sl st) in first ch-1 sp; to join, ch 3, sl st in top ch 4, **turn.** *(174 tr, 58 ch-4 sps) [192 tr, 64 ch-4 sps; 210 tr, 70 ch-4 sps]*

Rnds 3-25: For **beginning (beg) diamond,** 2 tr evenly spaced across first ch-4 sp, ch 4, sl st in top ch of same ch-4 sp; for **diamond,** 3 tr evenly spaced across next ch-4 sp, ch 4, sl st in top of same ch-4 sp; work diamond in each ch-4 sp around, join, **turn.** *(58 diamonds) [64 diamonds, 70 diamonds]*
Row 26: For **back,** working in rows, beg diamond, diamond 28 [31,34] times leaving last 29 [32, 35] diamonds unworked, turn. *(29) [32, 35]*
Rows 27-42 [27-44, 27-46]: For **half diamond, ch 1, (sc, hdc, dc) evenly spaced across first ch-4 sp, ch 4, sl st in top ch of same ch-4 sp;** diamond across, turn. *(28½ diamonds) [31½ diamonds, 34½ diamonds]*
Row 43 [45, 47]: For **first shoulder,** half-diamond, diamond 8 [9, 11] times; for **end diamond,** 3 tr evenly spaced across next ch-4 sp, tr in top ch of same ch-4 sp leaving last 18½ [20½, 21½] diamonds unworked, turn. *(9½) [10½, 12½]*
Row 44 [46, 48]: Diamond across, turn.
Row 45 [47, 49]: Ch 7, sc in top of first ch 4, (ch 3, sc in top ch of next ch-4) across. Fasten off.
Row 43 [45, 47]: Working across **back neck,** join with sl st in top ch of last worked ch-4 on row 42 [44, 46], (ch 3, sc in top ch of next ch-4) 9 [10, 10] times; for **second shoulder,** diamond 10 [11, 12] times, turn. *(10) [11, 12]*
Row 44 [46, 48]: Half-diamond, diamond 8 [9, 10] times, end diamond, turn.
Row 45 [47, 49]: (Ch 3, sc in top ch of next ch-4) across. Fasten off.
Row 26: For **front,** with wrong side of rnd 25 facing you, join with sl st in top ch of last worked ch-4 on rnd 25, diamond across, turn. *(29) [32, 35]*
Rows 27-29 [27-31, 27-33]: Half-diamond, diamond across, turn. *(28½) [31½, 34½]*
Row 30 [32, 34]: For **first side,** half-diamond, diamond 12 [14, 16] times, end diamond leaving last 14½ [15½, 16½] diamonds unworked, turn. *(13½) [15½, 17½]*
Row 31 [33, 35]: Diamond across, turn. *(13) [15, 17]*
Row 32 [34, 36]: Half-diamond, diamond across to last diamond, end diamond, turn. *(12½) [14 ½, 16½]*
Rows 33-37 [35-41, 37-45]: Repeat rows 31 and
Continued on page 118

Lacy V-Neck Vest

Continued from page 117

32 [33 and 34, 35 and 36] alternately, ending with row 31 [33, 35] and *(10) [11, 12]* diamonds.

Rows 38-43 [42-45, 46-47]: Half-diamond, diamond across, turn. *(9½) [10½, 11½]*

Bow 44 [46, 48]: Half diamond, diamond across to last diamond, end diamond, turn.

Row 45 [47, 49]: (Ch 3, sc in top ch of next ch-4) across. Fasten off.

Row 30 [32, 34]: For **second side,** with wrong side of row 29 [31, 33] facing you, join with sl st in top ch of last worked ch-4, diamond across, turn. *(14) [16, 17]*

Rows 31-38 [33-42, 35-44]: Repeat rows 32 and 31 [34 and 33, 36 and 35] of front first side alternately. At end of last row *(10) [11, 12]*.

Rows 39-44 [43-46, 45 -48]: Half-diamond, diamond across, turn. *(9½) [10½, 11½]*

Row 45 [47, 49]: Ch 7, sc in top ch of first ch-4, (ch 3, sc in top ch of next ch-4) across. Fasten off.
Sew shoulder seams.

Neck Ribbing

Rnd 1: With right side of neck edge facing you, join with sl st in left shoulder seam, ch 1; spacing sts evenly, 60 sc across to center front, 60 sc across right shoulder seam, 52 [56, 60] sc across back, join with sl st in first sc. *(172 sc made)* *[176 sc made, 180 sc made]*

Row 2: Ch 13, sc in second ch from hook, sc in each ch across, sl st in next 2 sts on rnd 1, turn. *(12)*

Row 3: Working this row in **back lps** *(see Stitch Guide),* skip sl sts, sc in each sc across, turn.

Row 4: Working in **back lps,** sc in each st across; working in **both lps** of sts on rnd 1 throughout, sl st in next 2 sts on rnd 1, turn.

Rows 5-50: Repeat rows 3 and 4 alternately.

Row 51: Working in **back lps,** skip first 2 sl sts, sc in each st across to last 2 sc, sl st in next st leaving last sc unworked, mark last sl st made, mark unworked sc, turn. *(10 sc)*

Row 52: Working in **back lps,** skip first sl st, sc in each st across, sl st in next 2 sts on rnd 1, turn.

Rows 53-59: Repeat rows 51 and 52 alternately, ending with row 51 and *(2 sc)*.

Row 60: Working in **back lps,** skip first sl st, sc in next st, sc last st on ribbing and next st on rnd 1 tog, sl st in next st on rnd 1, turn. *(2) Row 60 is center front.*

Row 61: Working in **back lps,** skip first sl st, sc in next 2 sts, sl st in marked sl st, move marker to last sl st made, turn.

Notes: *Mark front lp of each new sl st as it is worked.*

Remove marker as each marked st is worked.

Row 62: Working in **back lps,** skip first sl st, sc in each st across, sl st in next 2 sts on rnd 1, turn.

Row 63: Working in **back lps,** skip first 2 sl sts, sc in each sc across, sc in first marked sl st, sc in next marked sc, sl st in next marked sl st, turn. *(4)*

Rows 64-70: Repeat row 62 and 63 alternately, ending with row 62 and *(10 sc)*.

Row 71: Working in **back lps,** skip first 2 sl sts, sc in each sc across, sc in next marked sl st, sc in last marked st on row 50, turn. *(12)*

Rows 72-171 [72-175, 72-179]: Repeat rows 4 and 3 alternately.

Row 172 [176, 180]: Working in **back lps,** sc in each st across, sl st in last st on row 1. Leaving 6" end for sewing, fasten off.
Overlap first and last rows to form rib, sew together.

Armhole Trim

Rnd 1: With right side of armhole facing you, join with sc at underarm, sc 4 times across each half-diamond around, join with sl st in first sc.

Rnd 2-3: Ch 1, sc in each st around, join. At end of last rnd, fasten off.
Repeat on other armhole. ❧

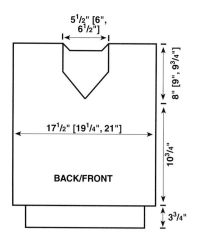

Victorian Snood

Designed by Elizabeth Ann White

Finished Size: 26" across.

Materials:
- ❏ 200 yds. ecru size 20 crochet cotton thread
- ❏ 1 yd. of ⅜" ribbon
- ❏ No. 8 steel hook or hook size needed to obtain gauge

Gauge: We are not responsible for lack of materials due to project not being worked to gauge. Gauge for this pattern: 37 chs = 4".

Basic Stitches: Ch, sc.

Snood
Row 1: For **base**, ch 10, sc in first ch to form ring; ch 130; for **base**, sc in tenth ch from hook; (ch 10, skip next 5 chs, sc in next ch) 19 times, ch 10, sc in base, turn. *(2 bases, 20 ch lps made)*

Row 2: Ch 5, sc in next ch lp, (ch 10, sc in next ch lp) 19 times, ch 5, sc in base, turn. *(21 ch lps)*

Row 3: Ch 10, skip next ch-5 lp, sc in next ch lp, (ch 10, sc in next ch lp) 18 times, ch 10, skip next ch-5 lp, sc in base, turn. *(21 ch lps)*

Rows 4-48: Repeat row 2 and 3 alternately, ending with row 2.

Row 49: Ch 5, skip next ch-5 lp, sc in next ch lp, (ch 5, sc in next ch lp) 18 times, ch 5, skip next ch-5 lp, sc in base. Fasten off.

Weave ribbon through ch lps around outer edge. Tie in bow. 🐾

Evening Purse

Designed by Anita Green

Finished Size: 7½" x 6½".

Materials:
- ❏ 600 yds. size 5 black pearl cotton thread
- ❏ Small amount white size 8 pearl cotton thread
- ❏ Small amount silver metallic thread
- ❏ ½ yd. black satin fabric
- ❏ 3 yds. black twisted cord
- ❏ 6mm. white pearl bead
- ❏ Black and white sewing thread
- ❏ Craft glue
- ❏ Sewing and tapestry needles
- ❏ No. 3 steel hook and E hook or hook size needed to obtain gauge

Gauge: We are not responsible for lack of materials due to project not being worked to gauge. Gauge for this pattern: **E hook and size 5 cotton,** 11 patterns sts = 2"; 9 pattern rows = 2".

Basic Stitches: Ch, sl st, sc, dc.

Purse
Back and Flap
Row 1: With E hook and two strands black held tog, beginning at **bottom,** ch 25, (sc, dc) in second ch from hook, (sc in next ch, dc in next ch) across to last ch, (sc, dc) in last ch, turn. *(25 sts made)*

Row 2: (Ch 3, sc) in first st; for **pattern, dc in each sc and sc in each dc** across to last st, (dc,

sc) in last st, turn. *(28)*

Row 3: Ch 1, (sc, dc) in first st, work pattern across with (sc, dc) in last st, turn. *(30)*

Rows 4-7: Repeat row 2 and 3 alternately. At end of last row, *(38)*.

Rows 8-42: Ch 1, work pattern across turn.

Row 43: Ch 1; for **decrease (dec), insert hook in first st, yo, pull through, yo, insert hook in next st, yo, pull through st, yo, pull through 2 lps on hook, yo, pull though all 3 lps on hook**; work pattern across to last 2 sts, dec, turn. *(36)*

Row 44: Ch 2, work pattern across to last 2 sts, yo, insert hook in next st, yo, pull through st, yo, pull through 2 lps on hook, insert hook in last st, yo, pull through st, yo, pull through all 3 lps on hook, turn. *(34)*

Note: Ch-2 is used as a decrease. Do not work into or count as a st.

Rows 45-49: Repeat rows 43 and 44 alternately, ending with row 43 and 24 sts. Fasten off.

Front

Rows 1-26: Repeat rows 1-26 of Back. At end of last row, fasten off.

Gusset

Row 1: Ch 5, sc in second ch from hook, dc in next ch, sc in next ch, dc in last ch, turn. *(4 sts made)*

Rows 2-68: Ch 1, sc in first st, dc in next st, sc in next st, dc in last st, turn. At end of last row, fasten off.

Flower Petal (make 5)

Row 1: With No. 3 steel hook and one strand each white and silver held tog, ch 2, sc in second ch from hook, turn. *(1 sc made)*

Row 2: Ch 1, 2 sc in next st, turn. *(2)*

Row 3: Ch 1, 2 sc in each st across, turn. *(4)*

Row 4: Ch 1, 2 sc in first st, sc in next 2 sts, 2 sc in last st, turn. *(6)*

Rows 5-8: Ch 1, sc in each st across, turn.

Row 9: Ch 1, sc in each st across to last 2 sts, sc last 2 sts tog, turn. *(5)*

Row 10: Ch 1, sc first 2 sts tog, sc in each st across, turn. *(4)*

Rows 11-12: Repeat rows 9 and 10. *(3, 2)*

Row 13: Ch 1, sc next 2 sts tog. Fasten off. *(1)*

With white sewing thread, sew Petals to Flap forming Flower *(see photo)*. Sew bead to center of Flower.

Finishing

Block Purse pieces. For lining, using crocheted pieces as pattern, cut two pieces satin ¼" larger on all edges than each Purse piece. Set lining aside.

With right sides of crocheted pieces facing you, sew one long edge of Gusset to sides and bottom of Front piece. Sew remaining edge of Gusset to rows 1-26 of Back.

For **edging**, working around opening and Flap, hold Purse with right side facing you; with two strands black held tog, join with sc in any st on Front, sc in each st and in end of each row around front, Flap an top edges of Gusset, join with sl st in first sc. Fasten off.

Shoulder Strap

Cut twisted cord in half. With both pieces held together, tie knot at each end. Pull tight and trim ends. Tie knot at center. Glue underside of knots to secure. Glue one end of Strap to Gusset on each side of Purse with knot 3" from top edge. When dry, using black sewing thread, sew to secure.

Lining

1: With right side facing you, allowing ¼" for seams, sew one long edge of one Guesst lining piece across sides and bottom of one front lining piece, easing slightly around corners. Sew other edge of gusset to bottom of back lining piece. Repeat with other lining pieces.

2: With right sides together, matching raw edges, place one lining inside the other. Sew pieces together leaving opening on flap for turning. Clip curves. Turn right side out. Sew opening closed. Place lining inside Purse and sew together around opening next to bottom of edging. ❧

Collared Vest

Designed by Mara Goodwin

Finished Sizes: Lady's small, fits 32"–34" bust. Finished Measurement: 38". **Lady's medium,** fits 36"–38" bust. Finished Measurement: 43". **Lady's large,** fits 40"–42" bust. Finished Measurement: 48".

Materials:
- ❑ Amount needed of size 10 crochet cotton thread stated for size:
  - 2,250 yds. for small
  - 2,550 yds. for medium
  - 2,800 yds. for large
- ❑ 8 decorative shank ⅝" buttons
- ❑ Crochet stitch markers
- ❑ Sewing needle and thread
- ❑ No. 8 for small, No. 6 for medium and No. 4 steel hook for large or hook size needed to obtain gauge for size

Gauges: We are not responsible for lack of materials due to project not being worked to gauge. Gauge for this pattern: **No. 8 hook,** Large Motif is 3¾" across. **No. 6 hook,** Large Motif is 4¼" across. **No. 4 hook,** Large Motif is 4¾" across.

Basic Stitches: Ch, sl st, sc, hdc, dc.

Special Stitches: For **beginning popcorn (beg pc),** ch 3, 4 dc in same st as ch-3, drop lp from hook, insert hook in top of ch-3, pull dropped lp through ch, ch 1.

For **popcorn (pc),** 5 dc in st, drop lp from hook, insert hook in top of first dc of group, pull dropped lp through st, ch 1.

For **reverse popcorn (rpc),** 5 dc in next st, drop lp from hook, insert hook from back to front in top of first dc of group, pull dropped lp through st, ch 1.

Large Motif (make 56)
Rnd 1: Ch 5, sl st in first ch to form ring, ch 3, 11 dc in ring, join with sl st in top of ch-3. *(12 dc made)*

Rnd 2: Beg pc *(see Special Stitches)* in first st, ch 1, **(pc—see Special Stitches, ch 1)** in each st around, join with sl st in top of beg pc.

Rnd 3: (Ch 3, dc) in first st, 2 dc in next ch sp, dc in next st, 2 dc in next ch sp, (2 dc in next st, 2 dc in next ch sp, dc in next st, 2 dc in next ch sp) around, join with sl st in top of ch-3. *(42 dc)*

Rnd 4: (Ch 3, dc) in first st, dc in next 5 sts, 2 dc in next st, ch 2, (2 dc in next st, dc in next 5 sts, 2 dc in next st, ch 2) around, join. *(54 dc, 6 ch sps)*

Rnd 5: (Ch 3, dc) in first st, dc in next 3 sts, pc in next st, dc in next 3 sts, 2 dc in next st, ch 2, (2 dc in next st, dc in next 3 sts, pc in next st, dc in next 3 sts, 2 dc in next st, ch 2) around, join. *(66 sts, 6 ch sps)*

Rnd 6: (Ch 3, dc) in first st, dc in next 9 sts, 2 dc in next st, ch 3, (2 dc in next st, dc in next 9 sts, 2 dc in next st, ch 3) around, join. *(78 dc, 6 ch sps)*

Rnd 7: (Ch 3, dc) in first st, (dc in next 3 sts, pc in next st) 2 times, dc in next 3 sts, 2 dc in next st, ch 4, *2 dc in next st, (dc in next 3 sts, pc in next st) 2 times, dc in next 3 sts, 2 dc in next st, ch 4; repeat from * around, join. *(90 sts, 6 ch sps)*

Rnd 8: (Ch 3, dc) in first st, dc in next 13 sts, 2 dc in next st, ch 5, (2 dc in next st, dc in next 13 sts, 2 dc in next st, ch 5) around, join. Fasten off. *(102 dc, 6 ch sps)*

Half Motif (make 8)
Row 1: Ch 5, sl st in first ch to form ring, ch 3, 7 dc in ring, turn. *(8 dc made)*

Row 2: Ch 4 *(counts as first dc and ch-1 sp)*, pc in next st, (ch 1, pc in next st) 5 times, ch 1, dc in last st, turn. *(8 sts, 7 ch sps) Front of row 2 is right side of work.*

Row 3: Ch 4, (2 dc in next ch sp, 2 dc in next st, 2 dc in next ch sp, dc in next st, ch 1) 3 times, skip last ch sp, dc in last st, turn. *(23 dc, 4 ch sps)*

Row 4: Ch 4, (*2 dc in next st, dc in next 5 sts, 2 dc in next st*, ch 2) 2 times; repeat between **, ch 1, skip last ch sp, dc in last st, turn. *(29 dc, 4 ch sps)*

Row 5: Ch 4, *[2 dc in next st, dc in next 3 sts, **rpc** *(see Special Stitches)* in next st, dc in next 3 sts, 2 dc in next st], ch 2; repeat from * one time; repeat between [ ], ch 1, skip last ch sp, dc in last st, turn. *(35 dc, 4 ch sps)*

Row 6: Ch 5 *(counts as first dc and ch-2 sp)*, (*2 dc in next st, dc in next 9 sts, 2 dc in next st*, ch 3, skip next ch sp) 2 times; repeat between **, ch 2, skip last ch sp, dc in last st, turn. *(41 dc, 4 ch sps)*

Row 7: Ch 5, *[2 dc in next st, (dc in next 3 sts, rpc in next st) 2 times, dc in next 3 sts, 2 dc in next st], ch 4, skip next ch sp; repeat from * one time; repeat between [ ], ch 2, skip last ch

Continued on page 124

Collared Vest

Continued from page 122

sp, dc in last st, turn. *(47 dc, 4 ch sps)*

Row 8: Ch 6 *(counts as first dc and ch-3 sp),* (*2 dc in next st, dc in next 13 sts, 2 dc in next st*, ch 5) 2 times; repeat between **, ch 3, skip last ch sp, dc in last st. Fasten off.

Vest Assembly

Working through both thickness in **back lps** *(see Stitch Guide),* sl st in each st and in each ch as needed to work Large and Half Motifs together *(see illustration).*

Fill-In

Row 1: With right side facing you, join with sl st in last st of 17-dc group before ch sp *(see red arrow on illustration)* on one Large Motif *(see red lines on illustration),* ch 5, skip next ch sp, sl st across next 17 sts, turn.

Row 2: Ch 1, skip first st, hdc in next st, dc in next 13 sts, dc next 2 sts tog, ch 4, skip next ch sp, dc next 2 sts tog, dc in next 13 sts, hdc in next st leaving last st unworked, turn.

Row 3: Ch 1, skip first st, sc in next st, hdc in next st, dc in next 2 sts, pc in next st, dc in next 3 sts, pc in next st, dc in next 3 sts, dc next 2 sts tog, ch 3, skip next ch sp, dc next 2 sts tog, dc in next 3 sts, pc in next st, dc in next 3 sts, pc in next st, dc in next 2 sts, hdc in next st, sc in

next st leaving last st unworked, turn.

Row 4: Ch 1, skip first st, sl st in next 4 sts, sc in next st, hdc in next st, dc in next 4 sts, dc next 2 sts tog, ch 2, skip next ch sp, dc next 2 sts tog, dc in next 4 sts, hdc in next st, sc in next st, sl st in next st leaving last 4 sts unworked. Fasten off.

Repeat Fill-In on sides, back and shoulder *(see red lines on illustration).*

Trim

Working around outer edge, with right side of right shoulder facing you, join with sc in ch-5 sp of last rnd on Half Motif; *work the following steps to complete the rnd:*

A: Working across sts on Fill-In, ch 1, sc in next unworked st on row 2, sc in next 4 sts on row 3, sc in next 5 sts on row 4, hdc in next 3 sts, 2 dc in next ch sp, hdc in next 3 sts, sc in next 8 sts, sc in next unworked st on row 3, sc in next unworked st on row 2; *(29 sts counting joining sc across shoulder)*

B: **Armhole trim starts here;** working across next Half Motif, ch 1, 5 sc in next ch sp, 2 sc in each end of next 7 rows, sc in ring, 2 sc in each end of next 8 rows;

C: (Ch 5, skip next 2 ch sps, sc in next 17 sts of Large Motif) 4 times, ch 5, skip next 2 ch sps.

D: Working across next Half Motif, 2 sc in each

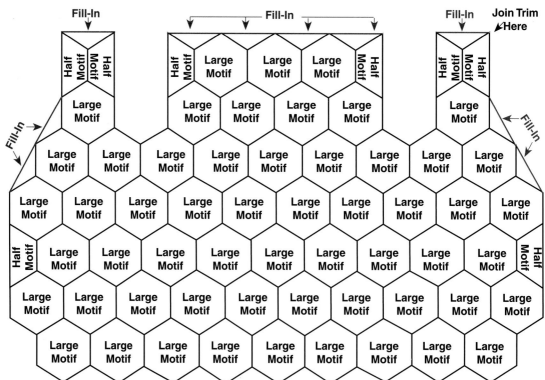

end of next 8 rows, sc in ring, 2 sc in each end of next 7 rows, 5 sc in end of last row; *(140 sts across armhole)*

E: Working across back, repeat step A; (ch 2, dc in next ch sp, ch 2, sc in next unworked st on row 2 of next Fill-In, sc in next 4 sts on row 3, sc in next 5 sts on row 4, hdc in next 3 sts, 2 dc in next ch sp, hdc in next 3 sts, sc in next 8 sts, sc in next unworked st on row 3, sc in next unworked st on row 2) 3 times; *(115 sts across back)*

F: Repeat steps B, C, D and A; *(168 sts across armhole and left front shoulder)*

G: Working down left front neckline, repeat step B, (ch 2, dc in next ch sp, ch 2, sc in next unworked st on row 2 of next Fill-In, sc in next 4 sts on row 3, sc in next 5 sts on row 4, hdc in next 3 sts, 2 dc in next ch sp, hdc in next 3 sts, sc in next 8 sts, sc in next unworked st on row 3, sc in next unworked st on row 2) 2 times; mark third st from last st made; *(94 sts)*

H: Working down center front, ch 5, skip next ch sp of next Large Motif, sc in next 17 sts, ch 5, skip next ch sp, working across next Half Motif, 2 sc in each end of next 8 rows, sc in ring, 2 sc in each end of next 8 rows, ch 5, skip next ch sp of next Large Motif, sc in next 17 sts; *(67 sts)*

I: Working across bottom of Large Motifs, 3 sc in next ch sp, mark last st made, 2 sc in same ch sp as last st made, (sc in next 17 sts, 5 sc in next ch sp) 4 times, *5 sc in next ch sp, (sc in next 17 sts, 5 sc in next ch sp) 2 times; repeat from

* 6 more times, 5 sc in next ch sp, (sc in next 17 sts, 5 sc in next ch sp) 3 times, sc in next 17 sts, 3 sc in next ch sp, mark last st made, 2 sc in same ch sp as last st made; *(529 sts)*

J: Working across center right front, sc in next 17 sts of next Large Motif, ch 5, skip next ch sp; working across last Half Motif, 2 sc in each end of next 8 rows, sc in ring, 2 sc in each end of next 8 rows, ch 5, skip next ch-5 sp of Large Motif, sc in next 17 sts, ch 5; *(67 sts)*

K: Working up right front neckline, (sc in next unworked st on row 2 of Fill-In, sc in next 4 sts on row 3, sc in next 5 sts on row 4, hdc in next 3 sts, 2 dc in next ch sp, hdc in next 3 sts, sc in next 8 sts, sc in next unworked st on row 3, sc in next unworked st on row 2, ch 2, dc in next ch sp of next Large Motif, ch 2) 2 times; working across last Half Motif, 2 sc in each end of next 8 rows, sc in ring, 2 sc in each end of next 7 rows, 4 sc in last row, join with sl st in first sc. Fasten off. *(93 sts across neckline)*

Match and sew sts on shoulders together.

Armhole Trim

With right side facing you, working around one Armhole, join with sc in any st, sc in each st around with 5 sc in each ch sp, join with sl st in first sc. Fasten off. Repeat on other armhole.

Right Placket

Row 1: With right side facing you, join with sc in first marked st at top left center front, remove

Continued on page 130

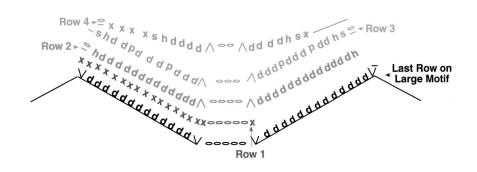

Row 4 ► / Row 3
Row 2 ► / Last Row on Large Motif
Row 1

V = 2 Dc in next st
d = Dc
○ = Ch
x = Sl st
— = Skip st or leave remaining sts unworked
h = Hdc
∧ = Dc next 2 sts tog
s = Sc
p = Pc

Rose Hat

Designed by Nancy Whitman

Finished size: One size fits preteen to adult.

Materials:
- ❏ 3½ oz. woven acrylic sport yarn
- ❏ Tapestry needle
- ❏ E hook or hook size need to obtain gauge

Gauge: We are not responsible for lack of materials due to project not being worked to gauge. Gauge for this pattern: Rnds 1-2 = 2" in diameter.

Basic Stitches: Ch, sl st, sc, hdc, dc, tr

Note: Work with two stands sport yarn held together as one throughout entire pattern.

Hat

Rnd 1: Ch 5, sl st in first ch to form ring, ch 4, (dc, ch 1) 7 times in ring, join with sl st in third ch of beginning ch-4. *(8 ch sps made)*

Rnd 2: (Sl st, ch 4, dc) in first ch sp, (dc, ch 1, dc) in each ch sp around, join.

Rnd 3: (Sl st, ch 4, dc, ch 1, dc) in first ch sp, (dc, ch 1, dc, ch 1, dc) in each ch sp around, join.

Rnd 4: (Sl st, ch 4, dc) in first ch sp, (dc, ch 1, dc) in each ch sp around, join.

Rnd 5: (Sl st, ch 4, dc) in first ch sp, (dc, ch 1, dc, ch 1, dc) in next ch sp, *(dc, ch 1, dc) in next ch sp, (dc, ch 1, dc, ch 1, dc) in next ch sp; repeat from * around, join.

Rnd 6: (Sl st, ch 4, dc) in first ch sp, (dc, ch 1, dc) in each ch sp around, join.

Rnd 7: (Sl st, ch 4, dc, ch 1, dc) in first ch sp, (dc, ch 1, dc) in next 3 ch sps; *(dc, ch 1, dc, ch 1, dc) in next ch sp, (dc, ch 1, dc) in next 3 ch sps; repeat from * around, join.

Rnd 8: (Sl st, ch 4, dc, ch 1, dc) in first ch sp, (dc, ch 1, dc) in each of next 5 ch sps; *(dc, ch 1, dc, ch 1, dc) in next ch sp, (dc, ch 1, dc) in each of next 5 ch sps; repeat from* around, join.

Rnds 9-15: (Sl st, ch 4, dc) in first ch sp, (dc, ch 1, dc) in each ch sp around, join.

Rnd 16: Ch 1, sc in each st and in each ch sp around, join with sl st in first sc.

Rnd 17: Ch 1, sc in each st around, join. Fasten off.

Rose

Rnd 1: Ch 4 *(counts as first dc)*, 5 dc in fourth ch from hook, join with sl st in top of ch-4. *(6 dc made)*

Rnd 2: Ch 1, sc in first st, ch 3, (sc in next st, ch 3) around, join with sl st in first sc.

Rnd 3: (Sl st, ch 1, sc, hdc, 3 dc, hdc, sc) in first ch sp, (sc, hdc, 3 dc, hdc, sc) in each ch sp around, join.

Rnd 4: Working behind petals, ch 1, sc in joining sl st of rnd 2, ch 5, (sc in next unworked st on rnd 2, ch 5) around, join.

Rnd 5: (Sl st, ch 1, sc, hdc, dc, 7 tr, dc, hdc, sc) in first ch sp, (sc, hdc, dc, 7 tr, dc, hdc, sc) in each ch sp around, join. Fasten off.

Sew Rose to rnd 15 of Hat for front. 🍃

Open Shell Jacket

Continued from page 106

3 chs, 7dc in next ch) 6 times, ch 1, skip next 3 chs, dc in last ch, turn. *(Seven 7-dc groups, 8 dc made) Front of row 1 is right side of work.*

Rows 2-49: Repeat rows 2-5 of Back consecutively.

Row 50: For **neck shaping,** beg V st, ch 1, skip first 2 sts of first 7-dc group, dc in next 3 sts of same group, ch 1, skip last 2 sts of same group, V st, (ch 1, skip first 2 sts of next 7-dc group, dc in next 3 sts of same group, ch 1, skip last 2 sts of same group, V st) across to last 7-dc group, ch 1, skip first 2 sts of last 7-dc group, dc in next 3 sts of same group, ch 1, skip last 2 sts of same group, dc in last st, turn.

Row 51: Ch 3, dc in center st of first 3 dc group, ch 1, (7 dc in ch sp of next V st, ch 1, dc in center st of next 3-dc group) across to last V st, ch 1, 4 dc in ch sp of last V st, turn.

Row 52: Ch 3, dc in next st of first 4-dc group, ch 1, skip next 2 sts of same group, V st, (ch 1, skip first 2 sts of next 7-dc group, dc in next 3 sts of same group, ch 1, skip last 2 sts of same group, V st) across to last 7-dc group, skip first 2 sts of last 7-dc group, dc in next 3 sts, skip last 2 sts of same group, skip next dc of last 2-dc group, dc in last st, turn.

Row 53: Ch 3, dc in center st of first 3-dc group, ch 1, 7 dc in ch sp of next V st, (ch 1, dc in center st of next 3-dc group, 7 dc in ch sp of next V st) across to last 2 sts, ch 1, skip next st, dc in last st, turn.

Rows 54-57: Repeat rows 50-53.

Rows 58-70: Repeat rows 2-5 of Back consecutively, ending with row 2. At end of last row, fasten off.

Sleeve (make 2)

Row 1: Starting at wrist, ch 52, 7 dc in eighth ch from hook *(counts as dc and ch-1),* (ch 1, skip next 3 chs, dc in next ch, ch 1, skip next 3 chs, 7 dc in next ch) 5 times, ch 1, skip next 3 chs, dc in last ch, turn. *(Six 6-dc groups, 7 dc made) Front of row 1 is right side of work.*

Row 2: Skip ch-1 sps throughout, beg V st, (ch 1, skip first 2 sts of next 7-dc group, dc in next 3 sts of same group, ch 1, skip last 2 sts of same group, V st) across, turn.

Row 3: Ch 3, 4 dc in ch sp of first V st, ch 1, dc in center st of next 3-dc group, (ch 1, 7 dc in ch sp of next V st, ch 1, dc in center st of next 3-dc group) across to last V st, ch 1, 5 dc in ch sp of last V st.

Row 4: Ch 3, dc in next 2 sts of first 5-dc group, ch 1, skip next 3 sts of same group, (ch 1, skip first 2 sts of next 7-dc group, dc in next 3 sts of same group, ch 1, skip last 2 sts of same group, V st) across to last 5-dc group, ch 1, skip first 3 sts of last 5-dc group, dc in last 3 sts, turn.

Row 5: Ch 4, dc in next dc, ch 1, 7 dc in ch sp of next V st, (ch 1, dc in center st of next 3-dc group, ch 1, 7 dc in ch sp of next V st) across to last 3-dc group, ch 1, skip next st of last 3-dc group, dc in next st, ch 1, dc in last st, turn.

Row 6: Ch 4, V st, (ch 1, skip first 2 sts of next 7-dc group, dc in next 3 sts of same group, ch 1, skip last 2 sts of same group, V st) across to last st, ch 1, dc in last st, turn.

Row 7: Ch 4, 7 dc in ch sp of first V st, (ch 1, dc in center st of next 3-dc group, ch 1, 7 dc in ch sp of next V st) across to last st, ch 1, dc in last st, turn.

Next Rows: Repeat rows 2-7 consecutively, ending with row 2 or to desired length needed. At end of last row, fasten off.

Sleeve Edging

Row 1: With wrong side of one Sleeve facing you, working on opposite side of starting ch on row 1, skip first ch and ch sp, join with sc in ch where first 7-dc group was made, 2 sc in same ch as last sc, (3 sc in each of next 2 ch sps, 3 sc in next ch where 7-dc group was made) 5 times leaving last ch sp and last ch unworked, turn. *(63 sc made)*

Row 2: Working in **back lps** *(see Stitch Guide),* ch 1, sl st in each st across, turn.

Row 3: Working in **back lps,** ch 1, sl st in first st, ch 3, (sl st in next 4 sts, ch 3) around to last 2 sts, sl st in last 2 sts. Fasten off.

Repeat on other Sleeve.

Finishing

For shoulder seams, match and sew sts on last row of Left and Right Front to last row on Back.

Match and sew ends of rows 10-46 on each side edge of each Front to each side edge of Back leaving rows 47-70 unsewn for armhole. Fold one Sleeve in half, center fold at shoulder seam, sew last row on Sleeve to ends of rows at armhole. Sew ends of rows on Sleeve and

Edging together. Repeat with other Sleeve.

Edging
Rnd 1: WIth wrong sides of Jacket facing you, working on opposite side of starting ch and in end of rows and in sts, join with sc in ch where first 7-dc group was made on Right Front, 2 sc in same ch as last sc, (4 sc in each of next 2 ch sps, 3 sc in next ch where 7-dc group was made) 6 times, 8 sc in first corner, 3 sc in each end of next 8 rows, working on Back, 3 sc in each end of next 8 rows, 8 sc in next corner, 3 sc in ch where next 7-dc group was made, (4 sc in each of next 2 ch sps, 3 sc in next ch where 7-dc group was made) 13 times, 8 sc in next corner, 3 sc in each end of next 8 rows working on Left Front, 3 sc in each end of next 8 rows, 8 sc in next corner, 3 sc where next 7-dc group was made, (4 sc in each of next 2 ch sps, 3 sc in ch where next 7-dc group was made) 6 times, 8 sc in next corner, 3 sc in each end of next 69 rows, working across sts and in ch sps, evenly space 30 sc across neck edge on Back, working on Right Front, 3 sc in each end of next 69 rows, 8 sc in last corner, join with sl st in first sc, **turn.** *(872 sc made)*

Rnd 2: Working in **back lps,** ch 1, sl st in each st around, join with sl st in first sl st, **turn.**

Rnd 3: Working in **back lps,** ch 1, sl st in first 2 sts, (ch 3, sl st in next 4 sts) 23 times, ch 3, sl st in next 14 sts, (ch 3, sl st in next 4 sts) 49 times, ch 3, sl st in next 14 sts, (ch 3, sl st in next 4 sts) 138 times, ch 3, sl st in last 2 sts, join. Fasten off. &

Collared Vest

Continued from page 125

marker, sc in each st across to next marker with 5 sc in each ch sp leaving remaining sts unworked, remove marker, turn.

Rows 2–5: Ch 1, sc in each st across, turn. At end of last row, **do not turn.** Fasten off.

Bottom Trim & Placket

Row 1: Join with sc in next unworked st at bottom of Trim, sc in each st across bottom edge to next marked st; for **Left Placket,** sc in marked st, remove marker, sc in next 19 sts, 5 sc in next ch sp, sc in next 33 sts, 5 sc in next ch sp, sc in next 17 sts, 5 sc in next ch sp leaving remaining sts and ch sps unworked on Trim at back, turn.

Row 2: Ch 1, 2 sc in first st, sc in next 84 sts leaving remaining sts unworked, turn. *(86 sc)*

Row 3: Ch 1, sc in first 2 sts; (for **buttonhole,** ch 4, skip next 4 sts; sc in next 5 sts; for **buttonhole,** ch 4, skip next 4 sts; sc in next 10 sts) 3 times; for **buttonhole,** ch 4, skip next 4 sts; sc in next 5 sts; for **buttonhole,** ch 4, skip next 4 sts; sc in last 2 sts, turn. *(54 sc, 32 chs)*

Row 4: Ch 1, sc in each st and in each ch across, turn. *(86 sc)*

Rows 5–6: Ch 1, sc in each st across, turn. At end of last row, fasten off.

Sew buttons to Right Placket opposite buttonholes.

Collar (make 2)

Row 1: Ch 29, working in **back bar of ch** *(see Stitch Guide),* sl st in second ch from hook, sl st in each ch across, turn. *(28 sl sts made)*

Rows 2–200: Working in **back lps,** ch 1, sl st in each st across, turn.

Row 201: Ch 1, sl st in each st across leaving last st unworked, turn. *(27 sl sts)*

Row 202: Ch 1, sl st in each st across, turn.

Rows 203–246: Repeat rows 201 and 202 alternately. At end of last row, fasten off.

Center short straight edges at center back of Vest, easing to fit, sl st long straight edges of Collars across back and neckline *(see photo).* ❧

Scarf, Hat & Gloves

Designed by Sandra Jean Smith of SJS Designs

Finished Sizes: Hat and Scarf; one size fits all. Gloves, 6½" circumference palm, 7" circumference palm and 8" circumference palm.

Materials:
- ❑ 10 oz. pompadour baby yarn
- ❑ 2" square cardboard
- ❑ Tapestry needle
- ❑ Hook stated for size or hook size needed to obtain gauge

Gauges: We are not responsible for lack of materials due to project not being worked to gauge. Gauge for this pattern: **For Hat and Scarf,** with G hook, 9 sts = 2"; 7 dcv rows = 2½". F hook, 5 sc = 1"; 5 ribbing rows = 1".
For **Gloves, 6½" circumference palm,** F hook, 5 sts = 1"; 3 dcv rows = 1". E hook, 11 sc = 2"; 11 sc rows = 2". D hook, 6 sc = 1"; 6 ribbing rows = 1". For **7" circumference palm,** G hook, 9 sts = 2"; 14 dcv rows = 5". F hook, 5 sc = 1"; 5 sc rows = 1". E hook, 11 sc = 2"; 11 ribbing row = 2". For **8" circumference palm,** H hook, 4 sts = 1"; 8 dcv rows = 3". G hook, 9 sc = 2"; 9 sc rows = 2". F hook, 5 sc = 1"; 5 ribbing rows = 1".

Basic Stitches: Ch, sl st, sc, dc.

Special Stitch: For **dc variation** *(dcv, see illustration),* insert hook under 3 bars at top of next dc, complete same as dc.

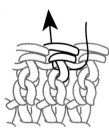

Scarf

Row 1: With larger hook, ch 47, dc in fourth ch from hook, dc in each ch across, turn. *(45 dc made)*

Row 2: Ch 3, **dcv** *(see Special Stitch),* (dcv in next st, ch 1, skip next st) 20 times, dcv in each of next 2 sts, dc in last st, turn. *(25 dc)*

Row 3: Ch 3, dcv in next 2 sts, *ch 1, skip next ch, (dcv in next st, dc in next ch sp) 2 times, dcv in next st, ch 1, skip next ch, dcv in next st; repeat from * 4 more times, dcv in next st, dc in last st, turn. *(35 dc)*

Rows 4-5: Ch 3, dcv in next 2 sts, (ch 1, skip next ch, dcv in next 5 sts, ch 1, skip next ch, dcv in next st) 5 times, dcv in next st, dc in last st, turn.

Row 6: Ch 3, dcv in next 2 sts, ch 1, skip next ch, *(dcv in next st, ch 1, skip next st) 2 times, (dcv in next st, dc in next ch sp) 2 times; repeat from * 3 more times; repeat between first ( ) 2 times, dcv in next st, ch 1, skip next ch, dcv in next 2 sts, dc in last st, turn. *(33 dc)*

Rows 7-8: Ch 3, dcv in next 2 sts, (ch 1, skip next ch, dcv in next st) 3 times, dcv in next 4 sts; * repeat between ( ) 2 times; dcv in next 4 sts; repeat from * 2 more times; repeat between ( ) 3 times, dcv in next st, dc in last st, turn.

Row 9: Ch 3, dcv in next 2 sts, ch 1, skip next ch, dcv in next st, (dc in next ch sp, dcv in next st) 2 times, *[ch 1, skip next st, dcv in next st] 2 times, (dc in next ch sp, dcv in next st) 2 times; repeat from * 3 more times, ch 1, skip next ch, dcv in next 2 sts, dc in last st, turn. *(35 dc)*

Rows 10-143: Repeat rows 4-9 consecutively, ending with row 5.

Row 144: Ch 3, dcv in next 2 sts, ch 1, (skip next st or next ch, dcv in next st) 20 times, dcv in next st, dc in last st, turn. *(25 dc)*

Row 145: Ch 3, dcv in next 2 sts, (dc in next ch sp, dcv in next st) 20 times, dcv in next st, dc in last st. Fasten off. *(45)*

For each **fringe,** cut four strands each 12" long. With all four strands held together, fold in half, insert hook in st, pull fold through st; pull ends through fold, tighten. Work fringe in every other st on first and last rows.

Hat

Row 1: With smaller hook, for **ribbing,** ch 25, sc in second ch from hook, sc in each ch across, turn. *(24 sc made)*

Rows 2-88: Working these rows in **back lps** *(see Stitch Guide),* ch 1, sc in each st across, turn.

Row 89: Matching sts on row 1 and row 88 tog, working through both thicknesses, sl st in each st across.

Rnd 90: Fold band in half with first and last st of each ribbing row tog; working in rnds through both thicknesses in ends of ribbing row, ch 1, sc in each row around, join with sl st in first sc. *(88)*

Rnd 91: With larger hook, ch 3, *dc in next 4 sts, (ch 1, skip next st, dc in next st) 2 times; repeat

Continued on page 134

Scarf, Hat & Gloves

Continued from page 133

from * 9 more times, dc in next 4 sts; repeat between ( ), ch 1, skip next st, join with sl st in top of ch-3. *(66 dc)*

Rnd 92: Ch 3, *dcv in next 4 sts, (ch 1, skip next ch, dcv in next st) 2 times; repeat from *9 more times, dcv in next 4 sts; repeat between ( ), ch 1, skip next st, join.

Rnd 93: Ch 4, skip next st, dcv in next st, ch 1, skip next st, (dcv in next st, dc in next ch sp) 2 times, *(dcv in next st, ch 1, skip next st) 2 times, (dcv in next st, dc in next ch sp) 2 times; repeat from * around, join with sl st in third ch of ch-4.

Rnd 94: Ch 4, skip next ch, dcv in next st, ch 1, skip next ch, dcv in next 4 sts, *(dcv in next st, ch 1, skip next ch) 2 times, dcv in next 4 sts; repeat from * around, join.

Rnd 95: Ch 3, *(dc in next ch sp, dcv in next st) 2 times, (ch 1, skip next st, dcv in next st) 2 times; repeat from * 9 more times, (dc in next ch sp, dcv in next st) 2 times, ch 1, skip next st, dcv in next st, ch 1, skip next st, join.

Rnds 96-98: Repeat rnds 92-94.

Rnd 99: Ch 3, dc in each ch sp and dcv in each st around, join. *(88)*

Note: *Beginning ch-2 is used as a decrease, do not count as a st.*

Rnd 100: Ch 2, (dcv in next 7 sts, dcv next 2 sts tog) 9 times, dcv in last 6 sts, skip ch-2, join with sl st in top of first dcv. *(78)*

Rnd 101: Ch 2, (dcv in next 6 sts, dcv next 2 sts tog) 9 times, dcv in last 5 sts, join. *(68)*

Rnd 102: Ch 2, (dcv in next 5 sts, dcv next 2 sts tog) 9 times, dcv in last 4 sts, join. *(58)*

Rnd 103: Ch 2, (dcv in next 4 sts, dcv next 2 sts tog) 9 times, dcv in last 3 sts, join. *(48)*

Rnd 104: Ch 2, dcv in next st, (dcv next 2 sts tog) around, join. Leaving 12" for weaving, fasten off. Weave end through sts of rnd 104, pull tight. Fasten off.

For **pom-pom,** wrap yarn around 2" cardboard 100 times. Slide loops off cardboard, tie separate strand yarn tightly around center of all loops. Cut loops, trim to 1½". Sew to top of Hat.

Gloves
Left hand

Row 1: For **cuff,** with smaller hook, ch 8, sc in second ch from hook, sc in each ch across, turn. *(7 sc made)*

Rows 2-32: Working these rows in **back lps,** ch 1, sc in each st across, turn.

Row 33: Match sts of row 1 and row 32 tog; working through both thicknesses, sl st in each st across.

Row 34: Working in ends of ribbing rows, ch 1, sc in each row around, join with sl st in first sc. *(32)*

Row 35: With larger hook, ch 3, *dc in next 4 sts, (ch 1, skip next st, dc in next st) 2 times; repeat from * 2 more times, dc in next 4 sts; repeat between ( ), ch 1, skip next st, join with sl st in top of ch-3. *(24 dc)*

Row 36: Ch 3, *dcv in next 4 sts, (ch 1, skip next ch, dcv in next st) 2 times; repeat from * 2 more times, dcv in next 4 sts; repeat between ( ), ch 1, skip next ch, join.

Row 37: Ch 3, *(ch 1, skip next st, dcv in next st) 2 times, (dc in next ch sp, dcv in next st) 2 times; repeat from * 2 more times; repeat between first ( ) 2 times, dc in next ch sp, dcv in next st, dc in last ch sp, join with sl st in third ch of ch-4.

Rnd 38: Ch 3, *(ch 1, skip next ch, dcv in next st) 2 times, dcv in next 4 sts; repeat from * 2 more times; repeat between ( ) 2 times, dcv in each of last 3 sts, join.

Rnd 39: Ch 3, dc in each ch sp and dcv in each st around to last 12 sts and ch, (dcv in next st, ch 1, skip next st) 2 times, (dcv in next st, dc in next ch sp) 2 times; repeat between first ( ) 2 times, join. *(28)*

Rnd 40: Ch 3, dcv in each st around to last 12 sts and chs, (dcv in next st, ch 1, skip next ch) 2 times, dcv in next 4 sts; repeat between ( ) 2 times, join.

Rnd 41: Ch 3, dcv in next 15 sts, *(dcv in next st, ch 1, skip next st) 2 times, (dcv in next st, dc in next ch sp) 2 times; repeat from * one time, join.

Rnd 42: Ch 3, dcv in next 15 sts, *(dcv in next st, ch 1, skip next ch) 2 times, dcv in next 4 sts; repeat from * one time, join.

Rnds 43-44: Repeat rnds 39-40.

Rnd 45: Ch 3, dcv in next 10 sts; for **thumb opening,** ch 4, skip next 9 sts; (dcv in next st, dc in next ch sp) 2 times, (dcv in next st, ch 1, skip next st) 2 times; repeat between first ( ) 2 times, join. *(21)*

Rnd 46: Ch 3, dcv in next 10 sts, dc in next 4 ch, dcv in next 5 sts, (ch 1, skip next ch, dcv in next st) 2 times; dcv in last 3 sts, join. *(25)*

Rnds 47-48: Repeat rnds 39-40.

Rnd 49: With middle size hook; for **little finger,** ch 1, sc in first st, sc in next 2 sts, ch 2, skip next 20 sts and ch sps, sc in last 4 sts and ch sps, join with sl st in first sc. *(7 sc, 2 chs)*

Rnd 50: Ch 1, sc in each st and ch around, join. *(9)*

Rnds 51-61: Or to desired length; ch 1, sc in each st around, join. At end of last rnd, leaving 6" for weaving, fasten off. Weave end through sts on last rnd, pull tight. Fasten off.

Rnd 49: For **ring finger,** join with sc in next unworked st on rnd 48, sc in next 2 sts, ch 2, skip next 14 sts and ch sps, sc in last 3 unworked sts, sc next worked st and side of sc worked in that st tog; working on opposite side of ch on last finger, sc in each ch across, sc in side of next sc on rnd 49 of last finger and st on rnd 48 below that st tog join. *(10 sc, 2 chs)*

Rnd 50: Ch 1, sc in each st and in each ch around, join. *(12)*

Rnds 51-63: Or to desired length; ch 1, sc in each st around, join. At end of last rnd, complete same as little finger.

Rnd 49: For **middle finger,** join with sc in next unworked st on rnd 48, sc in next 2 sts, ch 2, skip next 8 sts and ch sps, sc in last 3 unworked sts and ch sps, sc next worked st and side of sc worked in that st tog, working on opposite side of ch on last finger, sc in each ch across, sc side of next sc on rnd 49 of last finger and st on rnd 48 below that st tog, join. *(10 sc, 2 chs)*

Rnd 50: Ch 1, sc in each st and in each ch around, join.

Rnds 51-64: Or to desired length; ch 1, sc in each st around, join. At end of last rnd, complete same as little finger.

Rnd 49: For **index finger,** join with sc in next unworked st on rnd 48, sc in next 7 sts and ch sps, sc next worked st and side of sc worked in that st tog; working on opposite side of ch on last finger, sc in each ch across, sc side of next sc on rnd 49 off last finger and st on rnd 48 below that st tog, join. *(12)*

Rnds 50-63: Or to desired length; repeat rnds 50-63 of ring finger. At end of last rnd, complete same as little finger.

Rnd 45: For **thumb,** working in sts, ch and ends of rows around thumb opening, join with sc in first unworked st on rnd 44, sc in next 8 sts, sc in next row; working on opposite side of ch, sc in next 3 chs, sc last ch and next row tog, join. *(14)*

Rnds 46-47: Ch 1, sc in each st around, join.

Rnd 48: Ch 1, sc in first 11 sts, sc next 2 sts tog, sc in last st, join. *(13)*

Rnds 49-56: Or to desired length; ch 1, sc in each st around, join. Complete same as little finger.

Right Hand

Rnds 1-38: Repeat rnds 1-38 on Left Hand.

Rnd 39: Ch 3, *(dc in next ch sp, dcv in next st) 2 times, (ch 1, skip next st, dcv in next st) 2 times; repeat from * one time, dc in each ch sp and dcv in each st around, join with sl st in top of ch-3. *(28 dc)*

Rnd 40: Ch 3, *dcv in next 4 sts, (ch 1, skip next ch, dcv in next st) 2 times; repeat from * one time, dcv in each st around, join.

Rnd 41: Ch 3, *(ch 1, skip next st , dcv in next st) 2 times, (dc in next ch sp, dcv in next st) 2 times; repeat from * one time, dcv in each st around, join.

Rnd 42: Ch 3, *(ch 1, skip next ch, dcv in next st) 2 times, dcv in next 4 sts; repeat from * one time, dcv in each st around, join.

Rnd 43: Ch 3, *(dc in next ch sp, dcv in next st) 2 times, (ch 1, skip next st, dcv in next st) 2 times; repeat from * one time, dcv in each st around, join.

Rnd 44: Repeat rnd 40.

Rnd 45: Ch 3, (ch 1, skip next st, dcv in next st) 2 times, (dc in next ch sp, dcv in next st) 2 times; repeat between first ( ) 2 times, ch 4, skip next 9 sts and chs, dcv in last 10 sts, join. *(19 dc)*

Rnd 46: Ch 3, (ch 1, skip next ch, dcv in next st) 2 times, dcv in next 4 sts; repeat between ( ) 2 times, dc in next 4 chs, dcv in last 10 sts, join. *(23 dc)*

Rnd 47: Ch 3, (dc in next ch sp, dcv in next st) 2 times, (ch 1, skip next st, dcv in next st) 2 times; repeat between first ( ) 2 times, dcv in each st around, join. *(25 dc)*

Rnd 48: Ch 3, dcv in next 4 sts, (ch 1, skip next ch, dcv in next st) 2 times, dcv in each st around, join.

Rnd 49: With middle size hook; for **little finger,** ch 1, sc in first st, sc in next 2 sts, ch 2, skip next 20 sts and ch sps, sc in last 4 sts, join with sl st in first sc. *(7 sc, 2 chs)*

Rnds 50-61: Repeat rnds 50-61 of left little finger.

Rnd 49: For ring finger, join with sc in next unworked st on rnd 48, sc in next st, sc in next ch sp, ch 2, skip next 14 sts and ch sps, sc in each of last 3 unworked sts, sc next worked st and side of sc worked in that st tog; working on opposite side of ch on last finger, sc in each ch across, sc side of next sc on rnd 49 of last finger and ch sp on rnd 48 below that st tog, join. *(10 sc, 2 chs)*

Rnds 50-63: Repeat rnds 50-63 of left ring finger.

Rnd 49: For middle finger, join with sc in next unworked st on rnd 48, sc in next ch sp, sc in next st, ch 2, skip next 8 sts, sc in last 3 unworked sts, sc next worked st and side of sc

Continued on page 137

Crochet Fedora

Designed by Donna Jones

Finished Sizes: Small/Medium fits 19"-21" head. **Large** fits 21"-23" head.

Materials:
- ❑ 6 oz. black rug yarn
- ❑ 1 yd. of 1 1/2" wide grosgrain ribbon
- ❑ Floral wire
- ❑ H hook for Small/Medium or hook size needed to obtain gauge
- ❑ I hook for Large or hook size needed to obtain gauge

Gauges: We are not responsible for lack of materials due to project not being worked to gauge. Gauge for this pattern: **H hook,** 7 sc = 2"; 7 sc rows = 2". **I hook,** 13 sc = 4"; 13 sc rows = 4".

Basic Stitches: Ch, sl st, sc, hdc.

Note: Work in continuous rnds, do not join unless otherwise stated. Mark first st of each rnd.

Crown

Rnd 1: Ch 2, 8 sc in second ch from hook. *(8 sc made)*

Rnd 2: 2 sc in each st around. *(16)*

Rnd 3: (2 sc in next st, sc in next st) around. *(24)*

Rnd 4: (2 sc in next st, sc in next 2 sts) around. *(32)*

Rnd 5: (Sc in next 3 sts, 2 sc in next st) around. *(40)*

Rnd 6: Sc in next 2 sts, 2 sc in next st, (sc in next 4 sts, 2 sc in next st) 7 times, sc in each st around. *(48)*

Rnd 7: Sc in next st, 2 sc in next st, (sc in next 5 sts, 2 sc in next st) 7 times, sc in last 4 sts. *(56)*

Rnd 8: Sc in each st around.

Rnd 9: Sc in next 4 sts, 2 sc in next st, (sc in next 6 sts, 2 sc in next st) 7 times, sc in last 2 sts. *(64)*

Rnd 10: Sc in each st around.

Rnd 11: (2 sc in next st, sc in next 7 sts) around. *(72)*

Rnds 12-23: Sc in each st around. At end of last rnd, join with sl st in first sc. **Do not fasten off.**

Brim

Rnd 1: Working in sts of rnd 23 on Crown, ch 2, **hdc front post** *(see Stitch Guide)* around each st around, join with sl st in top of ch-2. *(72 hdc front posts made)*

Rnd 2: (Sc in next 8 sts, 2 sc in next st) around, **do not join.** *(80 sc)*

Rnd 3: Sc in next 4 sts, 2 sc in next st, (sc in next 9 sts, 2 sc in next st) 7 times, sc in last 5 sts. *(88)*

Rnd 4: (2 sc in next st, sc in next 10 sts) around. *(96)*

Rnd 5: Sc in each st around.

Rnd 6: Sc in next 6 sts, 2 sc in next st, (sc in next 11 sts, 2 sc in next st) 7 times, sc in last 5 sts. *(104)*

Rnd 7: Sc in each st around.

Rnd 8: Sc in next 10 sts, 2 sc in next st, (sc in next 12 sts, 2 sc in next st) 7 times, sc in last 2 sts. *(112)*

Rnd 9: Sc in each st around.

Rnd 10: (2 sc in next st, sc in next 13 sts) around. *(120)*

Rnd 11: Sc in each st around.

Rnd 12: Working around wire, **reverse sc** *(see Stitch Guide)* in each st around, join with sl st in first sc. Fasten off.

Finishing

For **crease in Crown,** tack top of first and fourth sts on rnd 1 together.

For **hatband,** cut ribbon ½" larger than base of Crown. Easing to fit, tack edge to rnd 23 on Crown.

For **bow,** cut 9½" ribbon. Trim ends for inverted "V". Fold as shown in illustration. Sew center to folds. Cut 3½" ribbon, place around center of bow *(see illustration)*, sew in place on back side. Sew to hatband, covering ends. ❧

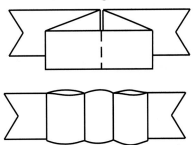

Scarf, Hat & Gloves

Continued from page 135

worked in that st tog; working on opposite side of ch on last finger, sc in each ch across, sc side of next sc on rnd 49 of last finger and ch sp on rnd 48 below that st tog, join. *(10 sc, 2 chs)*

Rnd 50-64: Repeat rnds 50-64 of left middle finger.

Rnd 49: For **index finger,** join with sc in next unworked st on rnd 48, sc in next 7 sts, sc next worked st and side of sc worked in that st tog; working on opposite side of ch on last finger, sc in each ch across, sc side of next sc on rnd 49 of last

finger and st on rnd 48 below that st tog, join. *(12)*

Rnds 50-63: Repeat rnds 50-63 of left index finger.

Rnd 45: For **thumb,** working in sts, ch sps, chs and ends of rows around thumb opening, join with sc in first unworked ch sp on rnd 44, sc in next 8 sts and ch sps, sc next row and first ch of ch-4 tog; working on opposite side of ch, sc in next 3 chs, sc in next row, join. *(14)*

Rnds 46-56: Repeat rnds 46-56 of left thumb. ❧

Drape Jacket

Designed by Carol Smith

Finished Sizes: Lady's 36", 40", 44" and 48".

Materials:
- ❏ Amount main color (MC) worsted needed for size:
  - 25 oz. for 36"
  - 26 oz. for 40"
  - 28 oz. for 44"
  - 30 oz. for 48"
- ❏ 4 oz. contrasting color (CC) worsted yarn for all sizes
- ❏ K hook or hook size size needed to obtain gauge

Gauge: We are not responsible for lack of materials due to project not being worked to gauge. Gauge for this pattern: 8 chs = 3". 8 hdc rows = 3".

Basic Stitches: Ch, sl st, sc, hdc.

Notes: Instructions are for size 36". Changes for sizes 40", 44", and 48" are in [ ].
Work in sps between sts unless otherwise stated.

Right Side

Row 1: Beginning at bottom sleeve with MC, ch 61 [61, 67, 73] to gauge, hdc in third ch from hook, hdc in each ch across, turn. *(60) [60, 66, 72] hdc made*

Rows 2-15: Ch 2, hdc in first sp, hdc in each sp across, turn. At end of last row, fasten off.
Note: To prevent puckering of motif panel, check ch gauge often.

Row 16: With row 16 as right side of work, join CC with sc in first st, sc in next 3 sps; for **first motif**, ch 7, sl st in fifth ch from hook to form ring, sl st in next 2 chs, sl st through center of last sc made, **do not turn,** bring yarn behind work to right of ch, with ring facing you, *for **long hdc, yo, insert hook in ring, yo, pull up 1" lp, complete as hdc;** repeat from * 14 more times, sl st through center of last sl st and last sc, sc in next 6 sps on row 15; for **motif, ch 7, sl st in fifth ch from hook to form ring, sl st in next 2 chs, sl st through center of last sc made, do not turn, bring yarn behind work to right, with ring facing you, 3 long hdc in ring, drop lp from hook, long hdc in ring, drop lp from hook, insert hook in 13th long hdc on**

last motif, pull lp through st, 12 long hdc in ring, sl st through center of last sl st and last sc; (sc in next 6 sps, motif) 8 [8, 9, 10] times, sc in each of last 2 sps, turn. Fasten off. *(10 motifs) [10 motifs, 11 motifs, 12 motifs]*

Row 17: With CC, ch 3, sc in eighth long hdc of first motif, (ch 5, sc in eighth long hdc of next motif) 9 [9, 10, 11] times, ch 3, turn. *(61 sts and chs) [61, 67, 73 sts and chs]*

Row 18: Sc in second ch from hook, sc in each st and ch across, **do not turn.** Fasten off. *(60) [60, 66, 72]*

Row 19: Join MC with sl st in first st, ch 2, hdc in each sp across, turn.

Rows 20-29 [20-29, 20-31, 20-31]: Ch 2, hdc in first sp, hdc in each sp across, turn. At end of last row, fasten off.

Row 30 [30, 32, 32]: Being careful to maintain gauge, with MC, ch 42 [42, 45, 42], hdc in first st on last row, hdc in first sp, hdc in each sp across, ch 43 [43, 46, 43], turn. *(145 sts and chs) [145 sts and chs, 157 sts and chs, 157 sts and chs]*

Row 31 [31, 33, 33]: Hdc in third ch from hook, hdc in each ch across to first hdc, hdc in first hdc, hdc in first sp, hdc in each sp across to next ch, hdc in each ch across, turn. *(144) [144, 156, 156]*

Rows 32-38 [32-40, 34-44, 34-46]: Ch 2, hdc in first sp, hdc in each sp across, turn. At end of last row, fasten off.

Row 39 [41, 45, 47]: For **end of row bar,** join CC with sl st in first st, ch 8, sc in second ch from hook, sc in each ch across to last ch, sc last ch and first sp on last row tog, sc in next 2 sps; for **first motif,** ch 6, sl st in fifth ch from hook to form ring, sl st in next ch, sl st through center of last sc made, bring yarn behind work to right, with ring facing you, 3 long hdc in ring, drop lp from hook, insert hook in fourth sc on bar, pull lp through st, 12 long hdc in ring, sl st through center of last sl st and last sc, (sc in next 6 sps, motif) across to last 2 sps, sc in last 2 sps, sc in top of ch-2, **do not turn.** Fasten off. *(24 motifs) [24 motifs, 26 motifs, 26 motifs]*

Row 40: [42, 46, 48]: For **end of row bar,** with CC, ch 7, drop lp from hook, with right side of last row facing you, insert hook in last sc on last row,

Continued on page 158

Reversible Cape

Designed by Richard Dowler

Finished Size: Adult's.

Materials:
- ❏ 15 oz. each of main color solid (MC) and contrasting color variegated (CC) worsted yarn
- ❏ G hook or hook size needed to obtain gauge

Gauge: We are not responsible for lack of materials due to project not being worked to gauge. Gauge for this pattern: 6 sts = 2" 6 rows = 2".

Basic Stitches: Ch, sl st, sc, hdc.

Cape

Note: Leave 15" strand for fringe at beginning and end of each row unless other wise stated.

Row 1: With MC, ch 161. Fasten off. Join MC with sc in first ch, hdc in same ch, *skip next ch, (sc, hdc) in next ch; repeat from * across to last 2 chs, skip next ch, sc in last ch, turn. Fasten off. *(81 sc made)*

Row 2: Join CC with sc in first sc, hdc in same st, (sc, hdc) in each sc across to last sc, sc in last sc, turn. Fasten off.

Row 3: Join MC with sc in first sc, hdc in same st, (sc, hdc) in each sc across to last sc, sc in last sc, turn. Fasten off.

Rows 4-55: Repeat rows 2 and 3 alternately.

Row 56: For **front opening**, join CC with sc in first sc, hdc in same st, (sc, hdc) in each of next 39 sc, sc in next sc leaving last 40 sc unworked, turn. Fasten off.

Row 57: With MC, ch 80, sl st in last st of last row. **Do not leave strand for fringe,** fasten off. Join MC with sc in first ch of ch-80, hdc in same ch, skip next ch, *(sc, hdc) in next ch, skip next ch;

repeat from * across ch (sc, hdc) in same sc as sl st, (sc, hdc) in each sc across to last sc, sc, in last sc, turn. *(81)*

Rows 58-111: Repeat rows 2 and 3 alternately.

Fringe

Working across one end of Cape, with two 15" strands held together, tie overhand knot *(see illustration),* tie next two strands together, across. Repeat across other end.

For extra **fringe,** cut 30" strand CC, fold in half, insert in hook in end of row between two overhand knots, pull fold through, pull ends through fold, tighten.

Repeat across each end of Cape. ❧

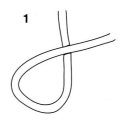

Shepherd's Coat

Designed by Arlyth Atkinson

Finished Size: Lady's; fits 32"-48" bust, or make to fit. Finished measurement: 60".

Materials:
- ❏ 40 ozs. of any combination of types and colors with a minimum of 12 yds. of each color
- ❏ ¼" metal bangles
- ❏ Decorative clasp
- ❏ Tapestry needle
- ❏ Q hook or hook size needed to obtain gauge

Gauge: We are not responsible for lack of materials due to project not being worked to gauge. Gauge for this pattern: 3 sc = 2"; 8 **back lp** rows = 5".

Basic Stitches: Ch, sc.

Notes: Hold as many strands of any yarn combination tog as needed to obtain gauge.

Change yarn types at end of row only; check gauge with every yarn change.

For **color change,** fasten off at end of row, join with sc in **back lp** *(see Stitch Guide)* of first st on next row.

Body Side (make 2)

Row 1: Ch 82 to measure 56", or to desired length from bottom edge on back to bottom edge on front, sc in second ch from hook, sc in each ch across, turn. *(81 sc made)*

Rows 2-24: Or to ¼ of desired finished measurement; working these rows in **back lps,** changing color at random as desired, ch 1, sc in each st across, turn. At end of last row, fasten off.

For **front and back seams,** holding pieces right sides together, sew 32 chs on one end of starting ch together for back; leaving center 21 chs unsewn for neck opening, sew last 28 chs together for front.

For **side seam,** fold in half with ends of rows touching, sew 22 sts on each end of last row together leaving center 37 sts unsewn for armhole. Repeat on other side.

Collar

*Note: Work entire Collar in **back lps.***

Row 1: Beginning at center back, ch 18, sc in second from hook, sc in each ch across, turn. *(17 sc made)*

Row 2: Ch 1, skip first st, sc in each st across, turn. *(16)*

Row 3: Ch 1, sc in each st across, turn.

Rows 4-15: Repeat rows 2 and 3 alternately. At end of last row *(10)*.

Rows 16-22: Ch 1, sc in each st across, turn.

Row 23: Ch 1, sc in each st across with 2 sc in last st, turn. *(11)*

Rows 24-36: Repeat rows 3 and 23 alternately, ending with row 3 and 17 sts. At end of last row, leaving long strands for sewing, fasten off.

Overlap edges of first and last rows to form rib, sew together. Matching seam to center back seam on body, with center front seam on body between rows 18 and 19, sew Collar to neck opening.

Finishing

For **bottom tie,** with several strands held together to make ¾" wide ch, leaving 6" end, ch tightly to measure 2 yds. Leaving 6" end, fasten off. Weave through ends of rows on bottom of body, tie in bow.

For **necklace,** work same as bottom tie to measure 36". Tie bangles to ends of strands of yarn as desired. With separate strand, tie ends of necklace tog; attach claps over knot. ꧂

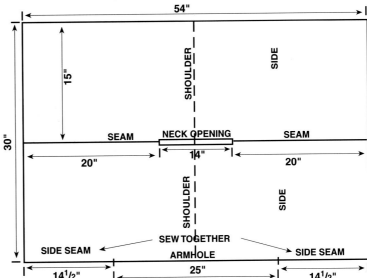

Herringbone Jacket

Designed by Ann Parnell

Finished Sizes: Girls's/lady's bust 30"-32", 34"-36", 38"-40", 42"-44", 46"-48" and 50"-52".

Materials:
- ❏ Amount of fingering yarn needed for size:
    8 oz. black, 7 oz. off-white for 30"-32"
    9 oz. black, 8 oz. off-white for 34"-36"
    10 oz. black, 9 oz. off-white for 38"-40"
    11 oz. black, 10 oz. off-white for 42"-44"
    11 oz. black, 10 oz. off-white for 46"-48"
    12 oz. black, 11 oz. off-white for 50"-52"
- ❏ 1½" button
- ❏ Shoulder pads
- ❏ Tapestry needle
- ❏ F and H hooks or hook sizes needed to obtain gauges

Gauges: We are not responsible for lack of materials due to project not being worked to gauge. Gauge for this pattern: **F hook,** 21 sc = 4". **H hook,** 19 pattern sts = 4"; 21 pattern rows = 4".

Basic Stitches: Ch, sl st, sc, dc.

Note: Instructions are for lady's bust 30"-32": changes for 34"-36", 38"-40", 42"-44", 46"-48" and 50"-52" are in [ ].

Back
Row 1: With H hook and off-white, ch 84 [92, 100, 108, 120, 128}, sc in second ch from hook, sc in next 2 chs, (dc in next ch, sc in next 3 chs) across, turn. *(83) [91, 99, 107, 119, 127] sts made*
Row 2: Ch 1, sc in each st across changing to black in last st made *(see Stitch Guide)*, turn. Drop off-white.
Note: *Work **dc front post** (fp—see Stitch Guide) around corresponding dc on row before last and skip next st on last row unless otherwise stated.*
Row 3: Ch 1, sc in first st, dc in next st, sc in next st, (fp, sc in next st, dc in next st, sc in next st) across, turn.
Row 4: Ch 1, sc in each st across changing to off-white in last st made, turn. Drop black.
Row 5: Ch 1, sc in first st, fp, sc in next st, (dc in next st, sc in next st, fp, sc in next st) across, turn.
Pattern is established in rows 2-5.

Rows 6-98 [6-102, 6-102, 6-102, 6-102, 6-104]: Work in pattern.
Row 99 [103, 103, 103, 103, 105]: For **armhole shaping,** sl st in first 4 [4, 6, 6, 8, 8] sts, sc in next st, work in pattern across leaving last 4 [4, 6, 6, 8, 8] sts unworked, turn. *(75) [83, 87, 95, 103, 111]*
Notes: *For **dec at beginning of row,** ch 1, skip next st, sc next 2 sts tog.*
*For **dec at end of row,** ch 1, skip next st, sc last 2 sts tog.*
Rows 100-101 [104-106, 104-106, 104-106, 104-107, 106-110]: Dec, work in pattern across to last 3 sts, dec, turn. At end of last row *(67) [71, 75, 83, 87, 91] sts.*
Rows 102-140 [107-144, 107-146, 107-148, 108-150, 111-152]: Work in pattern.
Row 141 [145, 147, 149, 151, 153]: For **first side,** work in pattern across first 22 [24, 24, 28, 30, 32] sts, dec leaving last 42 [44, 48, 52, 54, 56] sts unworked, turn. *(23) [25, 25, 29, 31, 33]*
Next row: Dec, work in pattern across, turn. *(21) [23, 23, 27, 29, 31]*
Last row: Work in pattern across, **do not turn.** Fasten off.
Row 141 [145, 147, 149, 151, 153]: For **neck,** skip next 17 [17, 21, 21, 21, 21] unworked sts on row 140 [144, 146, 148, 150, 152]; for **second side,** join with sl st in next st, dec, work in pattern across, turn. *(23) [25, 25, 29, 31, 33]*
Next row: Work in pattern across to last 3 sts, dec, turn. *(21) [23, 23, 27, 29, 31]*
Last row: Work in pattern across. Fasten off.

Right Front
Row 1: With H hook and off-white, ch 48, [52, 56, 60, 68, 72], sc in second ch from hook, sc in next 2 chs, (dc in next ch, sc in next 3 chs) across, turn. *(47) [51, 55, 59, 67, 71] sts made*
Rows 2-59: Work in pattern.
Row 60: Work in pattern across to last 10 sts; for **buttonhole,** ch 6, skip next 6 sts; work in pattern across, turn.
Row 61: Work in pattern across first 4 sts, sc in next 3 chs, dc in next ch, sc in next 2 chs, sc in next st, work in pattern across, turn.
Rows 62-66 [62-68, 62-66, 62-68, 62, 62]: Work in pattern.

Continued on page 146

*See Fedora pattern
on page 136*

Herringbone Jacket

Continued from page 144

Row 67 [69, 67, 69, 63, 63]: For **overlap edge**, dec, work in pattern across, turn. *(45) [49, 53, 57, 65, 69]*

Rows 68-98 [70-102, 68-102, 70-102, 64-102, 64-104]: Working dec at overlap edge on every eighth row, work in pattern. At end of last row *(39) [41, 45, 49, 57, 59] sts.*

Row 99 [103, 103, 103, 103, 105]: Continuing dec at overlap edge on every eighth row as established, work in pattern across leaving last 4 [4, 6, 6, 8, 8] sts unworked for **armhole**, turn. *(33) [37, 39, 43, 47, 51]*

Rows 100-101 [104-106, 104-106, 104-106, 104-107, 106-110]: Continuing dec at overlpa edge every eighth row as established and working dec at armhole edge on each row, work in pattern. At end of last row *(29) [31, 33, 37, 39, 41].*

Rows 102-131 [107-133, 107-139, 107-141, 108-143, 111-143]: Continuing dec at overlap edge on every eighth row as established, work in pattern. At end of last row *(21) [23, 23, 27, 29, 31].*

Rows 132-143 [134-147, 140-149, 142-151, 144-153, 144-155]: Work in pattern. At end of last row, fasten off.

Pocket Lining

Row 1: With H hook and off-white, ch 16, sc in second ch from hook, sc in next 2 chs, (dc in next ch, sc in next 3 chs) across, turn. *(15 sts made)*

Rows 2-14: Work in pattern. At end of last row, fasten off.

Left Front

Row 1: Repeat row 1 of Right Front.

Rows 2-66 [2-68, 2-66, 2-68, 2-62, 2-62]: Work in pattern.

Row 67 [69, 67, 69, 63, 63]: Work in pattern across to last 3 sts; for **overlap edge**, dec, turn. *(45) [49, 53, 57, 65, 69]*

Rows 68-98 [70-102, 68-102, 70-102, 64-102, 64-104]: Repeat same rows of Right Front.

Row 99 [103, 103, 103, 103, 105]: Continuing dec at overlap edge on every eighth row as established; for **armhole**, sl st in first 4 [4, 6, 6, 8, 8] sts, sc in next st, work in pattern across, turn. *(33) [37, 39, 43, 47, 51]*

Rows 100-101 [104-106, 104-106, 104-106, 104-107, 106-110]: Repeat same rows of Right Front. At end of last row *(29) [31, 33, 37, 39, 41] sts.*

Rows 102-110 [107-114, 107-114, 107-114, 108-118, 111-118]: Continuing dec at overlap edge on every eighth row as established, work in pattern. At end of last row *(27) [29, 31, 35, 37, 39] sts.*

Row 111 [115, 115, 115, 119, 119]: Continuing dec at overlap edge on every eighth row as established, work in pattern across first 8 [6, 8, 8, 12, 14] sts; to join Pocket Lining, with right side of lining and wrong side of Left Front held tog, skipping 15 sts of Left Front, work in pattern across row 14 of Pocket Lining, work in pattern across remaining sts of Left Front, turn. *(27) [29, 29, 35, 35, 37]*

Rows 112-131 [116-133, 116-139, 116-141, 120-143, 120-143]: Continuing dec at overlap edge on every eighth row as established, work in pattern. At end of last row *(21) [23, 23, 27, 29, 31] sts.*

Rows 132-143 [134-147, 140-149, 142-151, 144-153, 144-155]: Work in pattern. At end of last row, fasten off.

Sew shoulder seams.

For **buttonhole reinforcement,** with right side of work facing you, with F hook and black, working around buttonhole, join with sl st in any st, sl st in each st and in each ch around, join with sl st in first sl st. Fasten off.

Sew button on Right Front opposite buttonhole.

Pocket Edging

Row 1: With right side of work facing you, with F hook and black, working in unworked sts of pocket opening, join with sc in first unworked st, sc in each st across with fp in each dc on row before last, turn.

Rows 2-4: Working in **back lps** *(see Stitch Guide),* sl st in each st across, turn. At end of last row, fasten off.

Sew ends of rows to body.

With wrong side of work facing you, matching sts and ends of rows, sew Pocket Lining to body.

Body Edging

Rnd 1: With right side of work facing you, with F hook and black, working around entire outer edge, join with sc in first st at Back neck, sc in each st and in end of each row around with 3 sc in each bottom Front corner and 2 sc in end of row 67 [69, 67, 69, 63, 63] on each Front, join with sl st in first sc, **turn.**

Rnd 2: Working in **back lps,** sl st in each st around with (ch 1, sl st) in center st at each bottom Front corner, join with sl st in first sl st, **turn.**

Rnds 3-4: Working in **back lps,** sl st in each st and

in each ch around with (ch 1, sl st) in each bottom Front corner, join, **turn.** At end of last row, fasten off.

Sleeve (make 2)

Row 1: With H hook and off-white, ch 40 [40, 44, 44, 48, 52], sc in second ch from hook, sc in next 2 chs, (dc in next ch, sc in next 3 chs) across, turn. *(39) [39, 43, 43, 47, 51] sts made*

Rows 2-14 [2-10, 2-12, 2-12, 2-14, 2-10]: Work in pattern.

Note: A dash in place of the row number means not to work this row for that size.

Row 15 [11, —, —, 15, 11]: For **inc row,** ch 1, 2 sc in first st, (sc, dc) in next st, work in pattern across to last 2 sts, (dc, sc) in next st, 2 sc in last st, turn. *(43) [43, —, —, 51, 55]*

Row — [—, 13, 13, —, —]: For **inc row,** ch 1, (sc, dc) in first st, sc in next st, fp around same st on row before last, work in pattern across to last 2 sts, fp, sc in corresponding st as fp on last row, (dc, sc) in last st, turn. *(—) [—, 47, 47, —, —]*

Note: After working inc row, work each new st as needed to maintain pattern.

Rows 16-63 [12-71, 14-73, 14-69, 16-71, 12-75]: Work inc row every 12th [12th, 12th, 8th, 8th, 8th] row, work in pattern across, turn. At end of last row *(59) [63, 67, 75, 79, 87] sts.*

Rows 64-76 [72-80, 74-82, 70-82, 76-82]: Work in pattern.

Rows 77-79 [81-83, 83-85, 83-86, 83-86, 83-86]: Repeat rows 99-101 [103-105, 103-105, 103-106, 103-106, 105-108] of Back. At end of last row *(43) [47, 47, 51, 51, 59] sts.*

Rows 80-96 [84-97, 86-102, 87-101, 87-104, 87-100]: Work in pattern.

Row 97 [98, 103, 102, 105, 101]: For **dec row,** work in pattern across to last 3 sts, dec, turn. *(39) [43, 43, 47, 47, 55]*

Next rows: Work in pattern with dec row every second row until *15 [15, 19, 19, 19, 19] sts* remain.

Last row: Work in pattern across. Fasten off.

Edging

Row 1: With right side of row 1 on Sleeve facing you, with F hook and black, join with sc in first st, evenly space 43 [43, 47, 47, 51, 55] more sc across, turn.

Rows 2-4: Working in **back lps,** sl st in each st across, turn. At end of last row, fasten off.

Matching center of last row on Sleeve to shoulder seam, easing to fit, sew Sleeves in armholes. Sew side and Sleeve seams.

Sew shoulder pads in place. ♣

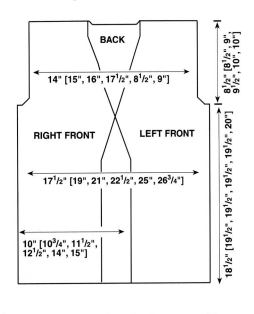

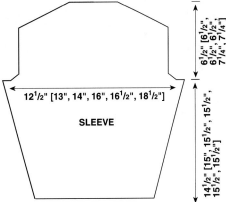

Winter Warmers

Designed by Sam Shubitz

FISHERMAN BRAID

Finished Size: Scarf is 10½" x 65½" without fringe. Hat is adult size.

Materials:
- ❏ 22 oz. mohair-type sport yarn
- ❏ Bobby pins or split stitch markers
- ❏ J hook or hook size needed to obtain gauge

Gauge: We are not responsible for lack of materials due to project not being worked to gauge. Gauge for this pattern: 5 post sts = 1"; 3 post stitch rows = 1".

Basic Stitches: Ch, sl st, dc.

Note: Begin pattern instructions with the Scarf using the following Special Cable Stitches which will be referred to as needed.

Special Cable Stitches

1: Special Stitch 1 (S1), skip next 3 sts, mark first skipped st, fp 3 times; bring hook behind sts just made and beginning with marked st, fp around each skipped st.

2: Special Stitch 2 (S2), skip next 3 sts, mark first skipped st, fp 3 times; bring hook in front of sts just made and beginning with marked st, fp around each skipped st.

3: Special Stitch 3 (S3), skip next 2 sts, mark first skipped st, fp 3 times; bring hook behind sts just made and beginning with marked st, fp around each skipped st.

4: Special Stitch 4 (S4), skip next 3 sts, mark first skipped st, fp 2 times; bring hook behind sts just made and beginning with marked st, fp around each skipped st.

5: Special Stitch 5 (S5), skip next 2 sts, mark first skipped st, fp 2 times; bring hook behind sts just made and beginning with marked st, fp around each skipped st.

6: Special Stitch 6 (S6), skip next 2 sts, mark first skipped st, fp 2 times; bring hook in front of sts just made and beginning with marked st, fp around each skipped st.

7: Special Stitch 7 (S7), skip next 2 sts, mark first skipped st, fp; bring hook in front of st just made and fp around each skipped st.

8: Special Stitch 8 (S8), skip next st, mark skipped st, fp 2 times; bring hook in front of sts just made and fp around skipped st.

9: Special Stitch 9 (S9), skip next st, fp around next 2 sts at same time; bring hook behind fp just made and bp around skipped st.

Scarf

Notes: Ch-2 at beginning of row is not used or counted as a st. Work first st of each row in same st as ch-2, leave ch-2 unworked at end of each row.

For ease in working, on note pad, write each row number with corresponding row of each panel beside it.

*For **dc front post (fp)** and **dc back post (bp)**, see Stitch Guide; work around post of next st unless otherwise stated.*

When working into marked sts, remove marker as each st is worked.

Foundation row: Ch 56, dc in third ch from hook, dc in each ch across, turn. *(54 dc made)*

Row 1: Ch 2, fp 2 times, *bp, S1 *(see Special Cable Stitches)*, fp 3 times, bp, fp 2 times; repeat from * across, turn.

Row 2: Ch 2, bp 2 times, (fp, bp 9 times, fp, bp 2 times) across, turn.

Row 3: Ch 2, fp 2 times, * bp, fp 3 times, S2 *(see Special Cable Stitches)*, bp, fp 2 times; repeat from * across, turn.

Row 4: Ch 2, bp 2 times, (fp, bp 9 times, fp, bp 2 times) across, turn.

Rows 5-196: Repeat rows 1-4 consecutively. At end of last row, fasten off.

For **fringe**, cut seven strands of yarn each 16" long. With all strands held together, fold in half, insert hook in sp between first 2 fp on one end of Scarf, pull fold through sp, pull ends through fold, tighten. Fringe between each pair of fp sts across each end of Scarf.

Hat
Top

Foundation rnd: Starting at bottom, ch 104, sl st in first ch to form ring, ch 2, dc in same ch, dc in each ch around, join with sl st in first dc, **turn.** *(104 dc made)*

Rnd 1: Ch 2, (fp 2 times, bp, S1, fp 3 times, bp, fp

Continued on page 150

2 times, bp, fp 3 times, S1, bp) around, join, **turn.**

Rnd 2: Ch 2, (fp, bp 9 times, fp, bp 2 times) around, join, **turn.**

Rnd 3: Ch 2, (fp 2 times, bp, fp 3 times, S2, bp, fp 2 times, bp, S2, fp 3 times, bp) around, join, turn.

*Notes: For **bp decrease (Bdec),** bp around next 2 sts at same time.*

*For **fp decrease (Fdec),** fp around next 2 sts at same time.*

Rnd 4: Ch 2, (fp, bp, Bdec, bp 6 times, fp, bp 2 times, fp, bp 6 times, Bdec, bp, fp, bp 2 times) around, join, **turn.** *(96)*

Rnd 5: Ch 2, (fp 2 times, bp, S3, Fdec, fp, bp, fp 2 times, bp, fp, Fdec, S4, bp) around, join, **turn.** *(88)*

Rnd 6: Ch 2, (fp, bp, Bdec, bp 4 times, fp, bp 2 times, fp, bp 4 times, Bdec, bp, fp, bp 2 times) around, join, **turn.** *(80)*

Rnd 7: Ch 2, (fp 2 times, bp, fp 2 times, S6, bp, fp 2 times, bp, S6, fp 2 times, bp) around, join, **turn.**

Rnd 8: Ch 2, (fp, bp 6 times, fp, bp 2 times) around, join, **turn.**

Rnd 9: Ch 2, (fp 2 times, bp, S5, fp 2 times, bp, fp 2 times, bp, fp 2 times, S5, bp) around, join, **turn.**

Rnd 10: Ch 2, (fp, bp 4 times, Bdec, fp, bp 2 times, fp, Bdec, bp 4 times, fp, bp 2 times) around, join, **turn.** *(72)*

Rnd 11: Ch 2, (fp 2 times, bp, Fdec, S7, bp, fp 2 times, bp, S8, Fdec, bp) around, join, **turn.** *(64)*

Rnd 12: Ch 2, (fp, bp 2 times, Bdec, fp, bp 2 times, fp, Bdec, bp 2 times, fp, bp 2 times) around, join, **turn.** *(56)*

Rnd 13: Ch 2, *fp 2 times, bp, fp around next 3 sts at same time, bp around next st; repeat from * around, join, **turn.** *(40)*

Rnd 14: Ch 2, (fp, Fdec, bp 2 times) around, join, **turn.** *(32)*

Rnd 15: Ch 2, (fp 2 times, Bdec) around, join, **turn.** *(24)*

Rnd 16: Ch 2, (Bdec, bp) around, join, **turn.** *(16)*

Rnd 17: Ch 2, Fdec 8 times, join. Fasten off. *(8)*

Band

Foundation row: Ch 15, dc in third ch from hook, dc in each across, turn. *(13 dc made)*

Row 1: Ch 2, fp 2 times, bp, S2, fp 4 times, turn.

Row 2: Ch 2, bp 10 times, fp, bp 2 times, turn.

Row 3: Ch 2, fp 2 times, bp, fp 3 times, S1, fp, turn.

Row 4: Ch 2, bp 10 times, fp, bp 2 times, turn.

Rows 5-63: Repeat rows 1-4 consecutively, ending with row 3.

Row 64: Hold row 1 and row 65 with right sides together, matching sts; working through both thicknesses, sl st in each st across. Fasten off. *(Edge of Band with bp ridge before cable is top edge).*

With right sides together, match top edge of Band to bottom edge of Hat; with wrong sides of Hat facing you, working through both thicknesses, with yarn in back, insert hook between any 2 sts on rnd 1 of Hat and through sp at end of corresponding row on Band, yo, pull lp through to front; for sl st insert hook in next sp and next row on Band, yo, pull lp through to front and through lp on hook; using one row on Band for every sl st, *(skip next sp on hat, sl st in next sp) 3 times, (sl st in next sp, skip next st, sl st in next sp) 2 times, sl st in next sp; repeat from * 6 more times, (skip next sp, sl st in next sp) 6 times, sl st in same sp as first st. Fasten off.

TAM & SCARF

Finished Sizes: Scarf is 9½" x 64" without fringe. Hat is adult size.

Materials:
❏ 20 oz. mohair-type sport yarn
❏ J hook or hook size needed to obtain gauge

Gauge: We are not responsible for lack of materials due to project not being worked to gauge. Gauge for this pattern: 5 post sts = 1"; 3 post sts rows = 1".

Basic Stitches: Ch, sl st, sc, dc.

Note: Begin pattern instructions with the Scarf using the following Special Cable Stitches which will be referred to as needed.

Special Cable Stitches
1: Special Stitch 1 (S1), skip first st, fp around next st; bring hook behind st just made and bp around skipped st.

2: Special Stitch 2 (S2), (yo, insert hook from front to back around post of next st, yo, pull through st, yo, pull through 2 lps on hook) 3 times, yo, pull through all 4 lps on hook.

3: Special Stitch 3 (S3), (fp, bp, fp) around next st.

4: Special Stitch 4 (S4), bp, fp; bring hook behind fp just made and bp around same st as first bp.

5: Special Stitch 5 (S5), skip next st, fp around next st; bring hook behind st just made and bp around skipped st, fp around same st as first fp.

6: Special Stitch 6 (S6), skip next st, fp around next 2 sts at same time; bring hook behind fp just made and bp around skipped st.

7: Special Stitch 7 (S7), skip next 2 sts, fp around next st; bring hook behind st just made and bp around 2 skipped sts at same time.

8: Special Stitch 8 (S8), fp, bring hook behind st just made and beginning ch-2 and bp around last st on last rnd.

Scarf
Notes: *Ch-2 at beginning of row is not used or counted as a st. Work first st of each row in same st as ch-2, leave ch-2 unworked at end of each row.*

For ease in working, on note pad, write each row number with corresponding row of each panel beside it.

*For **dc front post (fp)** and **dc back post (bp)**, see Stitch Guide; work around post of next st unless otherwise stated.*

When working into marked sts, remove marker as each st is worked.

Foundation row: Ch 44, dc in third ch from hook, dc in each ch across, turn. *(42 dc made)*

Row 1: Ch 2, fp 2 times, bp, * S1 (*see Special Cable Stitches*), bp 4 times, S1, S3 *(see Special Cable Stitches)*, bp 3 times; repeat from * 2 more times, S5 *(see Special Cable Stitches)*, fp, turn.

(49) Front of row 1 is right side of work.

Notes: *For **cluster st (cl)**, yo 2 times, insert hook in next st, yo, pull through st, (yo, pull through 2 lps on hook) 2 times, *yo 2 times, insert hook in same st, yo, pull through st, (yo, pull through 2 lps on hook) 2 times; repeat from * 3 more times, yo, pull through all 6 lps on hook.*

*For **fp decrease (Fdec)**, fp around next 2 sts at same time.*

*For **bp decrease (Bdec)**, bp around next 2 sts at same time.*

Row 2: Ch 2, bp 2 times, fp, (S1, fp 2 times, bp 3 times, fp, S1, fp 2 times, cl, fp) 3 times, S1, bp 2 times, turn.

Row 3: Ch 2, fp, Fdec, bp 2 times, sc in cl, bp, (*S1, bp 2 times, S2, bp, S1, bp 2 times*, sc in cl, bp) 2 times; repeat between **, fp 2 times, turn. *(42)*

Row 4: Ch 2, bp 2 times, fp 3 times, *S1, fp 4 times; repeat from * 4 more times, S1, fp 3 times, bp 2 times, turn.

Row 5: Ch 2, fp 2 times, bp 2 times, (S1, S3, bp 3 times, S1, bp 4 times) 3 times, fp 2 times, turn. *(48)*

Row 6: Ch 2, bp, S4, fp 2 times, cl, fp, (*S1, fp 2 times, bp 3 times, fp, S1*, fp 2 times, cl, fp) 2 times; repeat between**, fp, bp 2 times, turn. *(49)*

Row 7: Ch 2, fp 2 times, (S1, bp 2 times, S2, bp, S1, bp 2 times, sc in cl, bp) 3 times, S1, bp, fp 2 times, turn. *(43)*

Row 8: Ch 2, bp 2 times, fp 2 times, *S1, fp 4 times; repeat from * 5 more times, Bdec, bp, turn. *(42)*

Row 9: Ch 2, fp 2 times, bp 3 times, *[S1, bp 4 times, S1, S3], bp 3 times; repeat from * 2 more times; repeat between [ ], bp 2 times, fp 2 times, turn. *(48)*

Row 10: Ch 2, bp 2 times, fp 2 times, bp 3 times, fp, (*S1, fp 2 times, cl, fp, S1, fp 2 times*, bp 3 times, fp) 2 times; repeat between **, bp 2 times, turn.

Row 11: Ch 2, fp 2 times, bp (S1, bp 2 times, sc in cl, bp, S1, bp 2 times, S2, bp) 3 times, S5, fp turn. *(43)*

Row 12: Ch 2, bp 2 times, fp, *S1, fp 4 times; repeat from * 5 more times, S1, bp 2 times, turn.

Row 13: Ch 2, fp, Fdec, bp 4 times, *S1, S3, bp 3 times, S1, bp 4 times*; repeat between ** 2 more times, S1, S3, bp 3 times, S1, bp 2 times, fp 2 times, turn. *(48)*

Row 14: Ch 2, bp 2 times, fp, cl, fp, (*S1, fp 2 times, bp 3 times, fp, S1 fp 2 times, cl *, fp) 2 times; repeat between **, bp 2 times, turn.

Row 15: Ch 2, fp 2 times, sc in cl, bp, (S1, bp 2 times, S2, bp, S1, bp 2 times, sc in cl, bp) 3 times, fp 2 times, turn. *(42)*

Row 16: Ch 2, bp, S4, fp 4 times, *S1, fp 4 times;

Continued on page 152

Winter Warmers

Continued from page 151

repeat from * 4 more times, S1, fp, bp 2 times, turn. *(43)*

Row 17: Ch 2, fp 2 times, * S1, S3, bp 3 times, S1, bp 4 times; repeat from * 2 more times, S1, (fp, bp) around next st, fp 2 more times, turn. *(50)*

Row 18: Ch 2, bp 4 times, fp, (S1, fp 2 times, cl, fp, S1, fp 2 times, bp 3 times, fp) 3 times, Bdec, bp turn. *(49)*

Row 19: Ch 2, fp 2 times, bp, S2, bp, (*S1, bp 2 times, sc in cl, bp, S1, bp times*, S2, bp) 2 times; repeat between first*, Fdec, fp 2 times, turn. *(42)*

Row 20: Ch 2, bp 2 times, (fp 4 times, S1) 6 times, fp 2 times, bp 2 times, turn.

Rows 21-192: Repeat rows 1-20 consecutively, ending with row 13. At end of last row, fasten off.

For **fringe,** cut seven strands yarns each 16" long. With strands held together, fold in half, insert hook in sp between sts at one corner end of Scarf, pull folds through sp, pull ends through fold, tighten. Work five more fringe evenly spaced across end. Repeat on other end.

Tam

Rnd 1: Ch 4, sl st in first ch to form ring, ch 2, 12 dc in ring, join with sl st in top of ch-2, **turn.** *(12 dc made)*

Rnd 2: Ch 2, (bp, fp) around each dc, join, **turn.** *(24) Front of rnd 2 is right side of work.*

Rnd 3: Ch 2, (skip next st, 2 fp around next st; bring hook behind sts just made and bp around skipped st) around, join, **turn.** *(36)*

*Notes: For **bp increase (Binc),** work 2 bp around next st.*

*For **fp increase (Finc),** work 2 fp around next st.*

Rnd 4: Ch 2, S8 *(see Special Cable Stitches)*, Binc, *S1 *(see Special Cable Stitches)*, Binc; repeat from * around, join, **turn.** *(48)*

Rnd 5: Ch 2, S8, fp, Finc, (S1, fp, Finc) around, join, **turn.** *(60)*

Rnd 6: Ch 2, * bp 2 times, S1, S3 *(see Special Cable Stitches)*, bp 2 times, S4, bp; repeat from * around, join, **turn.** *(78)*

Rnd 7: Ch 2, **cluster** *(cl, see Notes after row 1 of Scarf)*, fp, S1, fp 2 times, bp 3 times, fp, S5, fp; repeat from * around, join, **turn.** *(84)*

Rnd 8: Ch 2, (bp, S1, bp 2 times, S2, bp, S4, bp 2 times, sc in cl) around, join, **turn.** *(78)*

Rnd 9: Ch 2, (fp 4 times, S1, fp 5 times, S5) around, join, **turn.** *(84)*

Rnd 10: Ch 2, (S1, bp, S3, bp 3 times, S4, bp 5 times) around, join, **turn.** *(102)*

Rnd 11: Ch 2, S8, fp around same st as first fp, *[fp 2 times, cl, fp 2 times, S1, fp 3 times, bp 3 times, fp 2 times], S5; repeat from * 4 more times; repeat between [ ], join, **turn.** *(108)*

Rnd 12: Ch 2, (bp 2 times, S2, bp 2 times, S4, bp 3 times, sc in cl, bp 2 times, S1, bp) around, join, **turn.** *(102)*

Rnd 13: Ch 2, (fp 2 times, S5, fp 6 times, S1, fp 5 times) around, join, **turn.** *(108)*

Rnd 14: Ch 2, (bp 4 times, S4, bp 7 times, S1, bp 2 times, S3) around, join, **turn.** *(126)*

Rnd 15: Ch 2, (bp 3 times, fp 3 times, S5, fp 2 times, cl, fp 4 times, S1, fp 4 times, S1, fp 4 times) around, join, **turn.** *(132)*

Rnd 16: Ch 2, (bp 3 times, S4, bp 5 times, sc in cl, bp 2 times, S1, bp 4 times, S2) around, join, **turn.** *(126)*

Rnd 17: Ch 2, (fp 6 times, S1, fp 8 times, S1, fp 3 times) around, join, **turn.**

Rnd 18: Ch 2, (bp, S7, bp 8 times, S1, bp 2 times, S3, bp 4 times) around, join, **turn.** *(132)*

Rnd 19: Ch 2, (fp 4 times, bp 3 times, fp 3 times, S6, fp 3 times, cl, fp 3 times, S1) around, join, **turn.** *(126)*

Rnd 20: Ch 2, fp; bring hook behind st just made and beginning ch 2 and bp around last 2 sts of last rnd at same time; *[bp 3 times, sc in cl, bp 2 times, S1, bp 4 times, S2, bp 2 times], S7; repeat from * 4 more times; repeat between [ ], join, **turn.** *(108)*

Rnd 21: Ch 2, S8, *[fp 7 times, S6, fp 6 times], S1; repeat from * 4 more times; repeat between [ ], join, **turn.** *(102)*

Rnd 22: Ch 2, (bp 5 times, S1, bp, S3, bp 4 times, S7, bp) around, join, **turn.** *(108)*

Rnd 23: Ch 2, (fp 2 times, S1, fp 3 times, bp 3 times, fp 2 times, S6, fp 2 times, cl) around, join, **turn.** *(102)*

Rnd 24: Ch 2, (sc in cl, bp, S1, bp 3 times, S2, bp, S7, bp 3 times) around, join, **turn.** *(84)*

Rnd 25: Ch 2, (fp 4 times, S1, fp 5 times, S6) around, join, **turn.** *(78)*

Rnd 26: Ch 2, (fp 3 times, S3, fp 2 times) around, join, **turn.** *(104)*

Rnd 27: Ch 2, (fp 2 times, bp 3 times, fp 3 times) around, join, **turn.**

Rnd 28: Ch 2, (bp 3 times, S2, bp 2 times) around, join, **do not turn.** *(78)*

Rnd 29: With two strands held tog, working from left to right in sps between sts, ch 1, **reverse sc** *(see Stitch Guide)* in next sp, skip next sp, (reverse sc in next sp, skip next sp) around, join with sl st in first sc. Fasten off. ❧

Cowl Hood

Designed by Deborah Levy-Hamburg

Finished Size: Teen or adult. Finished Measurement: 18" long.

Materials:
- ❑ 6 oz. worsted novelty yarn
- ❑ Stitch marker
- ❑ Tapestry needle
- ❑ I and M hooks or hook sizes needed to obtain gauges

Gauges: We are not responsible for lack of materials due to project not being worked to gauge. Gauge for this pattern: **I hook,** 11 extended sc = 4"; 5 rows = 2". **M hook,** 5 extended sc = 2"; 4 rows = 2".

Basic Stitches: Ch, sl st, sc.

Hood
Note: Do not join rnds. Mark first st of each rnd.
Rnd 1: Beginning at face edge, with I hook, ch 74, sl st in first ch to form ring, ch 1; working in **back bar of chs** *(see Stitch Guide),* for **extended sc (esc),** insert hook in next ch, yo, pull through, yo, pull through 1 lp on hook, yo, pull through 2 lps on hook; esc in each ch around. *(74 esc made)*

Rnds 2-11: Esc in each st around.

Rnds 12-16: With M hook, esc in each st around.

Rnd 17: Esc in first 6 sts; for **inc, 2 esc in next st;** (esc in next 11 sts, inc) around to last 7 sts, esc in last 7 sts. *(80)*

Rnds 18-20: Esc in each st around.

Rnd 21: For **neck shaping,** (esc in next st, skip next st) around. *(40)*

Rnds 22-29: Esc in each st around.

Rnd 30: (Inc, esc in next 9 sts) around. *(44)*

Rnds 31-32: Esc in each st around.

Rnd 33: (Inc, esc in next 10 sts) around. *(48)*

Rnds 34-35: Esc in each st around. At end of last rnd, fasten off. ❧

Aran Slippers

An Original by Annie

Finished Sizes: 4-5 (small), 6-7 (medium), 8-9 (large).

Materials:
- ❑ Worsted yarn:
  - 2½" oz. tan for all sizes
  - 10 oz. off white for medium and large sizes *(plus 2 oz. for high-top version)*
- ❑ 8 oz. off-white sport yarn for small size *(plus 2 oz. for high-top version)*
- ❑ Tapestry needle
- ❑ G hook or hook size needed to obtain gauge.

Gauges: We are not responsible for lack of materials due to project not being worked to gauge. Gauge for this pattern: With **worsted yarn**, 4 sc = 1", 4 sc **back lp** ribbed rows = 1"; 3-dtr cluster is 1¼" tall. With **sport yarn**, 3 dtr cluster is 1" tall.

Basic Stitches: Ch, sl st, sc, hdc, dc.

Special Stithes: For **3-dtr cluster** *(see illustration at right),* yo 3 times, insert hook around post of dc *(see arrow #1),* *yo, pull lp through, (yo, pull through 2 lps on hook) 3 times leaving last lps on hook*; yo 3 times, insert hook around post of same dc *(seee arrow #2)* and repeat between **; yo 3 times, insert hook around post of same dc *(see arrow #3)* and repeat between **, yo and pull through all lps on hook.

For **berry stitch (berry st),** insert hook in next st, yo,

pull lp through, ch 3, using first lp only, yo, pull through 2 lps on hook, pull chain to front of work.

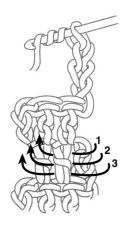

Note: Instructions are for small; changes for medium and large are in [ ].

Slipper (make 2)
Sole
Row 1: Beginning at heel, with tan, ch 8, sc in second from hook, sc in each ch across, turn. *(7 sc made)*

Rows 2-3 [2-3, 2-4]: Working these rows in **back lps** *(see Stitch Guide),* ch 1, 2 sc in first st, sc in each st across with 2 sc in last st, turn. At end of last row *(11) [11, 13].*

Rows 4-12 [4-14, 5-16]: Ch 1, sc in each st across, turn.

Row 13: [15, 17]: Ch 1, 2 sc in first st, sc in each st across with 2 sc in last st, turn. *(13) [13, 15]*

Rows 14-26 [16-30. 18-34]: Ch 1, sc in each st across, turn.

Rows 27-28 [31-32, 35-37]: Ch 1, sc first 2 sts tog, sc in each st across to last 2 sts, sc last 2 sts tog, turn. At end of last row *(9).* Fasten off.

Front Panel Center
Row 1: With off-white yarn for size, ch 4, 2 dc in fourth ch from hook, turn. *(3 dc made)*

Row 2: Ch 1, sc in next 3 sts, turn.

Row 3: Ch 3, **3-dtr-cluster** *(see Special Stitches)* around post of middle dc in second row below, dc in next 2 sc behind cluster just made.

Row 4: Ch 1, sc in next 3 sts, turn.

Row 5: Ch 3, 3-dtr cluster around post of middle dc in second row below *(it is hidden behind last cluster made),* dc in next 2 sc behind cluster just made, turn.

Rows 6-12 for Low-Top, Rows 6-20 for High-Top: Repeat rows 4-5 over and over, ending with row 4.

Last Row: Ch 3, 3-dtr cluster around post of middle dc in second row below, dc in next sc, ch 3, sl st in last sc. **Do not fasten off.**

Front Panel Border
Rnd 1: Working around outer edge of Front Panel Center, skipping ends of sc rows, sc in sp formed by the dc at the end of the next row, ch 2, 2 dc in same sp; *work following steps to complete rnd:*

A: 3 dc in sp at end of each dc row down first side to last sp, work 4 dc in last sp;

B: 4 dc in end st, 4 dc in first sp on opposite side;

C: Repeat A down other side;

D: 4 dc in end st;

E: 4 dc in remaining ch-3 sp on first side, join with sl st in top of ch-2;

Rnd 2: Ch 1, **sc back post (sc bp,** *see Stitch Guide)* around first st, ch 2; *work following steps to complete rnd:*

A: Using **hdc back post (bp) for small or medium** or **dc back post (bp) for large,** work bp around each dc down side to center 6 sts at end;

B: * Bp around next st; using **hdc for small or medium or dc for large,** work st in side of bp just made *(see illustration);* repeat from * 5 more times;

C-D: Repeat A-B down other side;

E: Bp around each of last 3 dc on first side, join with sl st in top of ch-2.

Rnd 3: Ch 1, sc in next st, **berry st** *(see Special Stitches); work following steps to complete rnd:*

A: (Sc in next st, berry st in next st) down side to center 8 sts at end;

B: In 8 end sts, work (2 sc in next st, berry in next st) 4 times;

C-D: Repeat A-B down other side;

E: (Sc in next st, berry st in next st) in remaining sts on first side *(last berry st will be worked over first ch-1 of this rnd and into joining sl st of last rnd),* join with sl st in first sc.

Rnd 4: *(The berry sts of this rnd will be staggered between the berry sts of the last rnd.)* Ch 1, (sc in next st, berry st in next st) around, ending with a berry st in joining sl st of st last rnd, join with sl st in first sc.

Rnd [5]: For **large size only,** ch 1, *(sc in next st, berry st in next) down side to center 8 sts at end; in end sts, work (2 sc in next st; berry st in next st) 4 times; repeat from * one time, (sc in next st, berry st in next st) in remaining sts on first side (last berry st will be worked over joining sl st of last rnd), join with sl st in first sc.

Rnd 5 [5, 6]: For **all sizes,** ch 2, *(hdc in each st down side to center 12 sts at end; in end sts, work (2 hdc in next st, hdc in next 2 sts) 4 times; repeat from * one time, hdc in each remaining

Continued on page 156

Aran Slippers

Continued from page 155

st on first side, join with sl st in top of ch-2.

Rnd 6 [6, 7]: Ch 1, sc bp around first st, ch 2, *dc bp around each st down side to center 12 sts at end; (dc bp around next st, dc in side of dc bp just made, dc bp around next st) 6 times; repeat from * one time, dc bp around each remaining st on first side, join with sl st in top of ch-2.

Rnd 7 [7, 8]: Ch 1, sc in next st; for **cable,** ch 3, skip next 2 sts, sc in next st *(see illustration #1),* **turn;** work 3 sc in ch-3 sp, sl st in next sc *(see illustration #2),* **turn;** working behind ch-3 sp, sc in 2 skipped sts *(see illustration #3),* you will reverse directed twice in completing each cable; *work following steps to complete rnd:*

A: *Ch 3, skip st where previous ch-3 was attached, skip next 2 sts, sc in next st, **turn,** work 3 sc in ch-3 sp, sl st in next sc, **turn;** working behind ch-3 sp, sc in each of 2 skipped sts; repeat from * down side to center 24 sts at end;

B: *Ch 3, skip st where previous ch-3 was attached, skip next st, sc in next st, turn, work 3 sc in ch-3 sp, sl st in next sc, turn; working behind ch-3 sp, 2 sc in skipped st; repeat from * 11 more times;

C-D: Repeat A-B.

E: Repeat A in remaining sts on first side, ending with ch 3, skip last 2 sts, sl st in st that is in front of first cable made, **turn;** 3 sc in ch-3 sp, sl st in next sc, **turn;** sc in 2 skipped sts behind ch-3 loop. Fasten off.

Back Panel Center
Rows 1-5: Repeat rows 1-5 of Front Panel Center.
Rows 6-11 for Low Top, Rows 6-19 for High Top: Repeat rows 4 and 5 of Front Panel Center over and over. At end of last row, **do not fasten off.**

Back Panel Border
Row 1: Working around outer edge of Front Panel Center, skipping ends of sc rows, sc in sp formed by the dc at the end of the last row, ch 2, 2 dc in same sp; *work following steps to complete row:*

A: 3 dc in sp at end of each dc row down first side to last sp, work 4 dc in last sp;

B: 4 dc in end st, 4 dc in first sp on opposite side;

C: 3 dc in each sp across, turn.

Row 2: Ch 1, sc front post around first st, ch 2; *work following steps to complete row:*

A: Using **hdc fp for small or medium or dc fp**

for **large,** fp around each dc down side to center 6 sts at end;

B: *Fp around next st; using **hdc for small or medium or dc for large,** work st in side of fp just made; repeat from * 5 more times;

C: Fp around each dc across, turn.

Row 3: Ch 1, sc in first st, berry st in next st; *work following steps to complete row:*

A: (Sc in next st, berry st in next st) down side to center 8 sts at end;

B: In 8 end sts, work (2 dc in next st, berry st in next st) 4 times;

C: (Sc in next st, berry st in next st) across with sc in last 2 sts, turn.

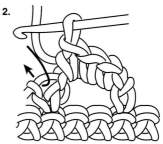

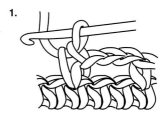

2 SKIPPED SC BEHIND CABLE

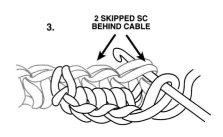

Row 4: *(The berry sts of this row will be staggered between the berry sts of the last row.)* Ch 1, sc in first st, (berry st in next st, sc in next st) across with sc in last st, turn.

Row [5]: For **large size only,** ch 1, (sc in next st, berry st in next st) down side to center 8 sts at end; in end sts, work (2 sc in next st, berry st in next st) 4 times, (sc in next st, berry st in next) st across, **do not turn.** Fasten off. Join with sl st in first st.

Row 5 [5, 6]: For **all sizes,** ch 2, hdc in each st down side to center 12 sts at end; in end sts, work (2 hdc in next st, hdc in next 2 sts) 4 times, hdc in each st across, turn.

Row 6 [6, 7]: Ch 1, sc fp around first st, ch 2, dc fp around each st down side to center 12 sts at end; (dc fp around next st, dc in side of dc fp just made, dc fp around next st) 6 times, dc fp around each st across, turn.

Row 7 [7, 8]: Ch 1, sc in next st; for **cable,** ch 3, skip next 2 sts, sc in next st, **turn;** work 3 sc in ch-3 sp, sl st in next sc, **turn;** working behind ch-3 sp, sc in 2 skipped sts; *work following steps to complete row:*

A: *Ch 3, skip st where previous ch-3 was attached, skip next 2 sts, sc in next st, **turn;** work 3 sc in ch-3 sp, sl st in next sc, **turn;** working behind ch-3 sp, sc in 2 skipped sts; repeat from * down side to center 24 sts at end;

B: *Ch 3, skip st where previous ch-3 was attached, skip next st, sc in next st, **turn;** work 3 sc in ch-3 sp, sl st in next sc, **turn;** working behind ch-3 sp, 2 sc in skipped st; repeat from * 11 more times;

C: *Ch 3, skip st where previous ch-3 was attached, skip next 2 sts, sc in next st, **turn;** work 3 sc in ch-3 sp, sl st in next sc, **turn;** working behind ch-3 sp , sc in 2 skipped sts; repeat from * across. Fasten off.

Gusset (make 2)

Row 1: WIth off-white for size, ch 10 [10, 14], sc in second ch from hook, sc in each ch across, turn. *(9 sc made) (9 sc made, 13 sc made)*

Rows 2-5: Working these rows in **back lps,** ch 1, sc in each st across, turn.

Row 6: Ch 1, sc first 2 sts tog, sc in each st across, turn. *(8) [8, 12]*

Row 7: Ch 1, sc in each st across to last 2 sts, sc last 2 sts tog, turn. *(7) [7, 11]*

Rows 8-12: Repeat rows 6 and 7 over and over, ending with row 6. At end of last row *(2) [2, 6].* Fasten off.

Sew Gusset to each end of last row on Back Panel Border *(see illustration).*

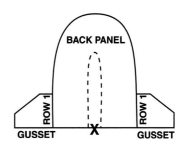

Assembly

Pin Back Panel Center at X to center of first row on Sole and over last rows on Gussets to ends of row 17 [17, 19] on Sole *(see illustration).*

Pin center of one end on Front Panel Border to center of last row on Sole.

Beginning at heel, sew Back Panel and Gussets to Sole one stitch from edges of Sole. Beginning at toe, working at base of cables and overlapping edges of Gusset, sew Front Panel to Sole, Gusset and Back Panel on each side leaving center top 12 cables on Front Panel and 14 cables on Back Panel unsewn. ❧

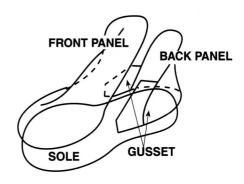

Drape Cape

Continued from page 139

pull lp through st, sc in first 3 chs, drop lp from hook , insert hook in 12th long hdc on last motif, pull lp through st, sc in last 4 chs, **turn;** with wrong side facing you, ch 1, sc in eighth long hdc on first motif, (ch 5, sc in eighth long hdc on next motif) across, ch 2, sl st in last sc on end of row bar, sl st in starting ch at bottom of same sc, turn.

Row 41 [43, 47, 49]: Ch 1, skip first sl st, sc in same st as next sl st, sc in each ch and each sc across to end of row bar, sc in side of last sc on bar, turn. Fasten off. *(144) [144, 156, 156]*

Row 42: [44, 48, 50]: Join MC with sl st in first st, ch 2, hdc in first sp, hdc in each sp across, turn.

Rows 43-46: [45-48, 49-52, 51-54]: Ch 2, hdc in first sp, hdc in each sp across, turn. At end of last row, fasten off.

Row 47 [49, 53, 55]: Skip first 70 [70, 76, 76] sps; for back, join MC with sl st in next sp, ch 2, hdc in each sp across, turn. *(73) [73, 79, 79]*

Row 48 [50, 54, 56]: Ch 2, hdc in first sp, hdc in each sp across to last 2 sps, hdc last 2 sps tog, turn. *(72) [72, 78, 78]*

Rows 49-51 [51-54, 55-58, 57-61]: Ch 2, hdc in first sp, hdc in each sp across, turn. At end of last row, fasten off.

Left Side

Row 1-38 [1-40, 1-44, 1-46]: Repeat rows 1-38 [1-40, 1-44, 1-46] of right side. At end of last row, **do not fasten off.**

Rows 39-52 [41-54, 45-58, 47-60]: Ch 2, hdc in first sp, hdc in each sp across, turn.

Row 53 [55, 59, 61]: For **back,** ch 2, hdc in first sp, hdc in next 70 [70, 76, 76] sps, hdc next 2 sps tog leaving last 70 [70, 76, 76] sps unworked, turn. *(73) [73, 79, 79]*

Row 54: [56, 60, 62]: Ch 2, hdc first 2 sps tog, hdc in each sp across, turn. *(72) [72, 78, 78]*

Rows 55-57 [57 -60, 61-64, 63-67]: Ch 2, hdc in first sp, hdc in each sp across, turn. At end of last row fasten off.

For **back seam,** sew last rows of Right Side and Left Side tog. Sew sleeve seam, sewing one st at center of end motifs tog to join motif row. Sew side seams leaving bottom 16 sts on each side unsewn for slit.

Collar

Row 1: Working in sps between sts across right front edge, join MC with sl st in first st, ch 2, hdc in first sp, hdc in each sp across to last sp; working ends of rows across neck and in back seam, 2 hdc in first row, (hdc in next row, 2 hdc in next row) 5 [6, 6, 7] times, hdc in next sp on left front, hdc in each sp across, turn. *(158 hdc) [161 hdc, 173 hdc, 176 hdc] made*

Rows 2-12: Ch 2, hdc in first sp, hdc in each sp across, turn. At end of last row, fasten off.

Finishing

For **bottom edge trim,** with right side facing you, beginning at left front corner, join MC with sc in end of row 12 on Collar; working in sts, ends of rows and on opposite side of starting ch, sc evenly across bottom edge with 3 sc in each outside corner at side slits ending with sc in row 12 at right front. Fasten off.

For **sleeve hem,** fold bottom of sleeve to outside at desired length; beginning at sleeve seam, working through both thicknesses, [holding yarn at back of work, insert hook in first ch of starting ch and between first 2 sts in corresponding row, yo, pull through to front; *working loosely, insert hook in next ch and between next 2 sts on corresponding row, yo, pull through to front and through lp on hook; repeat from * around, sl st through first sl st. Fasten off.]

For **sl st trim,** working between sts on corresponding row only, repeat between [ ] of sleeve hem.

Stitch Guide

Ounces to Grams	Grams to Ounces
1 = 28.4	25 = ⅞
2 = 56.7	40 = 1⅖
3 = 85.0	50 = 1¾
4 = 113.4	100 = 3½

Chain–ch: Yo, pull through lp on hook.

Single Crochet–sc: Insert hook in st, yo, pull through st, yo, pull through both lps on hook.

Slip Stitch–sl st: Insert hook in st, yo, pull through st and lp on hook.

Change Colors: Drop first color; with 2nd color, pull through last 2 lps of st.

Half Double Crochet: Yo, insert hook in st, yo, pull through st, yo, pull through all 3 lps on hook.

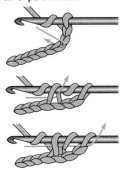

Double Crochet–dc: Yo, insert hook in st, yo, pull through st, (yo, pull through 2 lps) 2 times.

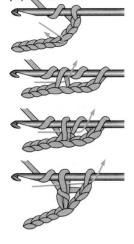

Treble Crochet–tr: Yo 2 times, insert hook in st, yo, pull through st, (yo, pull through 2 lps) 3 times.

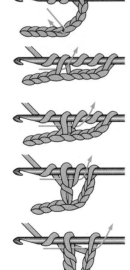

Reverse sc: Working from left to right, insert hook in next st to the right, complete as sc.

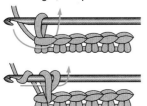

Double Treble Crochet–dtr: Yo 3 times, insert hook in st, yo, pull through st, (yo, pull through 2 lps) 4 times.

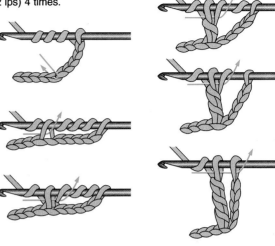

Front Post Stitch–fp Back Post Stitch–bp: Yo, insert hook from right to left around post of st on previous row, complete as dc.

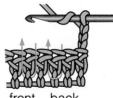

front   back

Back Bar of Chain

Front Loop Back Loop

front   back

Hook Sizes

U.S.	Metric	U.K.	U.S.	Metric	U.K.
14	0.60mm		6...G	4.50mm	7
12	0.75mm			4.75mm	
10	1.00mm		8...H	5.00mm	6
6	1.50mm		9...I	5.50mm	5
0...5	1.75mm		10...J	6.00mm	4
1...B	2.00mm	14		6.50mm	3
2...C	2.50mm	12	10½K	7.00mm	2
D	3.00mm	10	11	8.00mm	
4...E	3.50mm	9	13	9.00mm	
5...F	4.00mm	8	15..P	10.00mm	
			Q	16.00mm	

Standard Abbreviations

ch, chs . . . . . .chain, chains
dc . . . . .double crochet
hdc . . . . .half double crochet
lp, lps . . . . .loop, loops
rnd, rnds . . . .round, rounds
sc . . . . .single crochet
sl st . . . . .slip stitch
sp, sps . . . . . .space, spaces
st, sts . . . . . .stitch, stitches
tog . . . . .together
tr . . . . .treble crochet
yo . . . . .yarn over

sc next 2 sts tog—(insert hook in next st, yo, pull through st) 2 times, yo, pull through all 3 lps on hook.
hdc next 2 sts tog—(yo, insert hook in next st, yo, pull through st) 2 times, yo, pull through all 5 lps on hook.
dc next 2 sts tog—(yo, insert hook in next st, yo, pull through st, yo, pull through 2 lps on hook) 2 times, yo, pull through 3 lps on hook.